103

The Information Society
and the Black Community

The Information Society and the Black Community

Edited by
John T. Barber and Alice A. Tait

PRAEGER

Westport, Connecticut
London

Library of Congress Cataloging-in-Publication Data

The information society and the Black community / edited by John T. Barber and Alice A. Tait.

    p. cm.
  Includes bibliographical references and index.
  ISBN 0–275–95724–1 (alk. paper)
    1. Afro-Americans—Social conditions. 2. Afro-Americans—Economic conditions. 3. Information society—United States. 4. Information technology—Social aspects—United States. 5. Information technology—Economic aspects—United States. I. Barber, John T. II. Tait, Alice A.
  E185.86.I64 2001
  303.48′33′08996073—dc21   00–023547

British Library Cataloguing in Publication Data is available.

Library of Congress Catalog Card Number: 00–023547
ISBN: 0–275–95724–1

First published in 2001

Praeger Publishers, 88 Post Road West, Westport, CT 06881
An imprint of Greenwood Publishing Group, Inc.
www.praeger.com

Printed in the United States of America

The paper used in this book complies with the Permanent Paper Standard issued by the National Information Standards Organization (Z39.48–1984).

10 9 8 7 6 5 4 3 2

Copyright Acknowledgment

The editors and publisher gratefully acknowledge permission to reprint Oscar H. Gandy's "African Americans and Privacy" from *Journal of Black Studies* 24(2), pp. 178–195, copyright © 1989 by Sage Publications. Reprinted by permission of Sage Publications.

Contents

Acknowledgements

This work was inspired in part by the communications behaviors of two young black women: Rashida Gaston and the late Deshawn Mallory. Before we (the editors) started this project a few years ago, we noticed that they (and many others like them) seemed to always be working on personal computers, watching cable TV videos, talking on the cell phone, or checking answering machines or pagers for messages. It occurred to us that these young Black people were very much a part of the communications revolution that was taking place as the American Information Society evolved. It seemed reasonable that communication activities similar to theirs were taking place in Black communities across the nation. We realized, however, that all of this consumer type behavior was only the tip of the iceberg. There were deeper issues that needed to be addressed in any analysis of Blacks and communications systems in America. Issues such as equal access to cyberspace, ownership and control of telecommunication systems and creation and transmission of images and messages of and about African Americans would have to be a part of our research effort. We decided to look into these phenomena systematically and to try to describe their dimensions and characteristics in a way that might help us to understand how the emerging Information Age is impacting the Black community.

The work that needed to be done, however, would not have been possible without the assistance of a few institutions and several individuals. The financial support of the Office for Academic Affairs at Morgan State University and the Faculty Research and Creative Endeavors Committee at Central Michigan University allowed us to employ professional assistance in administrative, research, manuscript preparation and all of the activities that must be performed to produce a book. In the area of research, Drs. Stephen E. Jones and Marilyn K. Parr of the Library of Congress provided Humanities and Social Sciences Division timely and professional assistance in using the Library's technology to locate materials and verify citations. Brian White, a Morgan State University student, provided a tremendous amount of help in sorting out and locating Black web sites and documenting facts about the FCC and other communications agencies. In preparing the manuscript, the editorial advice and word processing assistance provided by Mirian Smith and Barbara Gaston was invaluable. The copy editing of Nina Duprey of Greenwood Publishing was superior and the indexing of Carol Jacob was incomparable.

We also wish to acknowledge Molefe K. Asante of Temple University and Steven G. Jones, Professional Head of the Department of Communication at the University of Illinois at Chicago for their reviews of the manuscript. They provided inspiration and insight that helped us to follow through with completing the project.

We wish to honor our parents: Nora L. Barber, and the late John T. Barber, Sr. and the late Corine Tait, and Lahoma Tait, Jr. After all, they are the reason that we are here to produce this publication. We dedicate our efforts, however, to our children and grand children: Jamila A. Barber and Ricardo J. Facey and Joseph Conrad Smith, II, Joseph Conrad, III, and Leiah, and Brigham Smith. And to all of the young people who are playing a leading role in making the coming age of hi-tech communications a reality in the Black community in America.

Introduction

John T. Barber and Alice A. Tait

Over the past 40 years, America has become a leading Information Society (Dordick & Wang, 1993). Conceptualists have characterized it as the "technological society" (Ellul, 1964), the "post-industrial society" (Bell, 1973), the "post-capitalist society" (Drucker, 1993), and the "network society" (Castells, 1997). Regardless of the name, there is general agreement that America is engaged in a massive transformation of its society from an industrial one to one that is based on the production and distribution of information (DeFleur & Ball-Rokeach, 1989). This transition is changing the future of information and communications systems in this nation and the way that our society functions in general.

The Information Society of which we speak is the contemporary societal condition of America as it transforms itself into a society that relies on information and its dissemination as a basis for sustaining the society itself. Speculations abound about how the emergence of the Information Society will affect the lives of Americans and others around the world. Some argue that it will improve the economic power of individuals as well as corporations (Baldwin, McVoy, & Steinfield, 1996; Gates, 1995); and others say a global democracy will emerge in which there will be electronic participation in government (Arterton, 1987). Many expect that there will be expanded educational opportunities because information and knowledge will be shared all over the world through vast computer and telecommunications systems such as the Internet (Gates, 1995). Still other predictions are that new employment opportunities will arise from the fields of information and communications (Dordick & Wang, 1993).

Other analysts have contradictory perspectives and see the Information Society as not enhancing the lives of everyone involved. Such pundits predict that the Information Society will be a society of controllers and controlled (Gandy, 1989) and the information-rich and the information-poor (Haywood, 1995). Castells (1989) argues that "people live in places, but power rules through flows" of electronic data. Information controllers, therefore, have become more concerned with worldwide networks of information flows than with communities, cities, or other locales. Castells sees the emergence of the Information Society as an opportunity for the organizations of power and production to continue to dominate society without submitting to its controls. He says: "In the end, even democracies become powerless confronted with the ability of capital to circulate globally, of information to be transferred secretly, of markets to be penetrated or neglected, of planetary strategies of political-military power to be decided without the knowledge of nations and of cultural messages to be marketed, packaged, recorded, and beamed in and out of people's minds" (p. 349). Castells concludes that the result of this process is that "there is no tangible oppression, no identifiable enemy, no center of power that can be held responsible for specific social ills."

Gillespie and Robins (1989) point out that new global communications systems are not established for the universal access of the members of various societies but are set up to expand the reach and centralize the interests of transnational corporations and government organizations. They comment that the "new electronic highways of the Information Society are not, therefore, public thoroughfares but are more akin to a myriad of private roads." This widening chasm of power between members of society and bureaucratic organizations is of critical importance in the information age. Gandy (1989) argues that the main function of the new technologies of the Information Society is surveillance of individuals in that society.

The emerging information order is replete with the contradictions discussed earlier. On one hand, analysts of the optimistic perspective see the Information Society as an enlightening, empowering, and egalitarian system that holds unlimited opportunities and potential for advancement for all within its boundaries. On the other hand, critical writers say that it is a system that is changing societal arrangements to the advantage of those who are already powerful and to the detriment of those who are less influential.

But what does all this mean to a historically disadvantaged people who are striving to maintain their well being and pursue advancement in the midst of the rapid changes taking place in American society? In this book, we explore America's Black community to find answers to this query.

The Black community of which we speak is the sector of American society that is populated by African Americans at the dawn of the twenty-first century. It should be noted at the outset that the terms "Black" and "African American" are used interchangeably throughout this book to refer to people who live in the Black community. During the 1980s the African American population grew to 30 million. This population continued to grow during the 1990's and as the year 2000 begins, the Black community is made up more than 35 million people (U.S. Census Bureau, March 1999). As the largest minority community in the leading Information Society in the world today, the Black community in

America is an excellent place to assess how well a historically disadvantaged societal group can cope with a society as it changes its socioeconomic configuration from one based on industry to one grounded in information production and distribution.

This transition is already having a devastating impact on large sectors of the Black community. Too often Blacks are concentrated in industries that are now on the decline (Marable, 1983). Wilson (1996) argues that the decline of the mass-production system, decreasing availability of lower-skilled blue-collar jobs, the growing importance of training and education in the higher-growth industries, and the growing suburbanization of jobs are having a dramatic, adverse effect on low-skilled Black workers. The nation's ghettos, which are occupied by nearly 6 million Blacks, are places where work and the ability to work are disappearing as the Information Society steadily advances.

Since the evolution of the Information Society is having serious impacts on some parts of the Black community, a serious discussion must take place about Blacks and the position that they will occupy in the new information order of this country and the world. The following questions seem pertinent to such a discussion. How large is the segment of the Black community that is ready to "go on-line" in a society that works best for a societal group's interests when it has the ability to "hook up" to the nation's information infrastructure using devices such as personal computers, cable television, cellular phones, satellite dishes, and other interactive equipment? To what extent do Blacks own major information industries such as telecommunications and broadcasting systems? To what extent are school systems, including historically Black colleges and universities, making use of the capabilities of new communications technologies to enhance the learning of young African Americans? How many Black people are working in information industries, especially in leading, decision-making positions? What amount of influence and power will Black Americans exert in transmitting messages and images about themselves and their culture in a society that is grounded in information development, processing, production, and distribution? This book looks at these issues and attempts to discuss them in a systematic way in order to provide a clearer picture of the position that the Black community occupies in the American Information Society.

Frank Webster (1995) provides a framework for systematically analyzing Information Societies in his book *Theories of the Information Society*. He distills the thinking of numerous researchers and analysts into key categories that define the concept "Information Society." He posits that the five contexts in which information societies have been analyzed include technological, economic, occupational, spatial, and cultural. The technological analysis deals with the application of information technology in all concerns of society, especially the proliferation of computers and the imbrication and convergence of telecommunications and computing. The economic analysis concerns the size and growth of information industries, especially those dealing with mass media and information services. The occupational analysis seeks to determine if the preponderance of occupations in a society is in the area of "information work." A major concern here is determining which jobs should be classified as information occupations because they are mainly engaged in the production, processing, and distribution of information. The spatial analysis focuses on the centrality of information networks in linking together locations within and between towns, regions, nations, continents, and the entire world. This linking has created an electronic environment commonly referred to as "cyberspace." The analytical focus is how these linking networks allow users to overcome the constraints of real time and space and deal with political, economic, and social enterprises rapidly and efficiently in cyberspace. Finally, the cultural analysis examines the explosion of images, messages, and symbolism in contemporary culture. The focus is the role of information technologies in increasing our abilities to record, transmit, and receive cultural images and messages about ourselves and others. These categories of analysis have been used to measure the informational dimensions of various nations to determine whether or not they should be classified as Information Societies.

We acknowledge the fact that America is an Information Society. In this book, we use Webster's (1995) categories to assess whether or not the Black community is progressing along the same lines as the American Information Society as a whole. In other words, we use them to assess the informational dimensions of Black America to determine if the Black community is an "information community." To this end, the book is divided into five parts: Part One deals with adoption of information technology by Black people as well as the use of information-gathering technology by the majority community to access personal information about people in the Black community; Part Two addresses economic factors that impact Black ownership and control of information industries; Part Three deals with professional training and employment patterns affecting Black people in the information era; Part Four deals with Blacks' abilities to enter cyberspace to solve social, political, and economic issues and to experience participatory democracy. Part Five concerns cultural issues in the American Black community and their connections to Africa and the rest of the world.

In this work, we seek to understand whether or not the Black community will progress in the Information Society, be left behind, or be left out. The contributing authors used research approaches that are quantitative, qualitative, and interpretive (Williams, Rice, & Rogers, 1988). Each writer or team has produced a chapter that deals with an issue that the editors feel is critical to understanding the relationship of the Black community to the American Information Society. In the final chapter, however, the editors draw some conclusions and make some predictions about the relationship of the Black community to the Information Society.

REFERENCES

Arterton, F. C. (1987). *Teledemocracy: Can Technology Protect Democracy?* Newbury Park, CA: Sage Publications.

Baldwin, T. F., McVoy, D. S., Steinfield, C. (1996). *Convergence: Integrating Media, Information & Communication.* Thousand Oaks, CA: Sage Publications.

Bell, D. (1973). *The Coming of Post-Industrial Society; A Venture in Social Forecasting.* New York: Basic Books.

Castells, M. (1989). *The Informational City: Information Technology, Economic Restructuring, and the Urban Regional Process.* Cambridge, MA: Basil Blackwell.

Castells, M. (1997). *The Information Age: Economy, Society and Culture. Vol. 2: The Power of Identity.* Madden, MA: Blackwell.

Cose, E. (1995). *The Rage of a Privileged Class.* New York: HarperPerennial.

DeFleur, M. L., & Ball-Rokeach., S.J. (1989). *Theories of Mass Communication.* 5th ed. New York: Longman.

Dordick, H. S., & Wang, G. (1993). *The Information Society: A Retrospective View.* Newbury Park, CA: Sage.

Drucker, P. F. (1993). *Post-Capitalist Society.* New York: HarperCollins.

Ellul, J. (1964). *The Technological Society.* New York: Knopf.

Gandy, O. H. (1989). The surveillance society: Information technology and bureaucratic social control. *Journal of Communication, 39,* 61-76.

Gates, W. H. (1995). *The Road Ahead.* New York: Viking Penguin.

Gillespie, A., & Robins, K. (1989). Geographical inequalities: The spatial bias of the new communications technologies. *Journal of Communication, 39,* 7-18.

Haywood, T. (1995). *Info-Rich-Info-Poor Access in the Global Information Society.* London: Bowkersaur.

Marable, M. (1983). How capitalism underdeveloped Black America: problems in race, political economy and society. Boston, MA: South End Press.

National Telecommunications and Information Administration (1998, July). *Falling Through the Net II: New Data on the Digital Divide.* [On-line]. Available: http://www.ntia.doc.gov/ntiahome/net2/.

National Telecommunications and Information Administration (1999, July). *Falling Through the Net: Defining the Digital Divide.* [On-line]. Available: http://ntiant1.ntia.doc.gov/ntiahome/fttn99/contents.html.

Rogers, E. M. (1986). Communication Technology: *The New Media in Society.* New York: Free Press.

U.S. Census Bureau (2000, February 14). Black population in the U.S. March 1999. [On-line]. Available: http://www.census.gov/population/socdemo/race/black/tabs99/tab01.txt

U.S. Department Of Commerce (1995, July). *Falling Through the Net: A Survey of the "Have Nots" in Rural and Urban America*. Washington, DC: Author.

Webster, F. (1995). *Theories of the Information Society*. New York: Routledge.

Wilson, W. J. (1996). *When Work Disappears*. New York: Alfred A. Knopf.

PART I

The Technological Dimension

With the diffusion of information innovations into every aspect of American life, there has been much concern about the ability of Blacks to adopt the various technologies and to access and use technological systems such as the Internet. Through three surveys entitled "Falling through the Net: A Survey of the 'Have-Nots' in Rural and Urban America," "Falling Through the Net II: New Data on the Digital Divide," and "Falling through the Net: Defining the Digital Divide", the federal government has determined that Blacks and other Americans have embraced the information age and brought technologies like personal computers and modems into their homes. It concludes, however, that the "digital divide" increased substantially between the years of the studies in 1995, 1998 and 1999, respectively. Although they were engrossed in the communications revolution like everyone else, Blacks lagged far behind Whites in telephone, personal computer, and on-line service usage. The Internet, however, is the major technology in the information age, and accessing it is key to the Black community's capability to use this technology to its advantage. Stephen Jones and John T. Barber explain in the first chapter how African Americans are using it to build a Black community in cyberspace.

In Chapter 2, John T. Barber and Willis G. Smith use consumer analysis surveys of the ten major media markets in America to determine the extent to which African Americans are adopting a wider range of information technologies than those dealt with by the government's "Falling through the Net" studies. Technologies examined include personal communication services, videocassette recorders, and cable television, as well as long distance telephone service, personal computers, and on-line computer services.

While information technology usage is expanding in the Black community, and the Internet is being used, there is another side to the technology issue. Many times information hardware and software are used as a surveillance mechanism to provide information about Black people to various agencies and corporations. Some writers have been concerned that the proliferation of huge information systems allows information controllers to impinge upon the personal privacy of individual Black citizens. In Chapter 3, Oscar H. Gandy Jr. addresses the questions of personal privacy and the orientation and concerns of African Americans about personal information-gathering technology and its impact on the Black community. This chapter is a reprint of an article entitled "African Americans and Privacy: Understanding the Black Perspective in the Emerging Policy Debate" that was published in the December 1993 issue of the *Journal of Black Studies*. It is included here because it leads an important perspective to run discussion of Blacks and information technology and there are hardly any other studies are to be found that deal with how the proliferation of information-gathering technology may impact the personal lives of African Americans.

CHAPTER 1

More Than You Think: African Americans on the World Wide Web

John T. Barber and Stephen Jones

INTRODUCTION

The Internet with all of its components and applications is probably the most visible and omnipresent mechanism of the Information Society. One of the leading discussions among pundits about this growing network is whether or not Blacks and others who have been historically disadvantaged in America can reap the benefits of this global network of information (Abrams, 1997; Holmes, 1997; Kahin & Keller, 1995; Novak, Hoffman, & Venkatesh, 1997). We feel that as they move into the twenty first century, African Americans are taking advantage of the many opportunities offered by the Internet and the World Wide Web. As Novak & Hoffman (1998) point out in their work on bridging the digital divide between Blacks and Whites in America, African Americans are making unrecognized progress in using Internet technology: "There are more African Americans on-line than you think. Our statistically derived estimate of the number of African American Web users is considerably larger than the current popular estimate of one million that is frequently reported in the popular media... Over five million African Americans have ever used the Web in the United States as of January 1997" (p. 11). The writers concluded that African Americans are already on-line in impressive numbers and predicted that continued efforts to develop on-line content targeted to African Americans would be successful.

This chapter outlines the development of the Internet and the Web, explains how the public came to use this network designed for military, scientific, and academic research, and discusses the kinds of information that is being published about Black people and their relationship to these technologies. It then focuses on African Americans as Internet users and the emergence of Web sites that are targeted toward the Black community. We present a classification of the types of African American-oriented sites that are proliferating on the Web and list more than 100 Black-oriented Web sites according to this classification. We also argue that by constructing these Web sites and using others that are targeted toward them, Black people are building and participating in a virtual community in cyberspace. Readers of this chapter can use the Appendix as a guide, visit some of these sites, and observe for themselves the growing array of places on the World Wide Web that are presented by, about, and for African Americans. We conclude that despite the growing gap between Blacks and Whites in Internet use, Blacks are making steady progress in mastering this technology and using it to the benefit of the Black community as the Information Society continues to evolve at the beginning of a new millennium in America. Finally, we recommend that Blacks begin to rely on Black institutions, businesses and corporations, churches, and community organizations to provide initiatives for closing the digital divide and informational gaps in the Information Society.

DEMYSTIFYING THE INTERNET AND WORLD WIDE WEB

Before discussing the participation of African Americans on the Internet and the World Wide Web, it would be well to give some background information on the nature and development of these computer technologies. The Internet was not initiated to be used by either Blacks or any other members of the general public but was set up by the Defense Department and private industry to carry out military research. In the 1960s and 1970s the U.S. Department of Defense's Advanced Research Projects Agency (ARPA) and a small group of computer programmers and electronic engineers who wanted to redesign the way computers were operated created a computer network called ARPANET (Rheingold, 1996). By the early 1980s scientists outside military-related research wanted to make use of such computer networks, and in the early 1980s ARPANET was divided into two parts: ARPANET for research and MILNET for military operational use. The system of networks that emerged in the 1980s was called ARPA Internet, then just Internet.

As time passed, many people who were originally unauthorized to do so wanted to make use of the Internet (Rheingold, 1996). At this point, the National Science Foundation (NSF) stepped in, established CSNET, a science-oriented network within Internet, set up BITNET for nonscientist scholars, and funded the development of other regional research networks. NSF also helped all universities in the nation to connect to supercomputers and funded the development of a backbone network called NSFnet, to which all regional networks were connected. This set of interconnected networks has come to be known as the Internet. This network of networks continues to grow fantastically, according to Baldwin, McVoy, and Steinfield (1996): "Moreover, analyses of the numbers of new hosts connecting to the Internet show it virtually doubling in size every year since 1988. At this rate, John Quartermann, a leading Internet analyst, has commented the world could be connected by the Year

2003!" (p. 70). The exponential growth of the Internet makes it difficult to keep up with the number of people who are users at any particular time.

For millions of people who are outside the military, scientific, academic, and general research fields, the Web has become the gateway to the Internet. The Web is not identical to the Internet but is one of many Internet-based communication systems (CERN, 1998). It was invented in late 1990 by Tim Berners-Lee, a computer scientist at CERN, a nuclear research center in Switzerland. Berners-Lee and Robert Cailliau wrote the first browser-editor and server for the Web, along with most of the communications software. They also defined the terms that are so familiar to users today: Uniform Resource Locator, (URL), Hypertext Transport Protocol (HTTP), and Hypertext Markup Language (HTML).

Although laypersons now use the Web, it was originally developed to be used so that physicists could collaborate on high-energy projects while working at different universities and institutes all over the world. Early in 1993 the National Center for Supercomputing Applications at the University of Illinois released the first version of the Mosaic browser (CERN, 1998). This was one of the most significant breakthroughs in making the Internet and the Web easy to use by home consumers (Baldwin, McVoy, & Steinfield, 1996).

Mosaic allowed users to point and click to retrieve text and other material without using complicated computer language. After the Mosiac and other browsers such as Netscape were introduced, the number of Web users began to rapidly increase. By late 1993 there were over 500 known servers, and the Web accounted for 1% of Internet traffic (CERN, 1998). By the end of 1994 the Web had 10,000 servers, of which 2,000 were commercial, and 10 million users. In 1997 there were more than 650,000 servers and 1,000 new ones appearing every day. The Web is now so big that it is difficult to find reliable statistics. It is generally thought that there are now more than 700,000 public information servers through which users can access over 50 million pages of information (CERN, 1998). It has also been estimated that the Web now represents as much as 60% of Internet traffic. Recent studies show that the number of Internet users over the age of 16 in the United State and Canada has reached 79 million, while the number of people buying products and services via the Web has hit 20 million (CommerceNet, August 1998).

CommerceNet and Nielsen Media Research, two major media market research firms, have collaborated on Internet demographics surveys since 1995. CommerceNet/Nielsen initial Internet Demographics Survey (IDS) was the first population-projectable survey regarding Internet usage (CommerceNet, 1996). The IDS was also the first Internet usage survey to provide information on Blacks and other ethnic groups. Over the past few years, releases of CommerceNet/Nielsen studies have provided valuable information about Internet usage for industry marketers and other interested researchers.

The CommerceNet/Nielsen reports also merit a brief review here before we move on to discuss Blacks' usage of the Internet and the World Wide Web. CommerceNet/Nielsen research reports projected that in 1995 the populations of the Internet and the Web were 22 and 14 million, respectively. Further studies revealed that Internet access in the United States and Canada population grew 50% from August/September 1995 to March/April 1996 (CommerceNet, August 1996).

In 1997 the two companies announced that the IDS for that time period revealed that the number of users had doubled and that a "startling increase" in Web users actively shopping on the Internet was taking place (CommerceNet, March 1997). CommerceNet/Nielsen, in the same year, also spoke of a significant narrowing of the gap between the number of male user and the number of female users. Later that year CommerceNet/Nielsen reported that in the United State and Canada, nearly 15 million people 16 years of age and older were frequent Web users. Frequent users were defined as persons having used the Web within the 24 hours prior to being surveyed (CommerceNet, April 1997). By the end of 1997, according to their reports, there were more than 58 million adults using the Internet in the United State and Canada (CommerceNet, December 1997).

The companies reported that 48 million people were using the Web in early 1997 and that the number of people who made purchases on the Web had reached almost 10 million. At this time, there were 59 million E-mail users age 16 and older in North America—26% of the total population—and four out of five of them were Internet users. By the summer of 1998 they reported that the number of Internet users over the age of 16 in the United States and Canada had reached 79 million and that the number of people buying products and services via the Web was 20 million (CommerceNet, August 1998). The study also projected that the number of people checking out or comparing products and services on the Web was 48 million.

Although the CommerceNet/Nielsen research material contains racial and ethnic data, no reports have been released that focus solely on African Americans' use of the Internet and the Web. Research on this topic is generally scarce, but what exists tends to fall into two categories. The first type, which we call "potential electronic consumer" research, is mainly concerned with the number and types of African Americans who can be targeted as buyers on the commercialized Internet and Web of the future. The second category, which we call "falling through the Net" research, deals with African Americans' lack of access to personal computers (PC) and the Internet and the growing gap between Blacks and Whites in PC and Internet usage. This gap is sometimes referred to as the "digital divide." Significant findings from both types of research are highlighted in the next two sections of this chapter.

TARGETING BLACKS FOR ELECTRONIC COMMERCE

Under the leadership of Donna Hoffman and Thomas Novak, Project 2000 at Vanderbilt University has done some insightful work on the relationship between African Americans and the Internet and the Web. Project 2000 is a five-year-sponsored research effort devoted to the scholarly investigation of the marketing implications of commercializing the Web and other emerging electronic environments. The researchers at Project 2000 used the CommerceNet/Nielsen research reports, performed analyses on them, and culled material that provides a clearer picture than had been previously available of African Americans and their relationship with the Internet and the Web. They emphasized the reasons that it is important to understand this relationship (Novak, Hoffman, & Venkatesh, 1997):

In 1997 Novak, Hoffman and Venkatesh found that African Americans were less likely than Whites to have ever used the Internet and the Web, from any location, including home, work, school, other, and to have used the Web in the previous 6 months. Blacks were also less likely than Whites to own a computer and have a PC access at work. They stated that the gap between Blacks and Whites in computer ownership might have been the key explanation for corresponding gaps in Internet and Web usage. They also found that there were 3.9 million African American Web users, of which 1.36 million stated they used the Web in the past week and concluded that there are more African Americans actively on-line than had been reported in the popular media up to that time.

In 1998 Novak & Hoffman asserted in their working paper entitled "Bridging the Digital Divide: The Impact of Race on Computer Access and Internet Use" that "race differences in Web use may diminish with experience." This time their research indicated, among many other findings, that Blacks and Whites were highly comparable in use of the Web and that there were no statistically significant differences between Black and White Web users in education, household income, gender, or presence of children in the home. The only exception was that Black Web users were more likely to be ages 16 to 24. Black users were also more likely to be both newer and less frequent users of the Internet. Finally, Blacks were more likely solely to rely on an on-line service rather than an Internet service provider as their only means of Internet access from home.

In 1999 Hoffman and Novak analyzed CommerceNet/Nielsen Internet Demographic Study data collected in 1996, 1997, and 1998 to determine if there were changes in Blacks' and Whites' Internet and Web use over time. In general, they found that Blacks were less likely than Whites to indicate that they had ever used the Web for business purposes. African Americans were more likely to state they used the Web most frequently at school and for academic use, and Whites were more likely to state they used the Web most frequently at home and for personal use. An interesting finding, however, was that African American Web users reported using multimedia Web applications slightly more frequently than White Web users. African Americans were also slightly more likely to state they frequently used the Web to perform audio/video conferencing, run Java applications, and receive audio/video.

In this study of overtime Internet use, the researchers also reported demographic profiles of Black and White Web users. African American Web users were more likely to be under 25, across all three surveys. Overall, Web users were more likely to be under 46 years of age. Web users were most likely to be professional, and white-collar, people and to be students, regardless of race. The percentage of African American Web users who were blue-collar workers more than tripled over time.

Where income was concerned, the researchers found that 59.73% of African American Web users had household incomes above $40,000 in 1997, compared with 71.01% of White Web users. This gap did not diminish over time. Of African Americans with no Internet access, 80.72% had household incomes less than $40,000 in 1997, compared with only 60.9% of Whites with no Internet access. Thus, among African Americans, the income-driven "digital divide" appeared larger than for Whites. Further, it did not diminish over time.

They found, however, that the number of Black Web users did change over time and that by 1998 almost 22% of African Americans had ever used the Web, amounting to over 5 million African Americans in June 1998 who had used the Web. Hoffman and Novak (1999) stated: "It is apparent that African American Web users have made significant gains in Web use. Indeed, the gaps are diminishing rapidly. The gap in Web use at home has decreased dramatically (even as the overall PC penetration rate among African Americans stagnates) and African Americans now appear to be more likely than Whites to have ever used the Web from work, school or other locations" (p. 18).

According to the researchers, gaps in general Web access and use between African Americans and Whites appeared to be driven by whether or not there was a computer present in the home. They concluded that access to a personal computer, whether at home, work, school, or somewhere else, was important because it was the dominant mechanism for getting on-line. Since individuals who own a home computer are much more likely than others to use the Web, they suggested that programs that encourage home computer ownership and the adoption of inexpensive devices that enable Internet access over the television be aggressively pursued, especially for African Americans.

FALLING THROUGH THE NET AND THE WEB

Although African Americans have been going on-line in increasing numbers over the past few years, a great deal of attention has been given to the fact that they lag behind European Americans in the use of the Internet. The National Telecommunications and Information Administration (NTIA), for example, reported in reports called "Falling through the Net" that while the ownership of personal computers has grown significantly among African Americans, they continue to lag far behind Whites in computer ownership and on-line access. The rates for on-line access are nearly three times as high for Whites as for Blacks (U.S. Department of Commerce, 1995; National Telecommunications and Information Administration 1998 and 1999). Consequently, this agency concludes that the "digital divide" between Blacks and Whites in America is increasing rather than decreasing as time goes on.

In an attempt to identify over 1 million African Americans who were active Internet participants, Net Genesis Corporation (1995) assessed the progress of African Americans on the Internet in 1995 and found that they were acquiring domain names and establishing their own sites with assistance from local service providers. Freedom Group, Inc., a Black-owned Web site development and Internet consulting firm, also implemented efforts to demonstrate that there were at least a million African American users on the Internet (EverythingBlack.Com, 1999). In 1997 and 1998 this company conducted investigations on their Web site: *EverythingBlack.Com*. The methodology for the research was on-line surveys that asked questions of visitors to the Web site. More than 5,000 people responded to each survey, and the findings from the later survey indicated that:

1. Most of the respondents were 26 to 40 years old.

2. Most respondents had been using the Internet two to four years.

3. The greatest number of respondents was female.

4. The greatest number of respondents had a college degree.

5. The household income of the greatest number of respondents was below $32,000.

6. The majority of respondents indicated that they did not make a purchase on the Internet in 1997.

7. Nearly 100% of the respondents considered themselves to be Black.

The EverythingBlack.Com (1999) survey results Web page states: "The good news is that there are over five million Black people on the Internet! The bad news is that we are behind in getting on the Internet and many folks, including us, don't seem to be concerned about catching up."

A DIFFERENT PERSPECTIVE

From all of this research, one could conclude that while Blacks lag behind Whites in Internet use, those who have access use the Internet and the Web in a fashion comparable to that of their White counterparts. Another way to summarize it is to say that those Blacks who have not fallen through the Net into the digital divide might be customers who are as viable on a commercialized Web as Whites or anyone else. In any case, researchers thus far seem to be mainly concerned with the extent to which African Americans can access the Internet and the Web and the probability that they will be consumers of goods sold on a commercialized Web.

Looking at it from a different perspective, we wish to pose another line of inquiry: To what extent are African Americans using the Internet and the Web to enhance the position of the Black community in the emerging Information Society? As African American educators, our day-to-day observations of Blacks and their interaction with Internet technologies inform us that many different types of Blacks are on-line and that they use Internet technologies for varied purposes in order to address issues and solve problems that they encounter in the real world (detailed examples of this are given in Chapter 11 of this book, where Jabari Simama expounds on the movement of African Americans from "Civil Rights to Cyberrights").

We have noticed that the types of African Americans on the Internet cover a broad spectrum. African American children are getting on-line at school and at home. They frequently use it as a resource for completing reports and school assignments and just to have fun. Children are also motivating their parents to purchase fun interactive software. African Americans are purchasing reading, writing, and math software to excite their children about learning. Free shareware software that helps children to learn according to their own unique learning style is abundant on the Internet.

African American teenagers are Internet users, too. They use E-mail messages to local friends and to their parents who are working. They receive messages and respond to them by the click of a button, and they search on-line libraries for information to complete school projects. Teenagers are searching for shopping opportunities as an alternative to spending time at a mall. One moment they are using the Internet to begin book reports or to start class projects, and in the next moment they transition to other kinds of fun activities.

African American adults are getting on the Internet to pay bills, organize social activities, and share information. African Americans realize the Internet can save them time and energy. The convenience of 24-hour payment services makes it attractive to pay on-line, and African Americans are banking on-line. The number of African American Internet users is small but is growing as more adults become less fearful about going on-line.

African American senior citizens won't be left behind in the Internet revolution. In fact, many African American senior citizens have more time to spend on-line than those who are less mature. Older Blacks are surfing the Internet to find information about senior programs and projects that are beneficial for their personal development. They may go onto a government Web site to learn about special benefits for seniors and to find information that may help them to receive discounts on health products. Seniors are not afraid to conduct business on the Internet and are establishing Web sites so they can communicate with the world.

ESTABLISHING A COMMUNITY IN CYBERSPACE

All of the aforementioned Internet activities by African Americans might well be expected. Howard Rheingold (1996) makes the point in his book *The Virtual Community* that "whenever Computer Mediated Communication (CMC) comes to a group of people anywhere in the world, they inevitably build virtual communities with it." CMC allows groups to use technology such as the Internet to create opportunities for education and learning, create new opportunities for participatory democracy, establish countercultures, and use machines to empower themselves (Jones, 1995). It also allows them to communicate social information, create group-specific meanings, form group-specific identities, form relationships, and create norms for interacting in these groups (Baym, 1998). Others have discussed how the Internet can be used as a vehicle for empowering and strengthening communities (Anderson, & Melchior, 1995).

In addition to facilitating community building at the global level, the Web facilitates neighborhood-level community building. Dertouzos, (1997) points out that virtual neighborhoods started three decades ago on time-shared computers as bulletin boards and persist until today as news groups. Novak, Hoffman, and Venkatesh, (1997) stated that in the future, neighborhood Web sites emerging as an important aspect of cyberspace should be expected and that these Web sites will parallel the ethnic profiles of the corresponding physical communities. There seems to be common agreement among writers that virtual communities and neighborhoods are built around real-world interests and needs that cause people to go on-line to share information and solutions to problems with others who have those needs and interests.

As the twentieth century closes, African Americans seem to be using CMC in this manner. African Americans are using the Internet and the Web, for example, to perform a variety of activities that are common to communities in the real world, including voicing political opinions, establishing social interactions, conducting business affairs, and dealing with health issues. They are also using the technology for activities such as artistic expression, storytelling, and entertainment and games. As with many other groups, they are using the Internet to establish their identity in cyberspace (Castells, 1997; Poster, 1998).

In the political arena, African Americans' opinions regarding federal, state, and local policies are critical to the representation of the public's total opinion on government decisions. For example, African Americans understand that there are many issues regarding the recent push to end affirmative action, and they have developed numerous Web sites to address this issue. African American organizations have also created Web sites in response to this attack on fair employment opportunity. For many Blacks, corresponding with politicians and government officials by telephone or mail is slowly becoming the activity of the past since all politicians at the federal level of government are accessible by the Internet (Hutting, 1997). Going on-line has increased the likelihood of an immediate response from senators and congresspersons. African Americans are sending thousands of messages to senators and congresspersons and letting government officials know their opinions.

The Internet allows African Americans to conduct political research without leaving their homes. They are making decisions based on current information, and they E-mail their responses to the appropriate public official. African Americans are E-mailing opinions on social, economic, academic, and moral issues critical to having a diverse population. African Americans are also gathering information from various government home pages and Web sites. African Americans conduct research using government data and reports. African Americans who are studying law or who practice as professional lawyers use their knowledge and technology, such as the Internet, to form critical opinions about the injustices that exist in the political system.

At the same time that using the Internet has changed the way Black people participate in political affairs, it has also changed the way that they socialize. Shields (1996) has elaborated on the various forms of Internet communication that Blacks and others can access when they go on-line, including interactive forums, E-mail, focus groups organized around particular issues of interest, and teleconferences that offer video discussions. African Americans are using such technology to let people in Africa know their circumstances immediately, and they respond with little difficulty. At no other time in history have we witnessed the tremendous explosion of technology used in African American communities. African Americans have cell telephones, pagers, fax machines, laptop computers, and computer hardware in their homes and business offices. African Americans communicate from cars, on the street, and while on airplanes.

Kahin and Keller (1995) say Internet communications have allowed African Americans to escape the barriers of geographic and physical location. African Americans who own businesses are decreasing travel and telephone expenses by using the Internet. Blackwood, Moore, and Yee (1997) predict that over the next ten years, most businesses will either be on the Internet or be connected through some general access method. African American businesspersons are already advertising their products on the Internet and creating a new electronic economy in the Black community. African American businesspersons, for example, who want to establish electronic storefronts recognize the high cost of establishing a local store and choose the Internet as an alternative business opportunity. They realize that the cost of advertising, renting space, and communication is less expensive on the Internet. Turlington (1995) points out that the main feature of the Internet is the ability to distribute information about products and services from anywhere in the world. When businesspersons leave their office, their establishment is closed for the day. On the Internet, a businessperson's store never closes. African Americans are recognizing that, in the future, their businesses may not exist if they do not establish a presence on the Internet. According to Donovan (1997), the ability of the Web to increase business opportunities is revolutionary. African Americans buy, sell, and advertise on the Internet by establishing their own Web sites and Web pages. By doing this, they are beginning to form communities in cyberspace.

THE FORMATION OF THE AFRICAN AMERICAN COMMUNITY ON THE WEB

A virtual community is a community of people sharing common interests, ideas, and feelings over the Internet. Rheingold (1996) defines "virtual communities" as "social aggregations that emerge from the Net when people carry on those public discussions long enough, with sufficient human feelings, to form Webs of personal relationships in cyberspace." Research concerning on-line communities usually analyzes Usenet news groups, mailing lists, chat rooms, Multi-User Domains (MUDS), and Multi-User Object Oriented (MOO) domains (Baym, 1998). Mitra (1997) relates, furthermore, that most of this research has centered around investigations of Internet text-based news groups. Much of this research has focused on such topics as the dynamics of virtual community formation with the use of computer-mediated networks, the various patterns of such communication, and emerging norms within such communities.

Mitra (1997) also makes it clear that the term "community" is taking on a larger meaning as diasporic people who have moved away form their places of origin now use the Internet and the Web to serve communicative and community-building processes. Mitra (1997) expresses the need for researchers to move beyond the narrow analysis of "cybercommunity" as being text-based news groups available on the Internet.

Mitra (1997) states: "Only recently, with the explosion in user groups and WWW [World Wide Web] sites, is it now possible to examine some of the specific WWW sites that are related to unique groups. Such directions of research begin to acknowledge the fact that the Internet is now a more mature forum for communication and there are specific aspects of the Internet that can be examined in greater depth to draw conclusions about the way in which the Internet is being used by the large community of users" (p. 162).

We feel that African Americans form one such "large" community of users and that it would be well if researchers would begin to view them in this way. Today, African Americans are creating and using hundreds of Web sites on the Internet. Recognizing the importance of the information age, African Americans are getting on the Internet to share information and to exchange products and services. They are also developing educational resources, and on-line communication, responding to political and social issues, and creating informative Web sites to address specific needs of the African American community. We believe that all of this is tantamount to the emergence of an African American community in cyberspace.

African American Web sites are visible and quantifiable evidence of African Americans' community building with Internet and Web technology. Over the past few years, the Internet has seen the number of African American Web sites steadily increase. *Everything Black.Com*, a Black-owned and -run Web site, provides a list of nearly 1,000 Black Web sites. In the spring of 1999, E-mail was circulating the Net that stated: "After surveying 42,000 African American citizens on their favorite sites, we have created the following list of top sites based on popularity, content, design, and navigation. Please forward this message to others who are in search of quality African American programming on the Web." The list included more than 50 sites including *Netnoir.Com*; *Blackvoices.Com*; *Essence.Com*; *Vibe.Com*; *Blackenterprise.Com*; and *Losnegroes.Com*. This E-mail was forwarded to us from students at Howard and Morgan State Universities who knew of our interest in Blacks and the Internet. Although we never found the original source of the E-mail, we took this as further evidence of growing participation and interest in the Internet on the part of African Americans.

We recognize, however, that at the same time that many African American sites are proliferating; many others on the Web have come and gone. This pattern makes it difficult to determine exactly how many sites on the Internet are oriented toward African Americans or how they can be organized and classified into a framework that helps us understand them. After viewing hundreds of sites, including the ones listed in the E-mail, the authors of this chapter decided that African American Web sites address five types of issues within the Black community: political, social, educational, and cultural.

To test our thinking, we, along with a research assistant, collected information on hundreds of Web sites by consulting printed lists, on-line listings and links, and E-mails from friends and colleagues. We then attempted to reduce this data to 100 sites that could be classified according to our five categories.

1. Those listed under *Social* are devoted to improving the welfare and well-being of the African American community by creating links between individuals, groups, and organizations.

2. Sites listed under *Political* are concerned about political empowerment of Black people in Africa, America, and the African diaspora.

3. *Economical* sites deal with wealth-building activities of the Black community, especially the production, and distribution of products and services that meet the needs and demands of African American people.

4. Sites entered under *Educational* present sources of news and information, educational opportunities, historical data, and other material that aid the African American community to increase its knowledge.

5. Finally, the sites that are categorized as *Cultural* pertain to concepts, customs, art, entertainment, and other cultural aspects of the African American community.

Many of these sites serve multiple purposes, and most sites are frequently updated to provide Internet participants with the most recent information about their search topic (Eskow, 1997). Therefore, the Web sites were categorized according to what we felt was their main purpose. After the sites were selected, they were briefly described, often using the language that was used by the producers of the Web site. As a result, an annotated list of more than 100 Web sites is presented in the Appendix as a sample of typical sites that appeared on the Internet in the spring of 1999.

CONCLUSIONS

The notion persists among many that African Americans are falling behind in the technology race. Yet, more than 5 million African Americans are using the Internet, according to the recent research reports that we have discussed here. Internet users in the Black community cover the spectrum of age, education, and income and compare favorably with Whites in their use of the Internet for seeking information, transmitting messages, and conducting personal and professional business. Since many Blacks are bridging the divide, one could argue that some Blacks are pioneers on the electronic frontier who are establishing small communities along the information superhighway. In view of this, it may be necessary to refocus the discussion about Blacks in the communication technology race from how they are falling through the Net, to how they can increase their skills and knowledge of computers, gain access to such technology, and make optimal use of it for improving their well-being and prosperity in the real world.

As Jones (1995) cautions, the connections between computer-mediated community and the social and political worlds that users are part of off-line are unclear at this time. Rheingold (1996) states, moreover, that virtual communities may be only pseudocommunities. Their connection to the real world and whether they are real or pseudo will continue to be debated for some time. What we have demonstrated in this chapter, however, is that African Americans are using the Internet to present hundreds of Web sites that address the political, social, educational, and cultural problems and concerns of African Americans. As the Internet continues to evolve, more Blacks go on-line, so it seems safe to predict that this pattern will continue and that the Internet will become a major communication source for the Black community.

The downside to all of this, however, is that the emergence of the Black cybercommunity is minuscule in comparison to the explosive growth of the Web in general. With more than 1,000 Web sites, the quantity of African American sites seems paltry in comparison to nearly a billion Web pages that may exist. Blacks obviously have enjoyed a small beginning and have a long way to go to keep pace in the cyberspace race. Nevertheless, researchers and analysts must recognize their small beginning if we are to completely understand the Internet and its impact on all communities in the Information Society.

At the same time, we are mindful of what Investigate the Internet (1996), an interdisciplinary working group that critically examines the Internet, and others have said, that "the Internet may be just another form of social control through the control of information." It is important to understand whether or not Blacks will use Internet technology to control their own communities and destinies or be victims of information controllers who control their communities through technology. In light of this, further investigations of Blacks and the Internet and the World Wide Web might include the following questions:

1. As the price of personal computers continues to decline, are more African Americans gaining access to the Internet?

2. Are there any African American Internet controllers who provide service or computer space for Web site production and presentation?

3. How many Black companies, groups, organizations, and so on are being established to train African Americans to use the Internet and World Wide Web?

4. How many and what kind of Black companies design and present Web sites that serve the African American community?

5. What groups and organizations are taking the lead in building the Black community in cyberspace?

These and many other questions must be answered if we are to fully comprehend how Internet and World Wide Web technology impacts the Black community. Understanding how the Black community performs in this regard instructs our understanding of how these technologies impact the society as a whole. It is hoped that this chapter and the remainder of this book serve as a point of departure for such work and discussion.

RECOMMENDATIONS

Clearly, there is a widening digital divide in the Black community itself. On one side are the Blacks who are falling behind their more cyber-savvy brothers and sisters and practically everyone in the information technology race. They perhaps form that group that has been described as the urban poor and the urban underclass that cannot participate in virtual communities of the Information Society because they lack the requisite finances and skills to do so (Rifkin, 1995; Wilson, 1996). The dangers of this state of affairs and the need to bring about remedies for the digital divide by offering governmental programs, corporate intervention, and a general sharing between the information-rich and the information-poor have been pointed out by Novak, Hoffman, and Venkatesh (1997), Dertouszos (1997), and others. On a practical note, however, we feel that the immediate responsibility for rescuing Blacks who are "falling through the net" rests on the shoulders of those African Americans who are among the technologically astute and information-wealthy. They would be those Blacks we have discussed here who are constructing neighborhoods and communities along the information highway. They must pause to make sure that they do not become guilty of "redlining" their own kith and kin. We offer a few recommendations in this regard:

1. Historically Black colleges and universities, especially urban ones, should take the lead in developing programs that would provide training and education to the information-poor in the Black community. Perhaps this can be accomplished through alliances with NSF and corporations that have an interest in seeing Blacks as viable consumers on the commercialized Web.

2. Large Black corporations and companies, especially those involved in media and information businesses, should develop projects that defray the cost of computers and other information technologies for less fortunate African Americans. This might be accomplished through partnerships with urban and rural school systems that result in tax write-offs for such companies.

3. National Black organizations should continue to push for policy initiatives that ensure that African Americans gain access to the Internet and the Web and all information technologies that will improve conditions in the Black community. This may be accomplished by pressing for legislation that ensures universal access to the Web.

4. Black churches and community organizations should become community information centers where information technologies can be accessed by the information-poor so that they are connected to information that can enhance their prosperity and well-being. This may be accomplished through volunteerism and grants from corporate foundations and other philanthropic institutions.

Dertouzos (1997) warns that, "left to its own devices, the Information Marketplace will increase the gap between rich and poor countries and rich and poor people." If the Black community in cyberspace is going to be self-empowering, and if information technology is going to be used effectively to advance the Black community in the real world, then information-rich Blacks will have to take the initiative in closing the digital divide. They will have to take the lead in ensuring that the information marketplace (called the Information Society in this work) is not "left to its own devices."

APPENDIX: SELECTED AFRICAN AMERICAN SITES

Social

AAGA Home Page-www.aaga.com/- The official Web site of the African American Golf Association.

ACG96 EHLB: African American Males- pharminfo.com/meeting/ACG/ acg_pr8.html- Informs African American males about cancer, tobacco, and alcohol use.

The Africa Ring and the Africa International Ring- http://www.eec.co.za/ africa- Provides links for people who live on the African continent and people who are expatriates of Africa. The Rings were created to support the African Internet community by providing a focal point for all African home pages and Web sites.

The Aframian Webnet-www.tawcnet.com- A collage of links to various sites of interest to African Americans.

African American Groups and Events-www.emf.net/cheetham/kafans-1.html- Lists groups and events for African Americans on the West Coast.

African American HIV/AIDS Program Public-www.crossnet.org/hss/hsfacts/ aapsa/index.html- The American Red Cross site highlighting African Americans and AIDS.

African American Home Page-www.lainet.com/~joejones/director. Htm- Provides links to Afrocentric resources.

African American Shopping Mall-www.bnl.com/aasm/- Cyberspace access to Afrocentric products.

African American Web Connection-www.aawc.com/aawc.html- A directory of topics from politics to culture as they relate to the African American community, especially the family.

African American Woman's Web Guide-http://robynma.simplenet.com/ nianet/index/htm- A Web site devoted to African American women.

Afrikan Frontline Web Cruiser-www.globaldrum.com- Offers Web hosting with database, E-mail, and Front Page 98.

AFRONET-http://www.afronet.com- Offers a wide variety of information about African American communities around the nation.

The Black Health Net-www.blackhealthnet.com- Provides health information for African Americans.

The Black Market.Com-www.theblacketmarket.com./blksites.html- Provides links to topics for and about African Americans.

Black Seek Search Engine-www.blackseek.com- Provides links to Black business.

Everything Black.Com-www.EverythingBlack.com- Comprehensive resource that lists 900 Black-oriented Web sites.

For the Black Male-mars.superlink.net/edeering- Emphasizes improving the lives of male descendants of people of the African diaspora.

International Black Index Source Directory-www.blackindex.com- Provides channel for promoting people, culture, and heritage of the African diaspora.

Melanet-www.melanet.com- Provides platform for intellectual, economic, and spiritual expression of peoples throughout the African diaspora.

The National Society of Black Engineers-www.jhuapl.edu/NAPD/Contents.htm- A point of contact for African Americans pursuing careers in engineering.

NetNoir-http://www.netnoir.com- Helps businesses establish a presence on the Internet and provides channels for culture, news, entertainment, politics, and shopping.

The Organization of Black Designers-http://www.core77.com/OBD/welcome.html- A resource for individuals with a common interest in reaching out to others who need help and information about design careers.

The Virtual Afrocentric Repository-www.tawcnet.com/~awe/virtualy.htm- A listing of Web sites covering a wide range of subject matter for and about African Americans.

Ujamaa Trading Company-www.utco.com- A catalog of items created by Blacks for Blacks.

Universal Black Pages-www.ubp.com- Lists many African diaspora-related Web sites at one central location.

Political

American Civil Rights Review Mailbox-www.anet-stlcom/~civil/mailbox. html- An electronic mailbox devoted to receiving and posting views on civil rights in America.

Congressional Black Caucus Foundation, Inc-www.cbcfnet.org.- Provides up-to-date information on the political agendas and programs of the U.S. congressional Black Caucus.

The Freedom Network-http://members.aol.com/freedomnwk- Promotes the reeducation, organization, unification, mobilization, and complete liberation of African people in America.

Joint Center For Political And Economic Studies-http://www.jointctr.org- Provides access to research on public policy issues of special concern to African Americans.

NAACP-www.naacp.org- The home page of the National Association for the Advancement of Colored People.

National African American Leadership Summit-www.melanet.com/naals/- Lists events and discussions of the National African American Leadership Summit. Presents the Audit Report of the Million Man march.

National Civil Rights Virtual Tour-http://www.mecca.org/~crights/ cyber.html- Provides brief descriptions of important events in civil rights history.

National Coalition on Black Voter Participation-www.bigvote.org- Provides information on increasing Black voter registration and turnout and eradication of barriers to full political participation for African Americans.

The National Urban League-www.nul.org- The home page of The National Urban League.

Notes on Overcoming Black People's Objections to Black reparations-http://208.240.252.134/Slavery.htm/Index.html- Presents issues and ideas related to Blacks receiving reparations in America.

Welcome to Ebon Phoenix-http://members.aol.com/Ebon11111/EbonCommunity.html- A consortium of individuals committed to the political, economic, and spiritual prosperity of the Black community.

Economical

The African American Marketplace-http://stonesartgallery.com- Features Stones Art Gallery, one of the largest collections of fine artwork by African American artists, and Damali African Wear, a collection of fine African clothes.

African American Shopping Mall-http://www.bnl.com/aasm/pubs.html- The mall was created to give the African American merchant a place to showcase his or her wares and to offer products and services of interest to the African American community.

Ashanti Kente Cloth Stoles and Fashion Accessories-http://ally.ios.com/~nogomo19- Products include commencement stoles, Greek-letter stoles, and religious/clergy stoles. All stoles are handmade in West Africa, and customized orders are available.

Black Access Marketplace-http://home.navisoft.com/bam/index.htm- An Internet marketing, networking, and Web site design company. Also a Web site, Cybermall, that provides a place for products, ads, services, and information.

Black Business Network-www.blackbusinesses.com- Developed to establish a foundation for networking for Black communities and Black businesses and to be a resource center for Black communities across the globe.

Blacksilk-www.blsk.com- A fully Black-owned ISP (Internet Service Provider) based in White Plains, New York, and specializing in Web hosting and design for businesses and consumers.

The Buy Black Network-http://www.ibuyblack.com/Buyblack.htm- Represents a unique private initiative to organize and register Black entrepreneurs to provide a mechanism that encourages and facilitates Black America's support of Black owned businesses.

Coalition of Black Investors-http://www.cobinvest.com/index.html- "The place where Black Investors Communicate." Provides conferences, advisers, and a newsletter for Black investors.

Collard Enterprises Ltd.-www.collard~cards.com- A new line of greeting cards that takes a lighthearted look at the unique culture and sense of style of today's African American.

Destee Design and Publishing-http://www.destee.com/http://www.destee.com- A Black-owned company offering a line of Web design services.

Gettosake Comics-http://gettosake.hypermart.net- An African American comic book publisher that presents the character Chocolate Thunder, a hero in the tradition of Spider Man and Batman.

Imanis Paradise-http://www.imanisparadise.com- An on-line collection of handmade gifts by African Americans and African Caribbeans.

Inner City Software-http://www.intellitech.net/samples/InnerCitySoftware/index.html- The Web site of Inner-City Software of Boston This company develops Afrocentric and general-purpose software.

Keepsake Expressions-http://www.viamall.com/babyblue- Gifts and collectibles for the entire family, figurines, ornaments, baby collectibles, African American children's collection, and more.

Maxxis 2000 Inc-http://www.maxxis2000.com- A consulting firm that helps create African American wealth.

Mays Chemical Company-http://www.mayschem.com- A fully integrated chemical distributor offering chemicals and other related raw materials, cleaning and sanitation products, outsourcing services, consolidation, and materials management programs.

Mind, Body & Soul Enterprises-http://www.mbs-enterprises.com- Educational services focusing on mental, physical, and spiritual development.

Mypheduh Films, Inc.-http://www.sankofa.com- Distributors of African and African American cinema.

SFI Simeus Food International-http://www.simeusfoods.com/index.htm- A manufacturer of over 80 high-quality food products.

13scribes-www.13scribes.com- A state-of-the-art software engineering firm that recently kicked off a comprehensive effort to reverse the trend of computer illiteracy in the Black community. "Computers in the Hood" is designed to equip 2 million African American households with computers.

True Essence-www.trueessence.com- Specializes in body oils, including designer type and originals.

Web Masterpieces-http://www.Webmasterpieces.com- A Black woman-owned and operated Web design company.

Educational

African American History-www.msstate.edu/Archives/History/USA/ AfroAmer/afro.html-Contains pages on African American genealogy, in addition to *Atlantic Monthly* articles in Black history.

AFRICA NEWS on the World Wide Web-www.Africanews.com- Presents news from around the continent of Africa.

African and African American Collections-www.lib.berkeley.edu/ Collections/Africana/-University of California at Berkeley's collection of African and African American articles and essays featuring over 100,000 volumes and over 1,000 serial titles.

African American Heritage Research-www.luc.edu/libraries/cudahy/aahm/ aahmres.html- Presents research on African American science, history, literature, and other subjects.

The African American Mosaic-http://lcWeb.loc.gov/exhibits/african/intro. html- Provides access to the Library of Congress African American mosaic collections.

Afro-Americ@-www.afroam.org/index.html- Features news and information from around the nation that are of interest to African Americans.

Black/African Related Resources-www.sas.upenn.edu/African_Studies/ Home_Page/mcgee.html- Lists information storage sites (FTP, Gopher, Telnet, WWW, BBS, and databases) that contain a significant amount of information about Black or African people.

Black Electronic Network-www.ben.net- A national on-line information and services provider serving the general population from an African American perspective.

Black Enterprise On-line-www.blackenterprise.com- Provides business news, strategies, and resources for African American entrepreneurs, corporate executives, managers, and professionals.

Black Excel-http://cnct.com/home/ijblack/BlackExcel.html- A college admissions, selection, and scholarship service for African Americans.

Black Facts on Line-www.blackfacts.com- A search engine providing a gateway to a wide range of Black facts.

The Black World Today-www.tbwt.com- Created by a group of journalists, writers, artists, communicators, and entrepreneurs to provide information that will empower Black people globally.

Diaspora.Com-www.diaspora.com/books.html- Provides links to significant and important works and books about people of African descent. This is a Web site dedicated to nurturing a global Black network.

Eso Won Books-http://host.scbbs.com/~esowon- The Web page of one of the nation's largest Black bookstores, providing over 10,000 titles about the African/African American experience.

Essence On-line-www.essence.com- An on-line magazine chronicling the lifestyle of contemporary African American women.

The Faces of Science: African Americans-www.lib.lsu.edu/lib/chem/display/faces.html- Provides hyperlinks to profiles of African Americans in the sciences and engineering.

Fisk University-www.fisk.edu- The Web site of one of the oldest historically Black colleges in the country.

First Science Ph.D.'s Awarded to African Americans-www.lib.lsu.edu/lib/chem/display/first_phds.html- Highlights the first science Ph.D.'s awarded to African Americans.

Frederick Douglas Institute for African American Studies-www.rochester.edu/College/AAS/index.html- Developed by the University of Rochester to promote the development of African and African American studies programs.

Granite Broadcasting Corporation-http://www.granitetv.com/gbc/home.htm-
An entrepreneurial group broadcaster that owns and operates ten network-affiliated television stations and one radio station.

Historically Black Colleges and Universities-eric-Web.tc.columbia.edu/hbcu/
index.html- Provides links to historically Black institutions across the nation.
There are more than 100 Black institutions listed.

Howard University-www.Howard.edu- The Web site of the flagship of
historically Black colleges and universities.

Johnson Publishing Company, Inc.-http://www.ebony.com- The world's
largest Black-owned publishing company is the home of *Ebony, Jet*, and *EM*
magazines.

MG Publishing, Co. Home Page-www.mgpublishing.com- An electronic
bookstore that features the Publishers Black Literary Catalog of African and
African American authors.

Share Newspaper-www.sharenews.com- The on-line version of Canada's
largest ethnic newspaper exploring issues relevant to their Caribbean, Black,
African, West Indian, and Jamaican populations.

Urbanbiz-http://www.urbanbiz.com- Publishes an Internet product that reports
on the entire urban business industry, focusing not only on industry leaders but
on their lesser-known emerging counterparts as well.

USAfrica On-line-www.usafricaon-line.com- Provides an information link
between America and Africa and features from news and commentary from
around the African continent.

World African Network On-line-www.worldafricannet.com- Presents news,
sports, entertainment, and lifestyle information that is relevant to the global
African community.

Cultural

African American Historical and Cultural Museum-http://www.libertynet.
org/iha/tour/_afro.html- Provides access to the cultural and historical record of
African Americans in Philadelphia.

African American Pamphlets Home Page-http://lcWeb2.loc.gov/ammem/aap/ aaphome.html- The Library of Congress presents the Daniel A. P. Murray of collection writings chronicling African American history and culture from the early nineteenth century through the early twentieth century.

African American Resources-www.wwar.com/literature/african_american. html- Provides numerous links to African and African American poetry.

African Americans and the Media-www.nyo.com/hype- A Web site that presents a chapter from the book *Don't Believe the Hype*. It provides information about countering cultural misinformation about Blacks often presented in the mainstream media.

African and African American Poetry-www.uct.ac.za/projects/poetry/africa. htm- A joint project of Microsoft and BET to provide access to African and African American literature and poetry from around the world.

African American Depictions in American Media-www.pomona.edu/ REPRES/BLACKS/BINTRO.HTML- Presents a critical analysis of Black portrayals in the four areas of the American media, including news/journalism, movies, music, and literature.

African American Poetry Editorial Policy-www.hti.umich.edu/english/daap/ ed-policy.html- A database and search engine providing a perspective of early America as seen through the eyes of Black poets during the eighteenth and nineteenth centuries.

The California African American Museum-www.caam.ca.gov/- Provides information about the galleries of the California African American Museum (CAAM) in Los Angeles, where there are living treasures of African American art, history, and culture.

Catch-A-Fire-www.catchafire.com- Provides a wide range of cultural, political, and social information on African Americans.

MSBET-www.betnetwork.com- This Web page is a joint venture of Microsoft Corporation and Black Entertainment Television. It provides material on entertainment, movies on cable television, and news and information.

Museum of African American History-www.detnews.com/1997/metrox/ maah- This Web site is described as "gathering place of African American culture."

Negro Leagues Resources-www.negroleaguebaseball.com- Provides information on various topics pertaining to the Negro League.

Schomburg Research Center-www.nypl.org/research/sc/sc.html- Provides access to a national research library devoted to collecting, preserving, and providing access to resources documenting the experiences of peoples of African descent throughout the world.

Yahoo-Society and Culture-http://dir.yahoo.com/Society_and_Culture/ Cultures_and_Groups/Cultures/American__United_States_/African_American/ History/- Yahoo's search engine and links to information on African and African American society and culture.

Zora Neale Hurston-pages.prodigy.com/zora- Provides links to stories, essays, photographs, and other material concerning Zora Neale Hurston.

REFERENCES

Abrams, C. (1997, June 26). Diversity and the Internet. *Journal of Commerce*. [On-line]. Available: http://www.joc.com/search97cqi/s97_cqi?... 26resultstart%3D181%26ResultCount%3D108.

Anderson, T. E., & Melchior, A. (1995). Assessing telecommunications technology as a tool for urban community building. *Journal of Urban Technology, 3* (1), 29-44.

Baldwin, T. F., McVoy, D. S., & Steinfield, C. (1996). *Convergence: Integrating Media. Information and Communication*. Thousand Oaks, CA: Sage.

Baym, N. K. (1997). Identity, body, and community in on-line life [Review of the books *Life on the Screen: Identity in the Age of the Internet; The War of Desire and Technology at the Close of the Mechanical Age; Cyberspace, Cyberbodies, Cyberpunk: Cultures of Technological Embodiment; Possible Worlds: The Social Dynamic of Virtual Reality Technology; Cultures of Internet;* and *Internet Culture*]. *Journal of Communication, 47* (4), 142-148.

Baym, N. K. (1998). The emergence of on-line community. In S. G. Jones (Ed.), *Cybersociety 2.0: Revisiting Computer-Mediated Communication and Community* (pp. 35-68). Thousand Oaks, CA: Sage.

Benson, J. M., & Gould, T. (1999, August). *Whither now? Five years of Internet research in mass communications, 1993–1995*. Paper presented at the Association for Education in Journalism and Mass Communication Convention, New Orleans.

Bettig, R. V. (1997). The enclosure of cyberspace. *Critical Studies in Mass Communication, 14*, 139-157.

Blackwood, F., & Yee, B. (1997). Compete using technology. *Home Office Computing*, 60-66.

Borland, J. (1998). Study: Blacks use Net less than Whites. *TechWeb the Technology News Site*. [On-line]. Available: http://www.techWeb.com/wire/story/TWB19980416S00 23.

Castells, M. (1997). *The Information Age: Economy, Society and Culture. Vol. 2: The Power of Identity*. Madden, MA: Blackwell.

CERN (1998). *A CERN Invention You Are Familiar With: The World Wide Web* [On-line]. Available: http://www.cern.ch/Public/ACHIEVEMENTS/Web.html.

CommerceNet (1996, August 13). Internet Hyper-Growth Continues, Fueled by New, Mainstream Users CommerceNet/Nielsen Announce Internet Study Results. The CommerceNet/Nielsen Internet Demographic Survey Press Releases. [On-line]. Available: http://www.commercenet.com/research/stats/7-13-96.html.

CommerceNet (1997, March 12). "Startling Increase" in Internet Shopping Reported in New CommerceNet/Nielsen Media Research Survey. Active Web Shoppers More than Double in the Past 18 Months. One-Third of All Web Users Have Made Purchases Based on Internet Information. The CommerceNet/Nielsen Internet Demographic Survey Press Releases. [On-line]. Available: http://www.commerce.net/research/stats/3-12-97.html.

CommerceNet (1997, April 8). Search Engines Most Popular Method of Surfing the Web. The CommerceNet/Nielsen Internet Demographic Survey Press Releases. [On-line]. Available: http://www.commerce.net/research/stats/4-8-97.html.

CommerceNet (1997, December 11). Electronic Commerce on the Rise according to CommerceNet/Nielsen Media Research Survey Number of Shoppers Increases; E-mail Usage Pervasive. The CommerceNet/Nielsen Internet Demographic Survey Press Releases. [On-line]. Available: http://www.commerce.net/news/press/121197.html.

CommerceNet (1998, August 24). Number of Internet Users and Shoppers Surges in United States and Canada. New Study Shows Users at 79 Million. Purchasers Double in Nine Months. The CommerceNet/Nielsen Internet Demographic Survey Press Releases. [On-line]. Available: http://www.commerce.net/news/press/19980824.html

CommerceNet (1998, October 8). Shoppers Filling On-Line Carts with Books, Computer Stuff. Study Shows Jump in Book, Hardware and Software Sales. The CommerceNet/Nielsen Internet Demographic Survey Press Releases. [On-line]. Available: http://www.commerece.net/news/press/19981008.html.

Dertouzos, M. L. (1997). *What Will Be: How the New World of Information Will Change Our Lives*. New York: HarperEdge.

Donovan, John J. (1997). *The Second Industrial Revolution: Reinventing Business on the Web*. Upper Saddle River, NJ: Prentice-Hall.

Elmer, G. (1997). Spaces of surveillance: Indexicality and solicitation on the Internet. *Critical Studies in Mass Communication, 14*, 182-191.

Eskow, D. (1997). Finding It Fast on the Web. *Home Office Computing*, 61-64.

EverythingBlack.Com (1999). [On-line]. Available: http://www. Everythingblack.com/Resources/survey/.html

Gaskins, J. E. (1997). *Corporate Politics and the Internet*. Upper Saddle River, NJ: Prentice-Hall.

Hoffman, D. L. & Novak, T. P. (1999, May 18). *The Evolution of the Digital: Examining the Relationship of Race to Internet Access and Usage Over Time*. Unpublished manuscript.

Holmes, Tamara E. (1997, February 20). Seeing a Future with More Blacks Exploring the Internet. *USA Today*.

Interrogate the Internet (1996). Contradictions in cyberspace: Collective response. In R. Shields (Ed.), *Cultures of Internet: Virtual Spaces, Real Histories, Living Bodies*. London: Sage, pp. 125-132.

Jones, S. G. (1995). Understanding community in the information age. In S. G. Jones (Ed.), *Cybersociety: Computer-Mediated Communication and Community*. Thousand Oaks, CA: Sage, pp. 10-35.

Kahin, B., & Keller, J. (1995). *Public Access to the Internet*. Cambridge: MIT Press.

Mitra, A. (1997). Diasporic Web sites: Ingroup and outgroup discourse. *Critical Studies in Mass Communication, 14*, 158-181.

National Telecommunications and Information Administration (1998, July). *Falling Through the Net II: New Data on the Digital Divide*. [On-line]. Available: http://www.ntia.doc.gov/ntiahome/net2/.

National Telecommunications and Information Administration (1999, July). *Falling Through the Net: Defining the Digital Divide*. [On-line]. Available: http://ntiant1.ntia.doc.gov/ntiahome/fttn99/contents.html.

Net Genesis Corporation (1995*). Building a World Wide Web Commerce Center*. New York: Wiley Computers.

Newhagen, J. E., & Sheizaf, R. (1996). Why communication researchers should study the Internet: A dialogue. *Journal of Communication, 46* (1), 4-13.

Novek, E. M. (1999, August). The virtual "good neighborhood": Tracking the role of communication in residential segregation. Paper presented at the Association for Education in Journalism and Mass Communication Convention, New Orleans.

Novak, T. P. & Hoffman D. L. (1998, February 2). *Bridging the gap: the impact of race on computer access and Internet use*. [On-line]. Available: http://www2000.ogsm.vanderbilt.edu/papers/race/science.html.

Novak, T. P., Hoffman, D. L. & Venkatesh, A. (1997, October 24). *Diversity on the Internet: the relationship of race to access and usage*. [On-line]. Available: http://www2000.ogsm.vanderbilt.edu/papers/aspen/diversity.on.the. internet.oct24.1997.html.

Parks, M. R., & Floyd, K. (1996). Making friends in cyberspace. *Journal of Communication, 46* (1), 80-97.

Poster, M. (1998). Virtual ethnicity: Tribal identity in the age of global communications. In S. G. Jones (Ed.), *Cybersociety 2.0: Revisiting Computer-Mediated Communication and Community*. Thousand Oaks, CA: Sage.

Rheingold, H. (1993). *The Virtual Community*. Available on-line:http:www. rheingold.com/vc/book/intro.html.

Rheingold, H. (1996). *The Virtual Community*. [On-line]. Available: http:// www.well.com/user/hlr/vcbook/.

Rifkin, J. (1995). *The End of Work: The Decline of the Global Labor Force and the Dawn of the Post Market Era*. New York: G. P. Putnam's Sons.

Shields, R. (1996). *Cultures of Internet: Virtual Spaces, Real Histories, Living Bodies*. Thousand Oaks, CA: Sage.

Turlington, S. R. (1995). *Walking the World Wide Web*. Chapel Hill, NC: Ventona Press.

U.S. Department Of Commerce (1995, July). *Falling Through the Net: A Survey of the "Have Nots" in Rural and Urban America*. Washington, DC: Author.

Wilson, W. J. (1996). *When Work Disappears: The World of the Urban Poor*. New York: Alfred A. Knopf.

CHAPTER 2

Blacks and Information Technology

John T. Barber and Willis G. Smith

The development of the Information Society is being driven, in large part, by advances in information technology. Castells (1989) has pointed out that it is in the electronic space of information systems and networks that those who utilize information technologies of the day will transact much of social, political, and economic enterprises of the future. *Black Enterprise* publisher Earl Graves in the magazine's March 1998 issue, summed up the implications of these developments for the Black community in an editorial entitled: "Staking a Claim on the Future": "As information remains the true currency of a capitalist, free-market economy, Black Americans must make every effort to master the information technologies that will be critical to our future—and more importantly, that of our children" (p. 11). The following analysis measures and describes the sector of the Black community that uses personal computers, cellular phones, cable TV, and other information technologies that are critical for this community to be a viable part of the Information Society.

BLACKS AND INFORMATION TECHNOLOGIES

Research on Blacks' adoption and use of information technologies falls into several categories. Some writers call attention to the gaps that exist between Blacks and other groups in accessing the information superhighway (Evans, 1995; Kahin, & Keller, 1995; Miller, 1996). Others emphasize that Blacks are at a socioeconomic disadvantage that impedes them from acquiring information technologies to improve their social condition (Red, 1988; Congressional Task Force on the Future of African Americans, 1989; Slater 1994; U.S. Congress, Office of Technology Assessment, 1995). They argue that Blacks' lack of capital renders them less likely to reap the benefits of the information age.

Still other researchers emphasize disparities in computer ownership by Blacks and Whites. The U.S. Bureau of the Census, for example, has reported in studies of computer use from 1984 to 1993 that Whites tended to have greater access to computers than Blacks. A more recent study by Quantum Electronic

Database Services (QED.), however, stated that factors other than race influence whether or not Blacks have computers in their homes (Parrish, 1997). The QED. findings demonstrate that income is a leading factor and that Blacks do purchase computers when they can afford them.

Different racial and geographic groups have concerned a few investigators of telephone penetration and computer and modem usage. The U.S. Department of Commerce's (1995) National Telecommunication and Information Administration's (NTIA) study on urban and rural American households that have telephones, modems, and computers, for example, reported that the Blacks in central cities and rural areas rank high among telephone and computer "have-nots."

Black Enterprise (BE), however, conducted a study of its readers and found that 88% of those surveyed rated themselves intermediate or expert in their computer skills and used a computer at home or work (Muhammad, 1996). They also used telephones, computers, and modems for conducting research on the Internet, E-mail, and other purposes. While limited to its readers, the BE survey suggests that Blacks are "more technologically savvy than they were given credit for" in the NTIA report.

Jorge Schement (1996) has pointed out in his study of minorities and new media that it is difficult to draw a concise picture of information technology adoption by Blacks and other minorities. Nevertheless, he made several general inferences. First, Whites, African Americans, and Latinos construct information environments in their homes that suit their needs but do not necessarily mirror each other. Second, ethnic groups are heavy users of media, and early adopters of products and subsidize the early growth of new service networks. Third, African Americans and Latinos continue to lag behind Whites in access to the National Information Infrastructure (NII) through the telephone and the PC. Fourth, extensive use of media among all groups tends to facilitate consumption patterns that assimilate them into mainstream American commercial culture.

In 1997, at the request of Vice President Al Gore, the NTIA revisited the "Falling through the Net" study of 1994 and came out with a new study: "Falling through the Net II: New Data on the Digital Divide." Some major findings of this study were that Blacks now lag even further behind Whites in their levels of personal computer ownership and on-line access. While the ownership of computers has grown among Blacks since 1994, White households are more than twice as likely to own computers as Black ones. White households also have a far higher telephone penetration level than Black ones.

A BROADER VIEW

Taken together, these studies do not provide simple answers to the question of how well African Americans are adjusting to the technologies of the information age. Too often the research is limited to whether or not Blacks have computers and telephones. We recognize a need to go beyond just looking at a few devices such as computers and telephones in analyzing the use of information technologies by Blacks. The U.S. government has described the nation's information infrastructure as one that includes a wide range of ever-expanding information equipment that builds foundations for living in the information age (Information Infrastructure Task Force, 1993). Such equipment includes cameras, scanners, keyboards, telephones, fax machines, computers, switches, compact discs, video- and audiotape, cable, satellites, optical-fiber transmission, microwavenets, TVs, monitors, printers, and much more. Mayer (1994) argues that the important new information technologies include cable TV (TV), interactive TV, compact discs, remote-control devices, satellite dishes, car phones, fax machines, telephone answering machines, video and teletext, and videocassette recorders, as well as modems and personal computers. Furthermore, the nation's telephone, cable, broadcast, and computer industries are rapidly moving to create an information system that integrates all of these technologies and allows users to interact in a variety of ways from any location at any time (Baldwin, McVoy, & Steinfield, 1996).

To determine if Blacks are mechanically equipped to participate equally with Whites in this type of environment, it is necessary to look toward a broad spectrum of technologies. It would be revealing to compare Blacks and Whites across their ownership and usage of a wide range of information technologies that will eventually be integrated in the emerging and expanding national information infrastructure. In this regard, the following questions seem pertinent:

1. To what extent do Blacks own information devices that allow them to make basic connections on the nation's information system in comparison to Whites?

2. To what extent are Blacks using information technologies that allow them to be interactive with the nation's emerging integrated information infrastructure in comparison to Whites?

3. Are Blacks keeping pace with Whites in the adoption of information technologies?

4. What are the demographic characteristics of Blacks that account for their adoption of information technologies in comparison to Whites?

The answers to such questions will help us to better understand the status of African Americans in the current technological environment as America continues to evolve as the world's leading Information Society.

A MARKET ANALYSIS APPROACH

To answer these questions, we analyzed telephone survey data collected on Black and White consumption of information technologies. The survey was conducted in 1996 in the top ten media markets in America by USA DATA, a firm specializing in media market research. Random residential service telephone numbers were obtained from these markets, and designated respondents living permanently in the contacted households completed telephone interviews. The data were collected as part of an extensive study of product and media use among adults age 18 or older residing in telephone households in New York, Los Angeles, San Francisco, Dallas, Philadelphia, Chicago, Detroit, Washington, Boston, and Atlanta. Large concentrations of Blacks and Whites live in these major urban markets, and they represent a geographical cross-section of the nation.

The survey was well suited to answering the queries of this study because the data collected provide a wide range of information technologies that are being used in the nation's expanding information environment. These technologies included cellular and car phones, long-distance telephone service, fax machines, telephone answering machines, basic cable TV service, cable pay-TV, videocassette recorders, personal computers, and on-line services.

In order to systematically describe the survey data in relationship to the questions posed here, the information technologies included in the survey were divided into two categories: connective and interactive. Each technology was classified according to its function, as illustrated in the following. "Connective" is a term coined here to refer to equipment that allows two users or machines to communicate with each other. Connective technologies allow the user to make basic connections to information systems and provide limited interactions, as in conversations between two parties. Interactive technologies allow the user to get a direct individual response from an information supplier such as a cable network or another user or users. Cable TV is included here because viewers can interact with cable services providers to get videos, movies, events, and other programs sent to them individually upon request. Cable TV is also a hybrid device, that can carry video and data and is sometimes used to carry computer services so that users can interact (Grant & Wilkinson, 1993). Interactive technologies also allow the users to interact with many users or information systems such as the World Wide Web.

Survey data on connective technologies were integrated with demographic data for each group to address the first question about Blacks' capability to make basic information connections. The demographic data, including gender, household income, and education, allowed us to look beyond a simple racial comparison of Blacks and Whites and their ownership of information technologies. The results are presented here in demographic profiles of Black and White owners of each connective and interactive technology (see Tables 2.1 through 2.4).

Before discussing the comparisons, it is important to note some fundamental differences in the two populations. As is the case with the nation as a whole, the number of Blacks in the top ten media markets is only a fraction of the number of Whites in those markets. Therefore, in the analyses of technologies presented here, the number of Whites who own information technologies is always far greater than the number of Blacks who own such information equipment. When reviewing the numbers, one should not take this to mean that the number of Blacks who own a particular technology is insignificant in comparison to the number of Whites. This is simply a function of the difference in the number of Blacks and Whites in the survey population.

TECHNOLOGY OWNERSHIP COMPARISONS

Our analysis revealed that Blacks in the nation's largest media markets own all of the connective technologies, including car and other cellular phones, fax

Information Technologies and Functions

Technologies	Functions
	Connective
Car or Cellular Phone	Connects two talkers without wires
Long-Distance Telephone Service	Connects two talkers over a distance
Fax Machine	Connects two machines for text transmission
Answering Machine	Connects a caller with a message recording device
	Interactive
Basic Cable TV	Presents video or data on request
Cable Pay-TV	Presents a specific show on request
Videocassette Recorder	Records a specific show when programmed
Personal Computer	Accesses computer networks on command
On-Line Service	Receives and sends text, sound, and data on request

machines, and answering machines, and they subscribe to long-distance telephone service (see Tables 2.1 through 2.4). Some interesting patterns emerge when the connective technologies are reviewed individually.

More than 2 million Blacks and 11 million Whites own car and cellular phones (see Table 2.1). In both racial groups, the majority of the owners are female. The largest age group among Blacks and Whites was the 35- to -54-year-old group. For both races, the largest income group was households earning $50,000 or more annually. In both racial groups, persons who had one to three years of college adopted more car and cellular phones than those in other educational groupings in this study.

Nearly 1 million Blacks in the survey paid $60 to $100 per month for long-distance (LD) telephone service, but around five times as many Whites paid the same amount for LD (see Table 2.4). Women, among both Whites and Blacks, outnumbered men in paying this amount for this service. In both racial groups, persons 35 to 54 years of age adopted LD at this price more than those in other age groups. Black households with incomes of $30,000 to $50,000 per year paid for this service the most among Black household income groups. Among Whites, however, households with an income of $50,000 or more per year adopted LD in greater amounts than other White households in the survey. In both racial groups, persons with one to three years of college adopted this amount of long-distance service more than others in educational groups in the survey.

More than .5 million Blacks in this survey adopted fax machines, and the majority of them were men (see Table 2.2). On the other hand, over 5 million Whites in the same population adopted such machines, with White men owning the greatest number. Black and White households with incomes of $50,000 or more adopted the most fax machines. In both racial groups, persons 35 to 54 adopted the most machines. Blacks with one to three years of college had the most fax machines, while White college graduates adopted the most fax machines in that group.

Over 5 million Blacks and 35 million Whites adopted answering machines, in the survey population. In both groups, women adopted more machines than men (see Table 2.3). Where age was concerned, in both racial groups, persons 35 to 54 years of age adopted the most answering machines. Black households that had incomes between $30,000 and $50,000 adopted the most machines, but White households that earned $50,000 or more had the most machines.

Table 2.1
Demographic Profile of Persons Who Own Car or Other Cellular Phones (Connective)

	Black	%	White	%
Total	2,021,840	100	11,827,770	100
Gender				
Men	967,080	47.8	5,767,200	48.7
Women	1,054,760	52.2	6,060,570	51.2
Age				
18 to 24	324,830	16.1	1,485,830	12.6
25 to 34	604,360	29.9	2,877,470	24.3
35 to 54	715,830	35.4	5,328,550	45.0
55+	376,820	18.6	2,135,920	18.0
Household Income				
<$10K	120,130	5.9	203,210	1.7
$10K to $30K	457,640	22.6	1,368,450	11.6
$30K to $50K	719,890	35.6	3,092,840	26.1
$50K Plus	724,180	35.8	7,163,270	60.6
Education				
HS Grad	673,110	33.3	3,389,880	28.7
Col 1 to 3	706,020	34.9	3,944,630	33.3
Col Grad	407,940	20.2	3,597,180	30.4
Postgrad	154,890	7.7	1,645,360	13.9

Table 2.2
Demographic Profile of Persons Who Have Long-Distance Telephone Service and Pay $60 to $99 per Month (Connective)

	Black	%	White	%
Total	958,050	100	5,253,100	100
Gender				
Men	466,660	48.7	2,509,010	47.8
Women	491,390	51.3	2,744,090	52.2
Age				
18 to 24	130,750	13.6	846,510	16.1
25 to 34	239,630	25.0	1,232,970	23.5
35 to 54	384,990	40.2	2,171,750	41.3
55+	202,680	21.0	1,001,870	19.1
Household Income				
<$10K	115,590	12.1	208,350	4.0
$10K to $30K	269,480	28.1	1,137,040	21.6
$30K to $50K	295,660	30.9	1,460,930	27.8
$50K Plus	277,320	28.9	2,446,780	46.6
Education				
HS Grad	368,280	38.4	1,446,980	27.5
Col 1 to 3	291,700	30.4	1,600,990	30.5
Col Grad	152,700	15.9	1,469,120	28.0
Postgrad	64,440	6.7	677,130	12.9

Table 2.3
Demographic Profile of Persons Who Own Home Fax Machines (Connective)

	Black	%	White	%
Total	520,920	100	4,834,660	100
Gender				
Men	287,900	55.3	2,759,950	57.1
Women	233,020	44.7	2,074,710	42.9
Age				
18 to 24	75,210	14.4	489,930	10.1
25 to 34	165,190	31.7	1,120,730	23.2
35 to 54	202,440	38.9	2,356,380	48.7
55+	78,080	15.0	867,620	17.9
Household Income				
<$10K	23,000	4.4	90,840	1.9
$10K to $30K	98,190	8.8	505,960	10.5
$30K to $50K	165,590	31.8	1,074,810	22.2
$50K Plus	234,140	44.9	3,16,3050	65.4
Education				
HS Grad	159,890	30.7	1,056,470	21.8
Col 1 to 3	178,470	34.3	1,692,730	35.0
Col Grad	140,750	27.0	1,839,640	38.0
Postgrad	62680	12.0	879,140	18.2

Table 2.4
Demographic Profile of Persons Who Own Telephone Answering Machines (Connective)

	Black	%	White	%
Total	5,766,060	100	35,911,010	100
Gender				
Men	2,714,580	47.1	17,857,380	49.7
Women	3,051,480	52.9	18,053,630	50.3
Age				
18 to 24	949,270	16.5	4,700,940	13.1
25 to 34	1,653,780	28.7	8,655,430	24.1
35 to 54	2,174,770	37.7	14,620,240	40.7
55+	988,240	17.1	7,934,400	22.1
Household Income				
<$10K	401,660	7.0	1,054,410	2.9
$10K to $30	1,668,620	28.9	6,775,140	18.9
$30K to $50K	2,015,170	34.9	11,128,750	31.0
$50K Plus	1,680,610	29.1	16,952,710	47.2
Education				
HS Grad	2,084,970	36.1	11,716,540	32.0
Col 1 to 3	1,980,740	34.3	11,368,730	32.0
Col Grad	1,033,330	17.9	9,824,710	27.3
Postgrad	382,170	6.6	4,501,220	12.5

Over 1 million Black people in the top ten markets surveyed had basic cable TV subscriptions, and 17 million Whites had such service (see Table 2.5). Black men outnumbered Black women in this category, while White women led White men in basic cable TV ownership. For both racial groups, persons 35 to 54 had the most subscriptions to basic cable TV. Black households with $30,000 to $50,000 in annual income adopted the most basic cable TV service, but White households with annual income of $50,000 or more had the most subscriptions. Persons who had one to three years of college had the most subscriptions in both racial groups.

As illustrated in Tables 2.5 and 2.6, far more Blacks subscribed to cable pay-TV (3.9 million) than those who had basic cable TV service (1.4 million). On the other hand, Whites subscribed to less cable pay-TV (15.7 million) than those who subscribed to basic cable TV (17 million). In both racial groups, women led men in the ownership of cable pay-TV. In both racial groups, persons 35 to 54 years of age subscribed to the most cable pay-TV. Among Black households, those that earned $30,000 to $50,0000 annually had the most cable pay-TV. White households that earned $50,000 or more had the most cable pay-TV services. In both racial groups, persons with one to three years of college had the most cable pay-TV.

Over 1.5 million Blacks and 7 million Whites adopted videocassette recorders (VCRs) in the survey population (see Table 2.7). More Black women than Black men adopted VCRs, but more White men adopted VCRs than White women. In both racial groups, persons 35 to 54 adopted the most VCRs. Black households that earned $30,000 to $50,000 annually had the most VCRs, while White households that earned more than $50,000 per year had the most machines. In both educational groups, persons with one to three years of college had the most VCRs.

Blacks in the top ten markets in America adopted all of the interactive technologies investigated in this study. Over 2 million Blacks in major media markets adopted personal computers (PCs) at the time of the survey, and, among this group, women adopted the most computers (see Table 2.8). The number of Whites in the survey who adopted PCs was ten times that of Blacks. White men adopted more computers than White women. In both racial groups, persons 35 to 54 years of age adopted the most computers. Black households with annual income of $30.000 to $50,000 adopted the most PCs and White households with an annual income of $50,000 or more had the most computers. Among Blacks and Whites, persons with one to three years of college adopted the most computers.

Although about 2 million Blacks adopted PCs, less than .5 million of them subscribed to on-line computer services (see Tables 2.8 and 2.9). While 20 million Whites adopted PCs, only 4 million of them subscribed to on-line computer services. In both racial groups, persons 35 to 54 years of age subscribed to the most on-line services. Among Blacks and Whites, households that earned $50,000 or more annually subscribed to the most on-line services. However, in the educational groupings, Black persons with one to three years of college adopted the most on-line services, while college graduates subscribed to the most on-line services in the White group.

Table 2.5
Demographic Profile of Persons Who Subscribe to Basic Cable TV (Interactive)

	Black	%	White	%
Total	1,448,970	100	17,074,470	100
Gender				
Men	797,900	55.1	8,480,550	47.9
Women	651,070	44.9	9,226,920	52.1
Age				
18 to 24	244,660	16.9	1,989,250	11.2
25 to 34	380,120	26.2	3,894,900	22.0
35 to 54	491,660	33.9	6,659,340	37.2
55+	332,530	22.9	5,232,980	29.6
Household Income				
<$10K	141,780	9.8	670,010	3.8
$10K to $30K	421,140	29.1	4,033,310	22.8
$30K to $50K	517,110	35.7	5,361,630	30.3
$50K Plus	368,940	25.5	7,642,520	43.2
Education				
HS Grad	480,530	33.2	6,074,050	34.3
Col 1 to 3	479,440	33.1	5,256,440	29.7
Col Grad	297,410	20.5	4,580,780	25.9
Postgrad	101,950	7.0	2,075,140	11.7

Table 2.6
Demographic Profile of Persons Who Subscribe to Basic Cable Plus Pay Channels (Interactive)

	Black	%	White	%
Total	3,997,430	100	15,724,860	100
Gender				
Men	1,760,130	44.0	7,647,150	48.6
Women	2,237,300	56.0	8,077,710	51.4
Age				
18 to 24	575,150	14.4	1,897,860	12.1
25 to 34	974,780	24.4	3,207,750	20.4
35 to 54	1,601,370	40. 0	6,898,180	43.9
55+	846,130	21.2	3,721,070	23.7
Household Income				
<$10K	259,010	6.5	444,980	2.8
$10K to $30K	1,203,630	30.1	2,834,070	18.0
$30K to $50K	1,379,180	34.5	4,805,410	30.5
$50K Plus	1,155,610	28.9	7,640,400	48.6
Education				
HS Grad	1,507,350	37.7	5,539,600	35.2
Col 1 to 3	1,337,130	33.4	4,698,890	29.9
Col Grad	649,610	16.2	3,907,960	24.8
Postgrad	243,760	6.1	1,709,970	10.9

Table 2.7
Demographic Profile of Persons Who Own a Videocassette Recorder
(Interactive)

	Black	%	White	%
Total	1,747,010	100	7,247,260	100
Gender				
Men	798,750	45.7	3,828,720	52.8
Women	948,260	54.3	3,418,540	47.2
Age				
18 to 24	288,150	16.5	1,210,220	16.7
25 to 34	521,540	29.8	1,821,440	25.1
35 to 54	652,710	37.4	2,832,530	39.1
55+	284,250	16.30	1,383,070	19.1
Household Income				
<$10K	119,730	6.8	253,260	3.5
$10K to $30K	557,080	31.9	1,520,600	21.0
$30K to $50K	571,400	32.7	2,221,750	30.7
$50K Plus	498,800	28.5	3,251,650	44.9
Education				
HS Grad	623,780	35.7	2,505,230	34.6
Col 1 to 3	591,880	33.9	2,157,080	29.8
Col Grad	304,690	17.4	1,697,780	23.4
Postgrad	105,540	6.0	744,970	10.3

Table 2.8
Demographic Profile of Persons Who Own a Personal Computer (Interactive)

	Black	%	White	%
Total	2,605,690	100	21,932,100	100
Gender				
Men	1,288,210	49.4	11,700,160	53.3
Women	1,317,480	50.6	10,231,940	46.6
Age				
18 to 24	447,460	17.2	2,836,550	12.9
25 to 34	830,290	31.9	5,132,930	23.4
35 to 54	1,050,610	40.3	9,973,630	45.5
55+	277,330	10.6	3,988,990	18.2
Household Income				
<$10K	177,240	6.8	490,540	2.2
$10K to $30K	633,760	24.3	3,132,420	14.3
$30K to $50K	942,410	36.2	6,283,270	28.6
$50K Plus	912,280	35.0	12,025,870	54.8
Education				
HS Grad	863,270	33.1	5,681,110	25.9
Col 1 to 3	894,440	34.3	7,369,860	33.6
Col Grad	605,290	23.2	7,208,000	32.9
Postgrad	247,180	9.5	3,436,860	15.7

Table 2.9
Demographic Profile of Persons Who Subscribe to an On-Line Information Service (Interactive)

	Black	%	White	%
Total	385,060	100	4,307,310	100
Gender				
Men	185,990	048.3	2,552,510	59.2
Women	199,070	51.7	1,754,800	40.7
Age				
18 to 24	58,260	15.1	619,420	14.4
25 to 34	116,230	30.2	1,156,660	26.9
35 to 54	148,470	38.5	1,929,290	44.8
55+	62,100	16.1	601,940	14.0
Household Income				
<$10K	17,200	4.5	90,680	2.1
$10K to $30K	62,250	16.2	403,550	9.4
$30K to $50K	114,910	30.0	1,039,100	24.1
$50K Plus	190,700	49.5	2,773,980	64.4
Education				
HS Grad	81,700	21.2	895,460	20.8
Col 1 to 3	145,870	37.9	1,492,180	34.6
Col Grad	118,770	30.8	1,662,760	38.6
Postgrad	52,010	13.5	796,590	18.5

RATE OF ADOPTION

To answer the question about Blacks' keeping stride with Whites in the adoption of information technologies, the percentage of ownership of connective and interactive technologies was calculated for each racial group (see Tables 2.1 through 2.9). The percentages demonstrate the proportion of each racial group that had adopted connective and interactive technologies at the time of the study. The percentages of ownership were further broken down into the demographic categories of gender, age, income, and education.

Calculating the proportions of each group that had adopted the connective and interactive technologies at the time of the study and comparing those proportions across demographic variables determined the rate of adoption. For example, 16.1% of Blacks 18 to 24 years of age adopted car or cellular phones at the time of the study, while only 12.6% of Whites of the same age adopted such technology (see Table 2.1). This age group of Blacks exhibited adoption rates of wireless phones in greater proportions than their White counterparts at the time of the study. Therefore, the adoption rate of Blacks was greater than that of Whites for this age group. The rate of adoption of connective and interactive technologies by each group was determined and compared in this manner, and the major findings are discussed next (see Tables 2.1 through 2.9).

Gender and Rate of Adoption of Connective Technologies. Black and White women had higher adoption rates than Black and White men in three connective technology categories: car and other cellular phones, long-distance service, and telephone answering machines (see Tables 2.1 through 2.4). For each of these technologies, women adopted more than 50% of the machines or services at the time of the study. Black and White men, however, led Black and White women in the adoption of fax machines, and these men adopted over 50% of fax machines at the time of the survey.

Age and Rate of Adoption of Connective Technologies. For both racial groups, persons 35 to 54 years of age adopted more connective technologies than persons in other age categories (see Tables 2.1 through 2.4). Blacks in this age category adopted connective technologies at a lesser rate than Whites in the same age category. It is worth noting, however, that Black youth, 18 to 34 years of age, outpaced Whites in the same age group in adoption of each connective technology except long-distance service (see Tables 2.1 through 2.4).

Household Income and Rate of Adoption of Connective Technologies. Black households in the $50,000 or more annual income category adopted the most car and cellular phones and fax machines among Black households at the time of the survey (see Tables 2.1 and 2.3). In this income category, Blacks had a lesser adoption rate than their White counterparts of car and cellular phones and fax machines. Black households in the $30,000 to $50,000 annual income category adopted the most long-distance service and answering machines among Blacks (see Tables 2.2 and 2.4). In this income category, Black households adopted long-distance service and answering machines at a greater rate than White households in the same income category. It should be noted, moreover, that at the less than $10,000 household income range, Blacks had a greater adoption rate in all connective technologies than their White counterparts (see Tables 2.1 through 2.4).

Education and Rate of Adoption of Connective Technologies. Black and White persons with one to three years of college adopted the most car and cellular phones and fax machines among their respective groups at the time of the study (see Tables 2.1 and 2.3). Blacks, however, with this amount of education had a greater rate of adoption for car and other cellular phones than their White counterparts. On the other hand, Blacks with one to three years of college had a lesser rate of adoption for fax machines than their White counterparts.

Black persons with a high school education adopted the most long-distance service among Black people at the time of the survey (see Table 2.2). Blacks with this amount of education had a greater adoption rate for long-distance service than their White counterparts. Whites with one to three years of college, however, adopted the most long-distance service among Whites. Whites with this amount of education had a slightly higher adoption rate for long-distance services than their Black counterparts.

Black and White persons with a high school education adopted the most answering machines in their respective groups at the time of the survey (see Table 2.4). Black people with this amount of education had a greater adoption rate for this technology than their White counterparts.

In summary, race is not the variable that determines the rate of adoption of connective technologies. The rate of adoption of connective technologies is similar among Blacks and Whites in some cases, and in others. For example, among persons with one to three years of college, there seems to be little difference (two percentage points or less) in the adoption rate of Blacks and Whites for technologies such as cellular phones, long-distance service, fax machines, and answering machines. In the demographic, group 18 to 24 years of age, Blacks led Whites in adoption rate by three or more percentage points in the adoption of cellular phones, fax machines, and answering machines. Let us now turn to the adoption of interactive technologies by each racial group according to gender, age, income, and education.

Gender and Rate of Adoption of Interactive Technologies. Black men had a higher adoption rate than White men in the adoption of basic cable TV (see Table 2.5). Black men adopted 55.1% of the basic cable TV service in the Black group, and White men adopted 47.9% of the basic cable TV service in the White group. Black women, however, had a lower adoption rate of basic cable TV than their White counterparts. Black women adopted 44.9% of the basic cable TV service, and White women adopted 52.1% of the service in their respective group.

For cable pay-TV, however, Black and White women had higher adoption rates than Black and White men (see Table 2.6). Black women adopted 56% of this service, and White women had 51.4% of this service. It should be noted that Black women outpaced all others in the gender category in the adoption of this technology. On the other hand, Black men had the lowest adoption rate of this technology in comparison to all others in the gender category.

For VCRs, Black women had a greater adoption rate than all others in the gender category (see Table 2.7). In the Black group, Black women adopted 54.3% of the VCRs, and Black men adopted 45.7% of these machines. In the White group, White men adopted 52.8% of the VCRs, and White women adopted the remainder.

Black women had a greater rate of adoption of PCs than their White counterparts (see Table 2.8). Black women adopted 50.6% of the PCs in the Black group, while White women adopted 46.7% of the PCs in the White group. Black men, on the other hand, had a lesser rate of adoption of PCs than White men. Black men adopted 49.4% of the PCs in the Black group, while White men owned 53.3%. It is noteworthy that Black men's adoption rate was less than that of Black women and White men and exceeded only that of White women in the gender category.

With on-line services, a similar pattern of adoption was found as with PCs. Black women had a greater adoption rate than their White counterparts (see Table 2.9). Black women adopted 51.7% of the on-line services, and White women adopted 40.7% of the services in their group. Black men had a lesser rate of adoption of on-line services than White men. Black men adopted 48.3% of the services, and White men adopted 59.3%. Black men's adoption of on-line services was less than that of Black women and White men and surpassed only White women in the gender category.

In summary, Black women's adoption of interactive technologies was noteworthy. Black women outpaced all others in the gender category in the adoption of cable pay-TV. Black women had a higher adoption rate than White women in four out of five interactive technologies, including cable pay-TV, VCRs, PCs, and on-line services. Black women had greater adoption rates than Black men in the same four technologies, and Black women outpaced White men in the adoption of cable pay-TV and VCRs.

Black men led everyone in the adoption of basic cable TV. Black men had a greater adoption rate than White women in the adoption of PCs and on-line services. Black men, on the other hand, lagged behind everyone in the gender category in the adoption of cable pay-TV and VCRs. Additionally, Black men had lesser adoption rates than White men in the adoption of PCs and on-line services.

Age and Rate of Adoption of Interactive Technologies. Black and White persons who were 35 to 54 years old adopted more of the interactive technologies at the time of the survey than any other age group (see Tables 2.5 through 2.9). In each technology, Blacks of this age had lesser adoption rates than did their White counterparts.

Blacks in the 35 to 54 age category adopted 33.9% of the basic cable TV, and Whites of this age adopted 37.2% of this technology. Blacks in this age range, therefore, had lesser adoption rates than Whites in the same age range in adopting basic cable TV (see Table 2.5). Moreover, in the over-55 years-old category, Blacks had a lesser adoption rate of basic cable TV than their White counterparts. It should be noted, however, that Blacks who were 18 to 34 years old had greater adoption rates of basic cable TV than their White counterparts (see Table 2.5).

A similar pattern to that of basic cable TV adoption was observed in the adoption rates of cable pay-TV. Blacks in the age group 35 to 55 years old and older had lesser adoption rates of cable pay-TV than their White counterparts (see Table 2.6). On the other hand, Blacks in the age range 18 to 34 had greater adoption rates than their White counterparts.

A similar pattern was observed in the adoption rates of videocassette recorders VCRs. Blacks who were 35 to 55 years old and older had a lesser adoption rate of VCRs than their White counterparts (see Table 2.7). Moreover, Blacks who were 18 to 24 years old had a lesser adoption rate of VCRs than their White counterparts. In the 25 to 34 years of age category, however, Blacks had a greater adoption rate of VCRs than their White counterparts.

The pattern that we have been discussing continues in the adoption rates of personal computers (PCs). Blacks who were 35 to 55 years old and older had lesser adoption rates of PCs than their White counterparts (see Table 2.8). At the same time, Blacks who were 18 to 34 years of age had greater adoption rates of PCs than their White counterparts.

The adoption rates of on-line services are slightly different from those for PCs. Blacks 35 to 54 years-old had lesser adoption rates of on-line service than their White counterparts (see Table 2.9). But Blacks had greater adoption rates of on-line services than their White counterparts in all other age categories.

To summarize, younger Blacks, 18 to 34 years of age, tended to have a greater rate of adoption of interactive technologies than their White counterparts. This age category of Blacks outpaced their White counterparts in the adoption of four out of five technologies, including basic cable TV, cable pay-TV, personal computers, and on-line service. It is noteworthy, furthermore, that Blacks 55 years old and older adopted on-line services at a greater rate than their White counterparts. Blacks in all other instances, however, fell behind their White counterparts in the adoption of the various interactive technologies.

Household Income and Rate of Adoption of Interactive Technologies. Blacks with annual household incomes of $30,000 to $50,000 annually adopted more interactive technologies than any other household income category among Blacks (see Tables 2.5 to 2.9). By comparison, Whites with annual household incomes of $50,000 or more adopted more interactive technologies than any other household income category among Whites. What follows are discussions of household incomes of Blacks and Whites and their rates of adoption of each interactive technology.

Blacks with annual household income of less than $10,000 to $50,000 adopted 74.6% of the basic cable TV service in the Black group and Whites with the same amount of income adopted 56.9% of this technology in the White group (see Table 2.5). Therefore, Blacks with household incomes of less than $10,000 to $50,000 had greater adoption rates of basic cable TV than their White counterparts. Blacks with annual household income of $50,000 or more, however, had a lesser adoption rate of basic cable TV than their White counterparts.

The same pattern as that for basic cable TV occurred in the adoption rates for the remaining interactive technologies, including cable pay-TV, VCRs, PCs, and on-line services. Blacks with annual household incomes of less than $10,000 to $50,000 had greater adoption rates of these technologies than their White counterparts (see Tables 2.6 through 2.9), and Blacks with annual household incomes of $50,000 or more had lesser rates of adoption of these technologies than their White counterparts.

To sum up, less wealthy Blacks seem to be more aggressive about adopting interactive technology than their White counterparts. In households with incomes of less than $50,000, Blacks led Whites in the adoption of interactive technologies in every instance. Blacks who are better off financially, however, may not be keeping pace with their White counterparts in the adoption of interactive technologies. In households with annual incomes of more than $50,000, Blacks fell behind Whites in the rate of adoption of interactive technologies in every instance.

Education and Rate of Adoption of Interactive Technologies. Blacks and Whites in the high school graduate category adopted more basic cable TV, cable pay-TV, and VCRs than Blacks and Whites in any other educational categories at the time of the survey (see Tables 2.5, 2.6, and 2.7). Blacks with a high school education had higher rates of adoption of cable pay-TV and VCRs than their White counterparts. Blacks led in the adoption of cable pay-TV in the education categories from high school to three years of college. On the other hand, Whites with college or postgraduate education led Blacks with the same amount of education in cable pay-TV adoption. Where VCR adoption is concerned, Blacks led Whites in the high school to three years of college groups (see Table 2.9). Whites with college and postgraduate education, however, led Blacks in adoption of VCRs.

Blacks and Whites with one to three years of college adopted more PCs than Blacks and Whites in any other age category at the time of the survey (see Table 2.8). Blacks with one to three years of college had a greater rate of adoption of PCs than their White counterparts. Blacks with a high school education also had a greater rate of adoption of PCs than their White counterparts. Black college graduates, however, had a lesser rate of adoption of PCs than their White counterparts (see Table 2.8). Furthermore, Blacks with a postgraduate education had a lesser rate of adoption of PCs than their White counterparts.

Blacks with one to three years of college adopted more on-line services than Blacks in any other educational category at the time of the survey (see Table 2.9). Whites with a college degree, on the other hand, adopted more on-line service than Whites in any other educational category. Blacks in educational levels from high school graduate to one to three years of college had greater rates of adoption of on-line services than their White counterparts. Blacks with college and postgraduate education had lesser rates of adoption than their White counterparts.

In summary, Blacks who had less than a college degree outpaced their White counterparts in the adoption of nearly all interactive technologies, including cable pay-TV, VCRs, PCs, and on-line services. Blacks who had college and postgraduate degrees had lesser rates of adoption of all interactive technologies than their White counterparts. This seems to indicate that less-educated Blacks are moving to make interactive technologies a part of their lives, perhaps at a greater pace than more educated Blacks and certainly more than their White peers.

IMPACT OF DEMOGRAPHIC VARIABLES ON ADOPTION OF TECHNOLOGIES

Now we turn our attention to the impact of different demographic characteristics on these groups' technology adoptions. The average measures of dispersion from the means for age, income, and education were calculated in order to determine which demographic factors accounted for the adoption of connective and interactive technologies (see Tables 2.10 and 2.11). It was assumed that the demographic variable that had the most dispersion from the mean was the variable that had the highest impact on adoption of a particular technology. The impact of each demographic variable on the adoption of a technology was classified as high, moderate, and low. High-impact demographics had the most deviation from the mean, and moderate and low demographics ranked second and third in deviation from the mean, respectively. Age, for example, had low impact on adoption of car and other cellular telephones because this variable had less deviation from the mean than income and education in the.adoption of this technology (see Table 2.10). The average mean deviations of the demographics for connective and interactive technologies are illustrated in Tables 2.10 and 2.11, and discussions of major findings are presented next.

Impact of Age on Adoption of Connective Technologies. Age did not have a high impact on the adoption of any connective technologies by Blacks or Whites (see Table 2.10). Age had a low impact on Blacks' adoption of car and other cellular phones and answering machines and a moderate impact on their adoption of fax machines and long-distance service. Age had only a moderate impact on Whites' adoption of all four connective technologies.

Impact of Household Income on Adoption of Connective Technologies. Income had a high impact on Blacks' adoption of two connective technologies: car and other cellular phones and fax machines (see Table 2.10). It had a moderate impact on the adoption of answering machines and a low impact on their adoption of long-distance service. Income, on the other hand, had a high impact on Whites' adoption of all four connective technologies.

Impact of Education on Adoption of Connective Technologies. Education had a high impact on Blacks' adoption of answering machines and long-distance services, moderate impact on their adoption of car and cellular phones, and a low impact on their adoption of fax machines (see Table 2.10). Education had a low impact on Whites' adoption of all four connective technologies.

Table 2.10
Average Deviations for Connective Technologies

	Blacks			
	Cell	L.D.	Fax	Answer
Age	7.65 (L)	7.6 (M)	10.29 (M)	7.14 (L)
Income	10.71 (H)	6.47 (L)	13.37 (H)	9.02 (M)
Education	10.09 (M)	11.56 (H)	6.98 (L)	11.49 (H)
Total	28.45	25.63	27.65	27.65
	Whites			
	Cell	L. D.	Fax	Answer
Age	10.03 (M)	8.17 (M)	11.87 (M)	7.86 (M)
Income	18.36 (H)	12.19 (H)	20.21 (H)	14.1 (H)
Education	6.34 (L)	5.91 (L)	8.26 (L)	6.76 (L)
Total	34.73	26.27	40.34	28.72
	Difference between			
Blacks and Whites	6.28	0.64	9.7	1.0
% Difference	22%	2%	32%	4%

Notes: Cell = car and cellular phone; Fax = fax machines; Answer = answering machines; L. D. = long-distance service; (H) = High; (M) = Moderate; (L) = Low.

In summary, for Blacks, no demographic variable appeared to have an overall impact on their adoption of all connective technologies (see Table 2.10). Income, however, had a high impact on their adoption of car and other cellular phones and fax machines, and education had a high impact on their adoption of answering machines and long-distance service. Income, on the other hand, appeared to be the determining factor in the adoption of all connective technologies by Whites. Now, let us review the impacts of the demographic variables on the adoption of interactive technologies by Blacks and Whites.

Impact of Age on Adoption of Interactive Technologies. Age had a high impact on Blacks' adoption of one interactive technology: personal computers (see Table 2.11). Age had a low impact on Blacks' adoption of most interactive technologies, including basic cable TV, cable pay-TV, and VCRs, and age had a moderate impact on their adoption of on-line services.

Age did not have a high impact on Whites' adoption of any interactive technologies (see Table 2.11). Age, however, had a moderate impact on Whites'

Table 2.11
Average Deviations for interactive technologies

	CATV	CATV Pay	VCR	PC	On-line
			Blacks		
Age	7.14 (L)	7.53 (L)	8.61 (L)	11.09 (H)	9.37 (M)
Income	9.02 (M)	9.26 (M)	9.07 (M)	10.10 (M)	14.68 (H)
Education	11.49 (H)	12.2 (H)	11.53 (H)	8.69 (L)	6.98 (L)
Total	27.65	28.99	29.21	29.88	31.03
			Whites		
	CATV	CATV Pay	VCR	PC	On-line
Age	8.8 (M)	9.43 (M)	7.11 (L)	10.24 (M)	5.08 (L)
Income	12.15 (H)	14.57 (H)	12.76 (H)	16.74 (H)	7.61 (M)
Education	7.09 (L)	7.35 (L)	7.66 (M)	6.22 (L)	9.67 (H)
Total	28.04	31.35	27.53	33.20	22.36
			Difference between		
Blacks and Whites	0.39	2.36	1.68	3.32	8.67
% Difference	1%	8%	6%	11%	28%

Notes: PC = personal computer; on-line = on-line services; CATV = basic cable TV; CATV pay = pay cable-TV; VCR = videocassette recorder; (H) = high impact; (M) = moderate impact; (L) = low impact.

adoption of three interactive technologies: PCs, basic cable TV, and cable pay-TV. Age had a low impact on Whites' adoption of on-line service and VCRs.

Impact of Household Income on Adoption of Interactive Technologies. Household income had a high impact on Blacks' adoption of one interactive technology: on-line services (see Table 2.11). Household income had a moderate impact on Blacks' adoption of the remaining interactive technologies, including PCs, basic cable TV, cable pay-TV, and VCRs. In contrast, household income had a high impact on Whites' adoption of all interactive technologies but one: on-line services. Household income had a moderate impact on Whites' adoption of on-line services.

Impact of Education on Adoption of Interactive Technologies. Education had a high impact on Blacks' adoption of three out of five interactive technologies, including basic cable TV, cable pay-TV, and VCRs but a low impact on their adoption of PCs and on-line services. In contrast, education had a low impact on Whites' adoption of three out of five interactive technologies, including PCs, basic cable TV, and cable pay-TV. Education had a high impact on Whites' adoption on-line services and a moderate impact on their adoption of VCRs.

To summarize, there is a great deal of difference in how demographic variables influence Blacks and Whites in the adoption of interactive technologies. Education appears to be the variable that influenced Blacks the most in their adoption of these technologies. Education had a high impact on Blacks' adoption of five out the nine technologies (connective and interactive) examined. For Whites, however, household income seemed to be the outstanding factor in their consumption of connective and interactive technologies. Household income had a high impact on Whites' adoption of eight out of the nine technologies (connective and interactive) reviewed.

CONCLUSION

Blacks in the major markets in America are moving to adopt a variety of information technologies that will allow them to connect to the nation's information infrastructure. Urban Blacks in all demographic categories own such devices as car and cellular phones and fax machines and pay a considerable amount of money for long-distance telephone service. Moreover, in most of the demographic categories, the proportion of Blacks who own such information technologies is greater than the proportion of Whites who own the same technologies and services.

In the same markets, Blacks are adopting personal computers and paying for interactive services such as on-line services, basic cable TV, and cable pay-TV. Our analysis indicates that even Blacks in the lower income sectors of major markets are purchasing such technologies. These findings are in line with the study reported by Parrish (1997), which states that, contrary to the NTIA and Census Bureau studies, Blacks tend to purchase PCs and other interactive technologies if they are able to do so.

Government and other research tends to indicate that Blacks are falling behind Whites and others in the technology race. Our most outstanding finding, however, is that, in many demographics, across all connective and interactive technologies, Blacks are adopting information technologies at a greater rate than Whites. One of the areas where this seems to be significant is among young Blacks 18 to 34 years of age. Their rate of adoption outpaced that of Whites of the same age for nearly all technologies examined here.

Our findings indicate that among age, household income, education, and gender, certain adoption characteristics stand out in each demographic. Here are some examples:

1. Black and White persons 35 to 54 years of age seem to dominate all categories of technology adoption.

2. Black households with annual income of $34,000 to $50,000 seem to be adopting the greatest amount of technology among Blacks.

3. White households with annual income of more than $50,000 seem to be significant adopters in the White community.

4. Black persons with one to three years of college seem to be significant information technology adopters, while Whites with college and postgraduate education seem to be adopting the most technology in their community.

5. Black women tend to lead Black men in the adoption of information technologies, but the opposite is true for members of the White community: White men lead White women.

More research is needed to ascertain greater detail about the impact of various demographics on the technology adoption of Blacks in comparison to

Whites and others. There were several shortcomings in the descriptive analysis presented here. It deals only with how well Blacks and Whites are doing with regard to adopting the prerequisite technologies for utilizing the information systems that will make up the Information Society of the future. It does not deal with how Blacks and Whites use those technologies, what their choices and decisions were in adopting them, what their level of awareness is about the Information Society of the future, what their attitudes are about technologies, or the social, economic, and political impacts that their information technology adoptions will have on the members of their communities.

Finally, despite the skepticism of some about Blacks' abilities to keep pace with the emerging information age, this analysis demonstrates that they are active participants in the adoption of technologies that are requisites for the Information Society. They are purchasing the products, subscribing to the services, and making a contribution to the formation of the information infrastructure of the nation. Our findings illustrate that Blacks are using the "information highways" and, therefore, helping to subsidize their construction. As a group, Blacks are neither "falling through the Net" nor falling behind in the information technology race. It's not that simple. Like Whites and others in the American Information Society, Blacks are caught in the throes of adjusting to rapid technological changes and developments and are allocating their resources to information technology adoption to the best of their abilities. This makes for a dynamic and complex phenomenon that demands the attention of forecasters, researchers, policymakers, and others who are concerned about ensuring that all groups in the Information Society are on equal footing in reaping the benefits of the information revolution. We trust that this chapter and the remainder of this book help to broaden our understanding of this phenomenon.

REFERENCES

Baldwin, T. F., McVoy, D. S., & Steinfield, C. (1996). *Convergence: Integrating Media, Information and Communication*. Thousand Oaks, CA: Sage.

Castells, M. (1989). *The Informational City: Information Technology, Economic Restructuring, and the Urban Regional Process*. Oxford: Basil Blackwell.

Congressional Task Force on the Future of African American. (1989). *The Future of African Americans to the Year 2000*. Washington, DC: Author.

Dervin, B. (1989). Users as research inventions: How research categories perpetuate inequities. *Journal of Communication, 39* (3), 216.

Dordick, H. S., & Wang, G. (1993). *The Information Society: A Retrospective View*. Newbury Park, CA: Sage.

Evans, V.T.P. (1995). Blackout: Preventing racial discrimination on the Net. *Library Journal, 120* (15), 44- 46.

Floyd, B. (1996). Program in Afro-American studies explores the racial gap in access to technology. *Chronicle of Higher Education, 43* (17), 19-20.

Grant, A. E., & Wilkinson, K. T. (1993). *Communication Technology Update: 1993–1994.* Austin, TX: Technology Futures.

Graves, E. G. (1998, March). Staking a claim on the future. *Black Enterprise, 28* (8), 11.

Information Infrastructure Task Force (1993*). The National Information Infrastructure: Agenda for Action.* Washington, DC: Author.

Kahin, B., & Keller, J. (1995). *Public Access to the Internet.* Cambridge: MIT Press.

LaRose, R., & Mettler, J. (1989, Summer) Who uses information technologies in rural America? *Journal of Communication, 58* (3), 48-58.

Mayer, W. G. (1991). Trends in media usage. *Public Opinion Quarterly, 57,* 593-611.

Mayer, W. G. (1994). The rise of the new media. *Public Opinion Quarterly,* 58, 124-146.

Miller, S. E. (1996). *Civilizing Cyberspace.* Reading, MA: Addison-Wesley.

Muhammad, T. K. (1996). B. E. Readers are cyber-ready. *Black Enterprise, 27* (5), 39.

Parrish, D. (1997). The story behind the numbers: Ethnicity plays little role in home computer purchasing. *Black Enterprise, 27* (6), 35.

Preparing for the information age. (1996). *Black Enterprise, 26* (8), 66.

Red, L. N. (1988). Telecommunication, economics, and Black families in America. *Journal of Black Studies, 19* (1), 111-123.

Schement, J. R. (1995). *Tendencies and Tensions of the Information Age: The Production and Distribution of Information in the United States.* New Brunswick, NJ: Transaction Publishers.

Schement, J. R. (1996, October). *Thorough Americans: Minorities and the new media.* Paper presented at the Aspen Institute Conference, Aspen, CO.

Slater, R. B. (1994). Will Blacks in higher education be detoured off the information superhighway? *Journal of Blacks in Higher Education, 3,* 96-99.

U.S. Congress, Office of Technology Assessment (1995). *The Technological Reshaping of Metropolitan America.* Washington, DC: U.S. Government Printing Office.

U.S. Department of Commerce (1995). *Falling through the Net: A Survey of the Have-Nots in Rural and Urban America.* Washington, DC: Author.

U.S. Department of Commerce (1997). *Falling through the Net II: New Data on the Digital Divide.* Washington, DC: Author.

U.S. Department of Commerce, Bureau of the Census. (1991). *Computer Use in the United States: Current Population Reports, Series P-23, 1989* (No. 171). Washington, DC: U.S. Government Printing Office.

CHAPTER 3

African Americans and Privacy: Understanding the Black Perspective in the Emerging Policy Debate

Oscar H. Gandy, Jr.

In January 1991 Lotus Development Corporation announced its intention to abandon efforts to develop a new software product because of what it understood to be a groundswell of public opposition. This product, Lotus Marketplace, was to have provided its customers with personal information about the resources and habits of the members of some 120 million U.S. households. The sorts of information Lotus would supply were already easily attainable from a host of information suppliers serving the direct marketing industry, but what made the Lotus product different was that it would be available on CD-ROM discs, which could be searched by anyone with an Apple Macintosh computer, a video disc player, and $695 for the first 5,000 names. Lotus and its partner, Equifax, had apparently lost an early battle in what promises to be a hotly contested war to determine who has the right to control the collection, sharing, and use of personal information.

The contemporary debate about privacy takes place in the context of substantial changes in the structure of the American political economy. The effort to rationalize the production, distribution, and sale of goods and services has involved the widespread computerization of many of the routine processes involved in these spheres. The coordination of these increasingly complex systems has come to require the collection, storage, and use of unimaginable amounts of information—much of which is information about identifiable individuals. Modern telecommunications systems provide reliable interconnection between computers within and between organizations. These telecommunications links facilitate the sharing of information, even across national borders.

The increasing importance of information as an input into the management process supports the development of a market for information as a producer's good. Not only is there substantial demand for information about individuals, but firms that collect information about employees and clients are frequently willing to sell or exchange this information with other organizations to improve the bottom line. Information of value to the management process is not limited to what is provided in response to direct inquiry but includes a broad array of data that are generated through transactions within product and labor markets. The collection, storage, and exchange of this information raise serious concerns about the privacy interests of the individuals described in these records.

The growing market for information also raises critical questions of public policy for the providers of telecommunications services. Traditional relationships with customers are being challenged as corporate managers seek to meet the demands of the more highly competitive environments in which these service firms now find themselves. The rapidly evolving policy terrain has come to represent a treacherous landscape, that these firms must negotiate as they develop national and international services. Some argue that the development of advanced fiber-optic systems has been placed at risk because of the uncertainty over the outcome of this debate (McManus, 1990; Shultz, 1990). Domestically, privacy policy has the character of a patchwork quilt, with different states pursuing their own unique visions of the best way to achieve the proper balance between the interests of commerce and government and the interests of individuals. Policy leadership at the national level is sadly lacking, and conflict in the international arena seems certain.

As the recent struggles over privacy-invasive technologies such as caller-ID and the expensive errors committed by Lotus in the development of its Marketplace database suggest, ignorance of what the citizen/consumer feels about privacy can have serious consequences. Even though Lotus and Equifax sought the advice of Alan Westin, the leading authority on informational privacy, they reported surprise at the magnitude of the negative response to their product (Miller, 1991). To the extent that public opinion serves to condition both corporate and government policies toward privacy, we can expect greater efforts to assess that opinion before product development proceeds too far. It will also be important for government and corporate decision makers to determine if there are critical differences within the population in terms of policy preferences.

From the perspective of the citizen/consumer, there are altogether different reasons for trying to assess the climate of opinion. To the extent that the opinions of African Americans depart from the opinions and policy preferences of the White majority, we can expect privacy to represent yet another area of social policy in which Black interests are subordinated to those of the mainstream. This chapter begins the process of examining these differences.

SOURCES OF PRIVACY ORIENTATIONS

It is rarely held that attitudes and opinions are genetically determined. Instead, we generally argue that concrete social experience is the source of the similarities and differences in attitudes that we find among people. It is generally assumed that individuals from similar backgrounds share similar experiences and that these experiences generate a common awareness and understanding. Thus, social categories perspectives assume that common experiences in the lives of women, African Americans, the poor, or the working classes explain the finding of greater variance between, rather than within, such groups. Recently, however, socioeconomic status has come under attack for its unreliability as a predictor of attitudes on a range of social issues. The expectation of an indirect or inverse relationship between socioeconomic status and conservatism is no longer supported with regard to a wide range of issues. According to Himmelstein and McRae (1998), the only consistent finding in their analysis of large national databases gathered in 1980 is that "liberalism on social issues tends to increase with education, but even here the relationship varies considerably from issue to issue." They conclude that "the lack of a consistent relationship reflects both the diversity of the social issues and the fuzziness of the social/economic distinction" (p. 492).

The social experience perspective implies a cumulative or additive process of attitude development. Each experience contributes in some way to the strength and clarity of any particular attitude, impression, or social perception. However, there is the sense that repeated exposure to a negative, aversive stimulus over time may result in a desensitization, a dulling of the perceptual response, that might eventually be reflected in a widening of the latitude of acceptance of some particular behavior. Thus, we might find the paradoxical result that the oppressed come increasingly to accept the oppression. The clearest examples are associated with the apparent impact of repeated exposure to pornographic or erotic material, not necessarily violent or aggressive. Such viewing under experimental conditions has been associated with more permissive attitudes toward rape among both males and females (Malamuth & Billings, 1986). Thus, we recognize the potential for a somewhat opposite impact to develop. Rather than desensitization, resentment may build up under the pressure of repeated assaults on one's sense of dignity. Victims of crime may be less persuaded by arguments about the social circumstances that cultivate a criminal lifestyle among urban youth, and as a result these victims may more readily support harsher punishment or greater restrictions on the freedom of those accused of crime.

ON THE QUESTION OF PRIVACY

The published literature on attitudes toward privacy as an issue of public policy is quite slim (Katz, 1988; Katz & Tassone, 1990; Laufer & Wolfe, 1977; McClosky & Brill, 1983). Although a search of the Roper Center database has identified a large number of opinion studies that have included one or more questions about privacy, very few of these studies have actually been introduced into the scholarly literature. Much of the survey research has been conducted on behalf of corporate sponsors presumably concerned about the implications of emerging policy on their lines of business. The most widely distributed and most frequently cited studies were financed by Sentry Insurance in 1979 (Harris & Westin, 1979), by Southern New England Telephone in 1993 (Harris and Associates, 1983), and, most recently, by Equifax (Equifax, 1990), a study that was again coordinated by Westin and the Harris organization.

Although the work on privacy as it relates to the practices of business and government is quite slim, there is considerably more work available that addresses the interpersonal dimensions of privacy (Derlega & Chairkin, 1977). One particularly interesting study examined the relationship between privacy preferences and the distance at which one sits from strangers on a bench (Kline & Bell, 1983).

Stone, Gueutal, Gardner, and McClure (1983) associated differences in attitudes toward privacy with an individual's differential experience with potential abusers of one's right to privacy. The correlations between individuals' experiences and their attitudes, beliefs, and intentions regarding privacy were quite low, but they were suggestive of the potential for either a direct or a mediated social influence on a person's awareness and beliefs about privacy.

SECONDARY ANALYSIS

In our attempt to discover the social origins of an individual's orientations toward privacy, a data set produced by Alan Westin and the Harris organization for Sentry Insurance (Harris & Westin, 1979) was acquired from the Roper Center. This comprehensive survey of public attitudes and opinions of some 1,500 adults involved more than 300 measured variables. The published analysis of this data set was limited to intergroup comparisons in terms of percentage agreement with statements about privacy concerns. The report was primarily descriptive and made little attempt to identify or explain the origins of these attitudes.

To reduce the number of variables to a manageable size, factor analysis was used to identify 25 constructs with reliabilities generally above .80 and never below .63. Analysis of variance was pursued as a means of identifying the relative importance of race, gender, type of employment, political ideology, age, and education as factors associated with particular orientations toward privacy. With regard to race, Whites and Blacks frequently anchored opposite ends of the distribution of index scores. Whites, for example, were significantly more supportive than Blacks of an individual's right to sexual privacy. Whites were also more likely to take the position that employers should not gather what they felt was irrelevant personal information; this included the traditional demographic information such as race, sex, age, and marital status.

An important reversal in position was identified with regard to government surveillance. Here, Blacks were significantly more willing than Whites to limit police use of surveillance techniques without a court order. Blacks were, however, less concerned about corporate use of information, despite the fact that

African Americans were significantly more likely than Whites to report having been turned down for jobs on the basis of inaccurate, unfair, or out-of-date information.

When we examined political orientation, we found support for the view that privacy concerns were generally seen to be matters of liberal social policy. Self-identified liberals and radicals always seemed to anchor the pro-privacy end of the attitudinal distributions, with conservatives often anchoring the opposite end. Those who did not identify a particular ideological label for themselves tended to be those who were most apathetic toward privacy protections. Black respondents were more likely than most to avoid identifying their ideological posture—a tendency that raises questions about the legitimacy of the ideological measure for all population groups (Conover & Feldman, 1981).

In any secondary analysis, one may find that questions have not been asked precisely as one would have liked them asked. Variables are not measured in ways that make it possible for one to pursue the complexities involved in informing an opinion or in taking action to preserve privacy or in resisting its further erosion. Before embarking on a national survey, we though it would be useful if we used a small sample to pretest and clarify some of our working hypotheses.

ORGANIZING THE FOCUS GROUPS

In the summer of 1988 five group interviews were conducted. The groups were organized on the basis of our loosely constructed theoretical expectations regarding concrete social experience as a basis for developing orientations toward privacy. Our review of the literature suggested that if we were to identify any social locations for privacy orientations, the most likely source would be employment experience. The experience of surveillance in the workplace was expected to be reflected in more generalized orientations toward privacy. Recent studies discussed by the U.S. Congress, Office of Technology Assessment (USOTA, 1987) suggested that telecommunications workers and office workers involved in computerized data entry experienced the highest levels of surveillance pressure. Therefore, we organized one group of eight workers who shared the telephone/computer experience. A group composed of managers and supervisors, many of whom were involved in marketing activities, was thought to provide some insights from the other side of the workplace-monitoring divide. Persons who had recently acquired a mortgage were expected to share the common experience of providing strangers with access to personal financial information, and a group of nine new mortgagees was organized. Similarly, because we thought that they shared a recent experience of something less than voluntary disclosure of personal experience, a group of six individuals who had recently been called for jury duty was organized.

Because our secondary analysis of Harris survey data indicated that African American respondents differed substantially from other groups in terms of their attitudes toward privacy and surveillance, one group was organized with five Black participants.

THE QUESTIONNAIRE

Each of the participants in the five groups ($n = 37$) was asked to complete a six-page questionnaire prior to arrival at the campus for the group interview. Respondents were assured that their answers to the questionnaire would be anonymous and that at no time would there be any attempt to associate their names with their answers. The questionnaire was designed to provide an individualized assessment of each participant's views on privacy outside the context of, and prior to, a group discussion on the issue. A variety of approaches was used to gather this information, from open-ended questions asking respondents to list what they thought were the three worst invasions of a person's privacy, to a variety of scaled responses measuring agreement with different statements. A ten-point scale was used to measure the extent to which they established limits on the privacy rights of others on the basis of their social status. Key status variables were related to employment or their responsibility for the safety or resources of others.

With only 37 respondents who had not been randomly selected but were volunteers, and who were purposely assigned to groups on the basis of presumed common experiences, inferential statistics would essentially be meaningless as statements about the general population. Instead, the analysis of this data has been directed toward describing the patterns or relationships between variables or responses that are indicative of types of responses or respondents. Such classification has been useful as an aid to understanding the conflicting impressions reported in other studies of public opinion regarding privacy. These correlational analyses also provide us with insights into the nature of the attitude clusters, which may be linked conceptually with unmeasured theoretical constructs. Information about the age, homeowner status, education, political ideology, interest, and involvement, as well as indications of involvement in the consumer economy, might also be shown to be related to particular attitude clusters and orientations but risks the temptation to generalize beyond the sample.

Open-ended responses had to be coded into response categories to be included in the analysis. Responses to the question about what were the worst invasions of privacy were coded into 16 categories. Responses to a question about justifications for gathering data were coded into 9 categories, and responses to a question about privacy invasions likely to increase in the future were coded into 12 categories. To pursue a correlation-based analytical model, responses were coded primarily as dichotomous dummy variables where zero was assigned if a particular response was not given, and one was assigned if the response was made. Ordinal-level responses that ranged from one to five or one to ten were treated as continuous for the purposes of identifying of associations between responses.

RACE

If we examine the correlations with being African American and claiming a particular political ideology, the data suggest that the strongest tendency was for Blacks in this sample to be identified as conservative ($r = .33$), whereas for Whites the strongest tendency was to choose "middle of the road" ($r = .18$). The African Americans in these groups were more highly educated than the general population, tending to have pursued graduate study ($r = .22$). This may explain, in part, their greater expressed interest in news and public affairs ($r = .15$) and their tendency to subscribe to a greater number of magazines and other periodicals ($r = .17$).

When we examine the correlations between being African American and assigning privacy rights to different kinds of people, a rather clear pattern emerged. Overall, with the sole exception of the privacy rights of minors, Blacks were more generous in this regard than were Whites. Ranked on the basis of the correlation with being Black, the following five types of persons are assigned the most comprehensive privacy rights by African Americans in this sample: workers who handle sensitive data or information ($r = .39$); workers responsible for the safety of others ($r = .35$); people who knock on your door ($r = .34$); government employees ($r = .33$); and workers who handle large sums of money ($r = .33$).

The differences between Blacks and Whites in their responses to the 26 attitudinal questions were not nearly as striking or consistent. If we take a correlation of $r = .30$ as the minimum relationship for comment with a group of this size, only 4 of the 26 correlations would qualify. The correlations suggest that the African Americans in this group believed that consumer research helps firms to develop better products ($r = .34$); and, consistent with such a view, they reject the position that the telephone numbers they call for information are their business alone ($r = -.33$), as well as the similar view that how they spend their money is their business and no one else's ($r = -.33$). Consistent with such a perspective on market-linked data gathering, there was also a tendency to agree with the view that "monitoring or surveillance has to be secret, otherwise it's meaningless" ($r = .32$). Thus, we find that these highly educated African Americans were quite willing to extend broad privacy rights to individuals and were also unlikely to see information gathering by businesses as falling within their definition of an objectionable invasion of privacy. This is consistent with research discussed earlier, that indicated that if African Americans express any concerns about privacy, they tend to focus on the relationships between individuals and the government.

FOCUS GROUP INTERVIEW

A somewhat different picture of how these individuals understood and felt about privacy can be derived from the focus group interview. Here, descriptive statistics are relatively unimportant. We were interested in the variety of experiences and emotional linkages people use to organize and clarify their views on a range of privacy-related issues.

Although focus groups are not meant to be representative of any actual or even conceptually distinct groups in the adult population, knowing something about the different focus groups helps to place them in a meaningful social context. All groups, even those constructed for the purposes of research, have a character and a personality of their own, influenced, in part, by the similarities and differences among their members. Comments made early in the interview by some members of a group are likely to affect the answers of those that follow. Some people may hesitate to repeat what someone has already said; others may use that fact as an excuse for limiting their own participation.

The African American group, had only five members. Three Black males and two Black females between ages 25 and 47 reported having voted in the last presidential primary, and all were employed full-time. Beyond these similarities, they differed greatly in terms of education and political orientation. Four of the five expressed a high degree of interest in news and public affairs.

As compared with the other groups, we sensed that members of the Black group were less willing to assume that the government would protect individuals against invasions of privacy. They also seemed to take current laws as given, rather than being a response to organized political pressure. Where members of other groups readily suggested that some action was illegal or that a person could be taken to court for asking for certain information, such comments were rarely heard in this African American group. Instead, participants talked about fairness or characterized certain institutional behaviors as reflecting a double standard or a conflict of interests. One respondent's expression of powerlessness is exemplary: "I can't control that, you know, as society exists today. If you don't put down your social security, you're not going to get to square one. That's the way it's set up. They're not going to let you they're going to reject that application, you know, and that's it." On the basis of impressions gained from the secondary analysis and focus group interviews, a questionnaire was developed for administration to a national sample.

TELEPHONE SURVEY

Between January 19 and February 8, 1989, 1,250 telephone interviews lasting an average of 15.7 minutes were conducted by professional interviewers employed by Maritz Marketing, a contractor for AT&T's Telecommunications Research and Analysis Center (TRAC) in Somerset, New Jersey. Because response rate is included so rarely in reports of privacy studies, we have no basis for comparing our participation rates with those obtained in other studies.

Readers will have to come to their own conclusions about the data and the analyses based on them in light of the fact that out of 5,401 randomly generated numbers actually dialed, 1,749 refused to begin the survey once contact was established, and an additional 231 terminated during the interview. Many of those terminations may have occurred when the focus of the survey became clear. Although we might suggest with some confidence that the underrepresentation of privacy preservers in the sample serves to underestimate the extent of privacy concerns in the population, there is no way for us to associate that concern with its specific expressions or, more importantly, with the social indicators that we hoped to identify as the origins of those views.

There is yet another problem with this and other telephone surveys. Although the supply of telecommunications services through a regulated monopoly was supposed to ensure "universal service," it is clear that not everyone has a telephone, and therefore some potential respondents have no chance of being included in the sample. An analysis of telephone coverage trends in the United States between 1963 and 1986 (Thornberry & Massey, 1988) finds strong inequities in coverage between geographic regions and urban and rural residences, as well as with regard to age, sex, race, and marital or employment status. African Americans remain the group with the highest probability of being without residential telephone service. The difference between Whites and Blacks in 1985 and 1986 was more than 10%, whereas the difference between men and women was less than 1%. The difference between those who were married and those who were separated was also a striking 13.8%, with 18.8% of those who were separated living in nontelephone households. Although nontelephone households are overwhelmingly poor, neither weighting nor continuing to sample until some predetermined quota of a demographic group has been reached is sufficient to represent those who do not have coverage. Thornberry and Massey note that nontelephone households tend also to include population segments that are characterized by a lower response rate than other segments. They represent a special population, which has systematically been excluded from this and other telephone surveys.

As a result, the 1,250 individuals who completed this survey cannot be thought of as fully representative of the population of adults over 18 in the United States. The sample underrepresented males, as there were proportionately more women reached and willing to participate. Despite reservations about the impact of weighting, previous research and a preliminary assessment of this sample suggest that there are significant relationships between gender and privacy. Thus, a weighting factor of .678 has been applied to each female in the sample, reducing the effective sample size to 1,002 and the number of African Americans to 76.

The resultant sample still underrepresents older adults, African Americans, and members of other minority groups—especially those for whom English is not their primary or preferred language. It also excludes the hundreds of thousands of adults in prisons, hospitals, barracks, and dormitories not considered to be part of a residential population. Yet, the data generated by this survey still provide a valuable window through which to observe some of the relationships between privacy orientations and the character of their origins.

THE CONTINUING SIGNIFICANCE OF RACE

To examine the contribution of racial identification to our understanding of privacy orientations, an analysis of correlations was developed. A dichotomous variable was created whereby being Black or African American was treated as a discrete measure that qualifies as a ratio level of measurement on its face. In the recent Equifax privacy report (Equifax, 1990), Blacks are identified as being more pro-privacy than Whites or Hispanics on 22 out of 46 questions covering a range of issues. For the 25 attitudinal measures used in this study, including an estimate of the extent of public concern, we find that being Black is a significant correlate or explanatory factor in nine of the comparisons (Table 3.1). Given the relatively small proportion of African Americans in the effective sample (7.6%), significant correlations with race may be treated with considerable confidence as indicators of orientations linked to common social experiences.

With regard to business practices, the strongest association with being Black is the tendency to agree that corporations gather only what they need to make good business decisions ($r = -.15$). This is consistent with the tendency among African Americans to believe that the more businesses know about them, the better they can meet their needs ($r = -.08$). This sense of trust did not extend, however, to decisions regarding potential employees. Here, Blacks tended to agree that employers should be limited in the kind of information they can gather about job applicants ($r = -.09$). This may reflect a difference in opinion about the utility of employment records as indicators of employee potential. African Americans in this sample tended to reject the view that how people behaved in the past was any indicator of how they would act in the future ($r = .11$).

When we controlled statistically for the influence of education and income, the relationship between being Black and being concerned about mailing lists remains significant ($r = .09**$). This finding is consistent with the Equifax report (equifax, 1990, p. 72), in which 66% of Whites reported finding the use of their names for direct marketing acceptable, whereas 70% of Blacks indicated acceptance.

Using a regression approach where education, gender, and ethnic identification are included, self-identification as African American retains its independent predictive power in several equations. With regard to the view that suggests that the only people concerned with privacy are those with something to hide (C2 in Table 3.1), the standardized beta ($-.12***$) suggests a significant tendency toward agreement that is not captured by educational differences. However, when we examine respondents' estimates of the extent of public concern about privacy (G1 in Table 3.1), being Black is positively associated with giving an estimate of extensive popular concern (*beta* = $.11***$). We might wish to interpret these responses as being consistent with the personal vision of victims. African Americans in this sample were more likely to agree that people with power

Table 3.1
Race as a Correlate of Privacy Orientations Correlation with Being Black (Spearman's Rho)

A. *Social Orientation*

1. The government can generally be trusted to look out for my interests. (.04)

2. There's very little an individual can do to improve the quality of his life. (-.01)

3. Most people with power try to take advantage of people like myself. (-.10***)

B. *Orientation toward Information and Power*

1. The more people know about you, the more control they have over your life. (.03)

2. Computers give big organizations an unfair advantage over the average person. (-.06)

C. *Privacy and Confidentiality*

1. You simply have to give up some of your privacy to enjoy the conveniences of the modern world. (-.02)

2. The only people who are concerned about their privacy are people with something to hide. (-.11***)

3. The government should not be able to open mail, tap phones, or examine bank records without a court order. (-.04)

4. Information provided to the Census Bureau is held strictly confidential. (-.02)

D. *Business Practices*

1. Banks, finance companies and credit bureaus should be doing more to keep personal information confidential. (-.08)

2. Insurance companies should be able to gather all the information they need in order to choose between applicants. (-.03)

3. Employers should be limited in the kinds of personal information they can collect about job applicants. (-.09**)

4. The more businesses know about me, the better they can meet my individual needs. (-.08*)

5. Companies rarely gather more information than they need to make good business decisions. (-.15***)

6. People can be denied credit cards if it doesn't look like they are going to spend very much. (-.04)

7. Having a social security number makes it easy for organizations to collect information about me from different places. (.-09**)

Table 3.1 (Continued)

Race as a Correlate of Privacy Orientations Correlation With Being Black (Spearman's Rho)

    8. Psychological testing helps employers select the best workers for the job.
        (.02)

    9. How a person behaved in the past is a good indicator of how they'll act in the
        future. (.11***)

E. *Marketing and Consumer List*

    1. Companies should seek your permission before they tell anyone else about
        products you buy, or the services you use. (-.03)

    2. There should be a way to keep your name off certain mailing lists. (.07*)

    3. You have a right to have your name removed from any mailing list. (.03)

F. *Telecommunication and Privacy*

    1. The numbers I call from my home are my business and no else's. (-.06)

    2. It would be good to know who is calling before I answer the phone. (-.06)

    3. Someone should invent a telephone that would screen out calls from people
        trying to sell you things. (-.07)

G. *Assessment of the Public Pulse*

    1. How concerned would you guess the average American is about threats to
        their privacy? (.14***)

Notes: *p<.05; **p<.01; ***p<.001.

tend to take advantage of people like themselves ($r = -.10$). In the context of social or political repression, individuals may quite properly believe they have something to hide, because disclosure may mean that they are excluded from employment or access to goods and services in the market. The fact that African Americans see these concerns as being so widespread is consistent with a tendency to project one's experience as representative of the population. Although this survey did not ask respondents to indicate how concerned they were personally about threats to privacy, data reported by Westin (Equifax, 1990, p. 2) indicate that 64% of Black respondents were very concerned, whereas only 43% of Whites were as concerned. This interpretation is supported by the finding that being Black is not significantly related to the belief that the loss of privacy is the price we pay for living in the modern world.

DISCUSSION AND CONCLUSION

The data we have gathered in this study through secondary analysis, focus group interviews, written questionnaires, and telephone interview responses all point to significant differences between African Americans and others in their response to what they perceive as invasions of privacy. Blacks are more concerned, believe others to be more concerned, and would seem to base that concern on inferences drawn from personal experience. African Americans appear to be concerned about privacy because the loss of control over personal information means greater susceptibility to discriminatory exclusion from employment, insurance, and credit. African Americans continue to be mistrustful of power, but they are apparently no more distrustful of government than are other citizens. This represents an important change that should be explored in future studies.

More important are the differences between African American and other respondents in terms of their trust in business. Much of the groundswell of public concern about privacy has been associated with annoyance about direct mail and telemarketing. Older respondents have become increasingly militant in their opposition to these practices, but African Americans seem to be little concerned. One interpretation of this difference may be found in the claim by Gandy (1989) that the new marketing technologies are inherently discriminatory (see also Novek, Sinha, & Gandy, 1990). Thus, the reason Blacks are not concerned about marketing pressure may be that they are not pressured; indeed, they are being ignored because demographic clustering models that predict likely customers systematically exclude the neighborhoods where Blacks are likely to live.

Future studies should explore the extent to which African Americans are aware of the variety of ways in which personal information may be used to reduce their access to goods and services. These studies may be helpful in developing much-needed programs of consumer education for African Americans.

REFERENCES

Altman, I. (1976). Theoretical and empirical issues with regard to privacy territorially, personal space, and crowding. *Environmental and Behavior, 8,* 3-29.

Altman, I. (1977). Privacy regulation: Culturally universal or culturally specific. *Journal of Social Issues. 33* (3), 66-83.

Bishop, G. (1976). The effect of education on ideological consistency. *Public Opinion Quarterly, 40,* 337-348.

Conover, P., & Feldman, S. (1981). The origins and meaning of liberal/ conservative self-identification. *American Journal of Political Science, 25,* 617-645.

Derlega, V., & Chairkin, A. (1977). Privacy and self-disclosure in social relationships. *Journal of Social Issues, 33* (3), 102-115.

Equifax, Inc. (1990). *The Equifax Report on Consumers in the Information Age.* (Louis Harris and Associates, Alan F. Westin, Survey Coordinators). Atlanta, GA: Author.

Fleishman, J. (1986). Trends in self-identified ideology from 1972 to 1982: No support for salience hypothesis. *American Journal of Political Science, 30*, 517-541.

Gandy, O. H. (1989). The surveillance society: Information technology and bureaucratic social control. *Journal of Communication, 39*, 61-76.

Groves, R. M., & Lyberg, L. E. (1988). An overview of nonresponse issues in telephone surveys. In R. Groves, P. Biemer, L. Lyberg, J. Massey, W. Nicholls, & J. Waksberg (Eds.), *Telephone Survey Methodology*. New York: Wiley, pp. 191-211.

Harris, L., & Associates (1983). *The Road after 1984: A Nationwide Survey of the Public and Its Leaders on the New Technology and Its Consequences for American life*. New York: Author.

Harris, L., & Westin, A. (1979). *The Dimensions of Privacy*. Stevens Point, WI: Sentry.

Himmelstein, J., & McRae, J., Jr. (1988). Social issues and socioeconomic status. *Public Opinion Quarterly, 52*, 492-512.

Jussawalla, M., & Cheah, C. (1987). Economic analysis of the legal and policy aspects of information privacy. In *The Calculus of International Communications*. Littleton, CO: Libraries Unlimited, pp 75-102.

Katz, J. (1988). U.S. Telecommunications privacy policy: Socio-political responses to technological advances. *Telecommunication Policy, 12* (4), 353-368.

Katz, J., & Tassone, A. (1990). Public opinion trends: Privacy and information technology. *Public Opinion Quarterly, 54 (1)*, 125-143.

Kline, L., & Bell, P. (1983). Privacy preference and interpersonal distancing. *Psychological Reports, 53*, 12-14.

Laufer, R., & Wolfe, M. (1977) Privacy as a concept and a social issue: A multidimensional developmental theory. *Journal of Social Issues, 33* (3), 22-41.

Linowes, D. F. (1989). *Privacy in America*. Chicago: University of Illinois Press.

Malamuth, N., & Billings, V. (1986). The functions and effects of pornography: Sexual communication versus the feminist models in light of research findings. In J. Bryant & D. Zillman (Eds.), *Perspectives on Media Effects*. Hillsdale NJ: Lawrence Erlbaum Associates, pp. 83-108.

McCloskey, H., & Brill, A. (1983). *Dimensions of Tolerance: What Americans Believe about Civil Liberties*. New York: Russell Sage Foundation.

McManus, T. E. (1990). *Telephone Transaction-Generated Information: Rights and Restrictions*. (Report P- 90-5). Cambridge: Harvard Program on Information Resources Policy.

Miller, M. (1991, January 23). Lotus is likely to abandon consumer-data project. *Wall Street Journal*, p. B1.

Novek, E., Sinha, N., & Gandy, O. (1990). The value of your name. *Media, Culture and Society, 12*, 525-543.

Rubin, M. R. (1988). *Private Rights, Public Wrongs: The Computer and Personal Privacy*. Norwood, NJ: Ablex.

Rule, J. B. (1974). *Private Lives and Public Surveillance: Social Control in the Computer Age*. New York: Schocken.

Shultz, P. (1990). *Caller ID, ANI & Privacy: A Review of the Major Issues Affecting Number Identification Technologies*. Washington, DC: Telecommunications Reports.

Stone, E., Gueutal, H., Gardner, D., & McClure, S. (1983). A field experiment comparing information-privacy values, beliefs, and attitudes across several types of organizations. *Journal of Applied Psychology, 68*, 459-468.

Thornberry, O., & Massey, J. T. (1988). Trends in United States telephone coverage across time and subgroups. In R. Groves, P. Biemer, L. Lyberg, J. Massey, W. Nicholls, & J. Waksberg (Eds.), *Telephone Survey Methodology*. New York: Wiley, pp. 25-49.

U.S. Congress, Office of Technology Assessment (1987). *The Electronic Supervisor: New Technologies, New tensions* (OTA-CIT-333). Washington, DC: U.S. Government Printing Office.

Weiss, A. (1967). *Privacy and Freedom*. New York: Atheneum.

Weiss, M. J. (1988). *The Clustering of America*. New York: Harper & Row.

PART II

The Economic Dimension

Information technology is having a major impact on the American economy. Yet African Americans hardly own or control any major hardware or software companies at this time. The major information enterprises in the Black community historically have been in the print and broadcasting industries, but as the information age develops, new Black information businesses are beginning to come on the scene. At the same time, advances in technology are affecting the way that Black information enterprises maintain their viability in the business world. In Chapter 4 George Sylvie examines a main source of information in the Black community for over a century—the African American newspaper. The issue here, however, is the economic capability of African American newspapers to adopt the information technology that will allow them to survive and continue to be viable sources of information for the Black community in the future. G. Thomas Wilson III, in Chapter 5 illustrates the decline of Black ownership of broadcast facilities and argues that the economic and political system in this nation hinders Blacks' ownership and control of broadcasting components of the Information Society. In Chapter 6, however, John T. Barber and Alice A. Tait examine a new model for Black entrepreneurship. The tremendous success of Robert Johnson and BET Holdings, Inc. is described as a paradox in the Black information business world. Chapter 7 investigates the ability of members of the Black community to participate in, and make profits from, new information businesses such as cellular phones. In this chapter, John T. Barber examines the inclusion and exclusion of African Americans in the recent sale of portions of the electromagnetic spectrum by the U.S. government to corporations for the purpose of operating personal communication services businesses.

CHAPTER 4

Technology and African American Newspapers: Implications for Survival and Change

George Sylvie

No industry can succeed if it does not meet the changing needs of its customers. This is doubly true for the Black press, which finds itself in the midst of an economic quandary. The Black press, since its beginnings in 1827, has attempted to serve, speak for, and fight for the Black minority population of the United States (Wolseley, 1990), and it has a long history of service and advocacy (Boyd, 1991). Throughout its history, there have been times of struggle, but none more serious than in the last 25 years.

As conditions improved for some Black citizens in the 1970s, the Black middle class began to grow (Rose, 1976; Landry, 1987). In addition, Black migration to suburbs began to accelerate (Logan & Schneider, 1984). At the same time, Black-owned and -operated newspapers began to decline. Critics pointed to outdatedness and irrelevance and the increasing need to depend on White advertisers for revenue (Ward, 1973). Editors, for their part, began to reexamine the function of the Black press to find out whether it was serving reader needs (LaBrie & Zima, 1971). As Black migration continued to show increased suburbanization (Winsberg, 1985; Johnson, 1990), it left an "underclass," to which advertisers did not want to send their message (Fitzgerald, 1986; Guzda, 1984). Talk of a Black newspaper "identity crisis" arose (Joseph, 1985), and Black newspaper publishers faced the 1990s threatened with extinction because of the loss of readers, journalists, and advertisers to other media (Fitzgerald, 1990).

To recoup such losses, many Black newspaper publishers feel a need to improve their product to attract more readers. That means hiring additional staff and purchasing more advanced (computerized) technology. But without large readerships, these newspapers have difficulty getting the advertising revenues that would help further and improve operations and the product. Therein lies the purpose of this chapter: to explore how and to what extent the Black press takes advantage of computerized technology—managerial approaches, technology adoption processes, and obstacles to adoption. In short, we examine how technology (or lack thereof) impacts the operations and survival of the Black newspaper. This study examines the use of technology at six Texas weeklies and how the changing winds of the Black newspaper industry influence that use. To do so, however, requires discussion of the realities of Black and small businesses as they encounter technology and the marketplace.

BACKGROUND

Most small businesses, such as the 200 to 300 individual Black newspapers, often do not adopt technology at the same rate as larger businesses. For example, whereas more than 80% of Canadian and American manufacturers with more than 500 employees used some new computerized technology, less than half of the small firms did (Statistics Canada, 1991). Although a majority of top managers at those small companies who use such technology rate it highly, one survey showed that many do not know what technologies would help them to better control and expand their businesses (Holzinger, 1993). Not surprisingly, this lack of technological knowledge probably helps explain why smaller companies are slow to adopt advanced tools (U.S. Department of Commerce, 1988).

Despite the relative lack of research into small business technology adoption, competing explanations abound. MacPherson (1994), for example, suggested that half his surveyed firms had not introduced any kind of new technology over a five-year study period because they were located in a declining geographic region "on the trailing edge of new technology adoption" (p. 159). More plausibly, inadequate resources and limited education about technology systems possibly inhibit adoption, as a case study showed (Cragg & King, 1993). But a second survey noted that quality, productivity, and price are the most important drivers of the small business adoption process (Taylor, Moore, & Amonsen 1994); this disputed earlier findings (Gatignon & Robertson, 1989) that adopters can be classified psychographically.

The Taylor, Moore, and Amonsen (1994) findings also lend credibility to other findings that small business owners look to technology mainly to control operating costs (Holzinger, 1993). Further support has come from studies that attempt to refine the classification of small business adopters. One survey (MacPherson, 1994) grouped innovators into those who adopt primarily to cut costs and those who aspire toward greater production flexibility. Another survey (Lefebvre Harvey, & Lefebvre, 1991) found that the more innovative small firms have an external orientation dominated by clients and suppliers and that they were more alert to the added flexibility that new technology brought. A third survey (Thong & Yap, 1995) revealed that small businesses tend to adopt information technology when their chief executives are more innovative, have a positive attitude toward adoption, and possess greater technology knowledge.

This latter area (of managerial behavior) may be the most revealing in terms of small business technology adoption. For example, a case study analysis (Gagnon & Toulouse, 1996) found that most managers, when adopting technology, act as entrepreneurs (intuitive and responsive) and not as administrators (rational and analytical); that is, they seize opportunities, disregarding the accompanying requisite planning involved. Another case study (Julien, 1995) suggests that the owner-manager steers a highly personalized, on-linear (iterative) adoption process and that small firms are more quick to adopt technology when the owner-manager is better educated and has mastered and/or fostered in subordinates technical information and an adequate technological culture.

But as small businesses, Black newspapers' adoption of technology must be placed in the context of the typical Black business, which has faced special obstacles in its attempts toward progressive operation. The earliest research on urban Black businesses showed the lack of financial capital as the largest barrier to successful operation (Pierce, 1947). But it was believed (Brimmer, 1966) and later shown (Brimmer & Terrell, 1971; Markwalder, 1981) that this lack of capital did not automatically exclude success.

Much of the responsibility went to segregation, which, while cutting Blacks off from many public services, created opportunities—however limited—for Blacks to serve their own segregated markets; the advance of desegregation was seen as a negative omen (Brimmer & Terrell, 1971). But Bates (1973) challenged such assumptions, suggesting that existing Black firms that are expanding should be examined in any attempt to assess the potential of Black entrepreneurship. Black firms with increased access to financial capital could escape the traditional lines of small, labor-intensive, service-oriented businesses.

So, it seems that such escape would be beneficial. For example, although Black-owned businesses grew from 1977 to 1982, firms declined in areas where Black businesses had traditional strongholds (Suggs, 1986). Historical exclusion from the general economy had rendered such firms unprepared to take advantage of desegregation's new markets. But other factors still make it difficult to exploit these opportunities; for example, disparities in personal wealth make Blacks ill fitted to navigate these opportunities' financial backwaters (Bradford, 1990). In fact, weaker Black business start-ups still have lesser access to capital (Bates, 1993). Heading into the 1990s, minority businesses—and Black enterprises in particular—faced additional problems: lack of successful business role models and minimal interest in terms of community patronage, investment, and labor (Chen, 1993).

Still, little is known about the technological adoption processes of Black businesses. In the earliest studies available, Hunte (1984, 1986) looked at Black farmers' use of farm technology and found little knowledge of current record-keeping technologies (1984) and an overall significant absence of basic modern farm equipment (1986). In one of the few generalized studies, the more viable Black businesses were, among others, those that had entered high-technology fields; also, successful Black entrepreneurs tended to have specialized training in high-technology fields (Smith & Moore, 1985).

This relative dearth of knowledge has been acknowledged in the popular press (Muhammad, 1996) and prompted calls for Black businesses to adopt new technology (Davidson, 1989). The Black press has not escaped such calls. To survive, popular wisdom goes, Black newspapers will have to invest in new technology and personnel—specifically, aggressive advertising campaigns, expanded coverage, and technologically enhanced face-lifts (Bernstein, 1989). All are considered a remedy for declining subscriptions and advertisers' claims that Black audiences are already being reached by mainstream media. Although Black newspaper managers report that they believe their newspapers will survive, one survey also showed great concern about advertising support (Lacy, Stephens, & Soffin, 1991). Nearly two-thirds of the managers agreed or strongly agreed that lack of reader support was a reason that African American newspapers fail. A later content analysis suggested Black newspapers' biggest advertising problem is the small amount of advertising from local retail and classified advertising (Lacy & Ramsey, 1994).

Thus, the present study seeks to know how Black newspapers, if they are to continue their tradition as a voice to and for the Black community, will meet and manage—through the use of communication technologies—the economic and marketing challenges they face. Although the general media have failed to provide either sufficient Black news or a Black perspective on the news (Caspari, 1983), and although the Black newspaper still serves the Black community (Hatchett, 1991; Boyd, 1991), Black suburban populations continue to grow (O'Hare, 1989; O'Hare & Frey, 1992) and continue to seek their own sense of identity and community (Durant & Louden, 1986).

Black newspaper trade group officials have pointed to increased circulation and renewed determination to attain a larger share of local advertising (Stein, 1990), but Black newspapers have lost many of their readers and much of their political niche (Strader, 1992). This mismatch of probable demand and supply may suggest a lack of outreach—which may translate into a lack of technological know-how—by the Black newspaper. It is doubtful that the reason for this discrepancy is lack of effort on the part of the Black newspaper, since the industry is attempting to help individual newspapers to deal with the problem (Bernstein, 1989), but the answer inherently lies in the direction, quality, and degree of that effort, particularly in terms of technological aids.

Finding the answer to this conundrum has implications for the survival of the traditional mission and role of the Black press. Though Black newspaper publishers feel the Black press is alive and well and that avenues toward prosperity exist (Bernstein, 1989), the documented lack of advertising constitutes a threat to the continued existence of many Black newspapers. Simultaneously, the interaction of the suburban exodus of the Black middle class and Black newspapers' circulation and advertising poses a vital area of inquiry for newspaper economic and communication theory. Only through direct querying and observation of Black newspaper management can these practical and scholarly interests be appeased.

This chapter represents an initial foray into the status of technology and technology adoption strategies in medium-sized and large Black newspapers as they concern potential suburban readers. An earlier study (Schweitzer, 1992) surveyed daily newspaper marketing research directors as to the role of marketing at their firms; no attempt was made to assess the qualitative impact at either dailies or Black newspapers. This study hopes to provide insight into the managerial decision-making processes as well as organizational culture and behavior of this long-ignored aspect of the print medium. Little research focuses on the economics of Black newspapers, let alone the specific strategy publishers need to deal with this advertising-circulation dilemma. In addition, existing studies have found Black publishers are reluctant to reveal much about their operations.

In short, this chapter attempts to answer three questions. (1) To what extent do Black newspapers take advantage of market-enhancing technology? (2) What managerial approach is taken, and how is such technology generally adopted at Black newspapers? (3) How does such technology (or the lack of it) impact the operations and survival of Black newspapers?

METHODS

The data for this study represent material gathered from the first phase of a three-phase project. For the first phase, medium-sized (circulation between 11,001 and 30,000) and large (circulation more than 30,000) Black newspapers were chosen because a recent content analysis (Lacy & Ramsey, 1994) indicated that large Black papers had fewer ads and less advertising linage than did medium-circulation papers. Although the difference was not statistically significant, it is large enough—more than 90% more ad space—to warrant further inspection.

As the earliest efforts (LaBrie & Zima, 1971) and the latest efforts (Lacy, Stephens, & Soffin, 1991) indicate, discovering the nature of the outreach to the suburban Black middle class by survey probably would be difficult. Low survey return rates are typical of a management class that tends not to share information well with outsiders. This phase employed a qualitative case study approach, since the purpose was to assess the quality of Black newspapers' technology adoption strategies. Six Black newspapers have thus far been visited, with plans to visit more in the near future. The six Black newspapers—one large and five medium-sized newspapers—are in Houston, Dallas, and Austin. Personal contacts with the publishers involved, the added prestige of the author's university affiliation, the personal nature of the inquiry, and the subject matter helped gain entry to each site.

Each visit included interviews with the publisher, editor, advertising manager, circulation manager, and marketing director (if available), as well as key marketing and circulation staff members. Where possible, employee behavior was observed as it regarded the issue under study. Visits generally lasted from a few hours to two days at each newspaper. Interviews were recorded, and extensive notes were taken. Selective follow-up phone interviews also were made after initial data were analyzed. Because each newspaper visited was in a competitive situation, anonymity was given in regard to specific settings, names, and circumstances. As a result, examples in the next section will seem somewhat general. But this concession to specificity yielded greater access to this relatively unstudied industry.

FINDINGS

Extent and Utility

Before assessing, as the first research question asked, the extent to which Black newspapers take advantage of market-enhancing technology, the possible types of technology need examination. Electronic technology has found great use and potential in the newspaper industry. Continuing computer developments will change newspapers' place in society and how they are marketed (Picard & Brody, 1997). Some of the tools that Black newspapers might consider using vary. They include pagination (an electronic editing system that allows pages to be designed and composed on computers), satellites (an extraterrestrial tool that allows the almost spontaneous transmission of information), facsimile (which speedily transmits images and text by satellite or telephone line), and the personal computer (which facilitates word processing as well as database construction, pagination, on-line communication, etc.) (Williams, 1987; Brooks, 1997).

None of the Black Texas publications could generally be considered an innovator or early adopter (Rogers, 1983); instead—depending on the technology—Moore's (1991) psychographic system might be used to classify them as anywhere from "early majority" (the last group of the first 50% to adopt, which seek references before making a substantial investment, and which generally are risk-averse), to "late majority" (the first of the last 50% to adopt, which generally don't like change), to "laggards" (which probably never will purchase a certain technology). For example, as a "late majority" user of word-processing computers, the editor-general manager of a leading Dallas weekly said that she did not know how to use the more advanced computers but that she relied on another staff member to do so. "There's no time to have someone teach us how to use [it]," she said. At the same time, this newspaper made competent use of personal computers to conduct billing and accounting functions. This pattern of fluctuation was typical at the papers observed. It might be more instructive to detail, technology by technology, the degree to which each tool was used.

Given such a selection, probably the most widely used (and the oldest) technology was facsimile (fax) transmission. All the Texas publications regularly used the fax, primarily as a vehicle to send messages, particularly advertising and billing materials. The pervasiveness of the fax came as no surprise, since one expects it—as the oldest of those new technologies available (surpassed only by the telephone)—to conform to traditional diffusion theory, which predicts that the longer a technology exists, the more widespread its adoption (Rogers, 1983).

After the fax, however, there was a considerable drop-off in the use of newer technologies. The next most widely used tool was the personal computer. Five of the six newspapers used personal computers in some manner, and use primarily included word processing. Computers and related equipment ranged in ages from new to 20 years old or older; many of the computers at the smaller newspapers were secondhand, discounted models.

In terms of word processing, at the typical paper the computers stored text and headlines (the one newspaper without a computer at the time of observation used a relatively archaic, automated typewriter that produced camera-ready copy, but in only one typeface; the publisher has since purchased a secondhand computer from a rival publisher). All computers were in fairly constant use, with a handful of employees constituting the more frequent computer users. In general, computer use at the Black newspapers was not distinguishable from use at any other weekly newspaper; heavier use occurred during peak production times, while more intermittent use occurred during off times.

However, in a sense, most of the newspapers still were at the mercy of an external typewriter. Each paper relied on freelance writers, and a majority were heavily dependent on syndicated, preprinted material (e.g., editorials and columns). Many freelancers worked without the aid of a personal computer. As a result, much freelance material, once submitted to the newspaper, had to be entered into the computer, causing some duplication of effort and schedule adjustments at those papers. The syndicated material often was "camera-ready," that is, required no additional handling before being placed on the page. Still, in most cases such material often was set in type that varied with the newspaper's predominant typeface. This was particularly true at the smaller newspapers, which were the heavier users of such nonstaff services. This combined to mitigate somewhat the personal computer's overall word-processing capabilities.

A word about nonjournalistic use of the personal computer: all those newspapers using the personal computer also employed it for business/accounting functions. Most of the time, these uses meant compiling a database of customers, as well as recording business transactions such as advertising and subscription requests (accounts receivable and accounts payable). Only one newspaper used the technology for more advanced administrative functions (computing tax returns, generating financial reports and forecasts, producing newsletters and extensive management information) or for possibly enhanced journalistic capabilities (electronic delivery, albeit in the development stages; one additional newspaper had plans to explore its on-line potential).

Black newspapers made little use of pagination technology. This tool, often shown to be a double-edged sword (e.g., Sylvie, 1995)—efficient, but with costs in terms of user satisfaction and change in work structure—is only recently making its way into Black newspapers. The inherent efficiency in the technology lies in its ability to design the page electronically and print out a camera-ready sheet, helping the newspaper to avoid the untidy and labor-intensive "backshop" process of waxing and pasting text onto a sheet in preparation for making the entire sheet camera-ready; the technology has the potential to make the copy editor and "backshop" editor one and the same. The problem in daily newspapers (where most large-scale pagination occurs) has come from copy editors who resent the mechanization of what they traditionally have perceived as a journalistic task (Sylvie, 1995). In the Black newspapers observed, only one newspaper used what's known as "full pagination," that is, designing complete pages on the computer. Two other papers were partially paginated, designing only parts or "sections" of pages (usually a story and its accompanying headline). The remaining papers used no pagination and were using their personal computers to produce text in the traditional cut-and-paste manner (often using files stored on computer disks, transferring the disks to typesetting machines, which then produced copy that had to be cut and pasted in the backshop).

Lastly, satellite transmission proved to be even more foreign than pagination to the observed Black newspapers. Only one newspaper used a satellite-transmitted "wire service" to provide nonlocal text; the same newspaper also receives advertising in this manner. This is not surprising, since most weeklies concern themselves with "local news"—issues and matters of local import or bearing on the immediate community of readers—and leave anything else to the purview of daily newspapers. The weeklies surveyed for this study primarily rely on the various postal services to receive and send material over extensive distances.

In summary, technology use at the observed Black newspapers varies, ranging from pervasive use of more common, relatively inexpensive technology (fax and personal computers), to lesser and, in some cases, almost universal nonuse of more select, recent technologies (pagination and satellite transmission).

Management Approaches and Adoption

Media organizations usually take one of the following approaches to technology: structural, technological-task, and sociotechnical (Lacy, Sohn, & Wicks, 1993). The structural approach focuses on technology as a planned, controlled instrument of management—a tool for managing people. The technological-task approach sees technology creating a certain observable, direct reaction in the organization. The sociotechnical approach combines the previous two approaches, focusing on the needs and actions of the users as well as the traits of the technology. In essence, then, the structural path looks at an organization's system or process of work and attempts to change it, whereas the technological-task method seeks to evoke a certain phenomenon or reaction *within* the process; it's then left to the sociotechnical manager to combine the two in a strategy that attempts systemic changes and specific, internal controls.

At the observed Black newspapers, the predominant managerial approach appeared to be a technological task. In each newspaper visited, the primary technology uses were task-related and only remotely connected to overall, systemic concerns. At almost every facility, technology was seen as a method to achieve a specific objective. For example, each newspaper used the personal computer for its more immediate benefits—namely, to ease word processing and facilitate numerical calculations in the form of accounting. Even in the case of the more advanced pagination users, the technology was viewed as a means to facilitate paste-up and control copy flow and copy manipulation—and not (as a structuralist might want) as a tool to revolutionize work routines and enact attitudinal change in the staff regarding the structure of work. In short, in the case of pagination and personal computers, most of the Black newspaper managers used them as new tools for old, ongoing tasks.

Within this approach was an adoption process, as set forth by Rogers (1983). The process involves agenda-setting, matching, redefining/restructuring, clarifying, and routinizing. Translated, this means that management first chooses to adopt the technology, which then is introduced to the organization, where interaction with the technology occurs. The nature of this interaction, in turn, influences management's perceptions regarding the technology, leading management to redefine its objectives and adjust and/or restructure the technology's role. Clarification ensues, employees' perceptions of the technology change, and a period of readjustment follows.

The observed Black newspapers were no exception to this process. At each publication, once a technology was adopted, employees—when possible— adjusted their skills to learn the technology. No employee upheaval or consternation was observed. Most training, by all appearances, was done in-house, with most employees learning by trial and error. In fact, several employees expressed ignorance in dealing with the computers or in describing their functions. Often, they would refer such questions to another, more knowledgeable authority; many times, this authority was considered the technologically competent individual on staff in regard to the technology. Other employees were unable to describe their training experiences in terms of their present employer, citing the fact that they had gained experience in previous jobs.

Only one newspaper went so far as to hire outside training consultants to train employees. Adjustment by this newspaper's employees was initially slow to pagination, for example. The critical employee was a woman in her mid-50s who had been laying out pages for ten years using the previous cut-and-paste technology. Computerization represented a fearful unknown and was resisted; but the woman realized she had no choice but to learn the technology if she wished to do her job. Now she proudly displays her proficiency with her new tool.

In summary, most technology at the Black newspapers was one-dimensional in terms of adoption and approach. Each technology was introduced from the standpoint of accomplishing one set of tasks, whether it be journalistic or administrative. As a result, the technological learning slope was linear and quick; single-task expectations led to familiarity, which then led to routine performance and, thus, adoption.

Impact

Williams (1987) argued that organizations, when implementing new technology, should emphasize creating a more effective organization rather than simply emphasizing the operation of the technology itself. Broadly, potential benefits include enhanced effectiveness of business operations, increased competitive advantage of the business, and enhanced value of the business. Such a categorization system works well, as the third research question asked, in assessing, the extent to which technology (or the lack of it) affects the operations and survival of the observed Black newspapers. Simply put, this issue deals with the technology's impact on the newspapers' market structure or the way the market is organized. This structure begins with the geographic limits of the market, followed by, among others, the nature of the product and the number of competitors (Lacy, Sohn, & Wicks, 1993). A general look at the newspapers studied follows, using the structural elements as organizing elements.

Geography. Technology often has the power to blur market boundaries, particularly on-line technology, with its capabilities of electronic delivery. But in the present study, none of the newspapers make but the most minimal use of this tool; as a result, no geographical blurring has occurred. So when it comes to technology, by and large the newspapers continue to retain their traditional geographic limits. There are two exceptions, however, one general and three specific.

The general exception occurs through the use of the fax, which allows the newspapers to occasionally garner advertisements or generate business with customers who are similarly equipped. However, such activity is not all that common, and the fact that all the newspapers have a fax means no one has a geographical advantage.

More specifically, pagination has proven an exception through its ability to facilitate one newspaper's attempt to publish an additional, youth-oriented publication that it delivers to local high schools. This gives the newspaper an additional geographic market to serve, as well as generating additional revenue via advertising. Conversely, those newspapers without the technology (or those not taking similar advantage of pagination) do not have such additional markets.

In addition, satellite transmission has greatly aided the same newspaper's ability to garner revenue from AdSend, an Associated Press service that sends materials directly to newspapers via satellite and digital technology. This tool provides the publication with the speed and capability to transmit advertising messages to its readers.

Finally, one newspaper has managed to use the personal computer to create a prototype publication or "pamphlet" that it intends to distribute to advertisers. The pamphlet would attempt to persuade advertisers as to the more promising, salient features of the newspaper in regard to potential audiences and exposure. This subtle public relations attempt has allowed the newspaper to go beyond the traditional "media kit/rate card" handout and attempt to expand its advertiser market.

Product Nature. Because Black newspapers provide an advertising as well as a news product, certain text-based technologies provide double-barreled potential in that regard. The previous section detailed the ability of pagination to enhance advertising revenue by helping to produce additional, related products. But the technology also enables its user to design a product that—to the casual eye—contains fewer errors, more appealing graphics, more appeasing typefaces, and nondisruptive textual variety, as well as to facilitate interdepartmental (electronic) handling of advertising space.

In the cases of two of the three Black newspapers using pagination, that promise remains largely unfulfilled, due mainly to the piecemeal approach employing the technology. Those newspapers' partial pagination methods (still largely in the trial-and-error stages) restrict this potential and confine the technology to its more basic, immediate role of layout enhancement tool. To be fair, much of this limited approach is entirely due to limited funding on the part of the publications, which—because of their size and financial limitations— could not afford additional personnel or resources required to reach pagination's potential.

Regarding the remaining technologies, however, they largely do not have product-altering potential. To give personal computers this power, for example, would require additional, expensive software, which most of the papers studied, again, could not afford. The same would be true for fax machines.

Number of Competitors. Technology often has the capacity to expand or diminish the number of competitors. Not to overdo a previous example, pagination has made one of the newspapers studied a new entry into the market for youthful readers. Technology aside, however, there have been few attempts to use the technologies studied to directly affect competitors. All the newspapers studied appear to be more concerned with packaging, distributing, and promoting their own products rather than trying to drive away competitors or enter new competitive markets.

This also appears to be a function of the small-staff nature of Black newspapers; unless the manager-owner makes a point of developing such a strategy, much of the staff's energy goes into daily tasks of routine production. For example, during the author's visit, one publisher's main concern was how to position his publication in a more visible place at the point of purchase. An entire staff meeting was devoted to this question; the publisher even took it upon himself to deliver a new rack to one location. There apparently was little thought given to changing or modifying the product for preparation into a new market.

In summary, then, the technologies studied have great potential to change the market landscape for their host newspapers. But those publications, with the exception of one, have chosen instead to pursue day-to-day, survival operations rather than to use the tools as strategic elements in an overall plan of change. In short, the market structure—the newspapers' effectiveness, competitive standing, and business value—has remained largely unchanged. A rationale for the status quo is examined in the next section.

DISCUSSION

Katzman (1974) proposed that new communication technologies would create new information gaps before old information gaps close. "Unless the gap in technological information and expertise is closed, traditionally marginalized groups like African Americans will be pushed even further to the sidelines," the leading U.S. Black business publication has stated (Muhammad, 1996). Besides being a public policy issue, observation shows this to be an organizational concern as well, particularly where it involves Black newspapers.

This chapter has shown that Black newspapers—beyond the routine operational structure—by and large remain largely unaffected by advanced technology. Manager-owners have chosen to use the technology as a method to improve internal procedures and strengthen the work flow. There certainly is nothing wrong with this decision—if the objective is to remain stationary. That obviously is not the goal of the publishers; they say they're constantly seeking additional advertising revenues and ways to improve.

But successful technological implementation requires a certain kind of action not witnessed in the typical publication. Meticulous planning is the hallmark of such success, but, as Gagnon and Toulouse (1996) suggest, most managers act as entrepreneurs (i.e., they lack the ability to plan), yet we know (Thong & Yap, 1995) that small businesses are more likely to adopt information technology when the chief executive officer is more innovative.

There certainly seemed to be no lack of innovation and planning during many of the author's visits to the Texas sites, but when it came to technology, this was not the case. Again, this is not a judgment, but a concession to the fact that Black newspapers—like many Black businesses and many non-Black businesses—lack the resources for successful planning. There is no shame in that; it is simply a fact of life for a small business. Many Black newspapers have, as one publisher put it, "internal problems" and don't have time for sound technological planning.

The problem comes when recalling the traditional vocal role that Black newspapers have exercised in the Black community's struggle for equality. To extend the metaphor, if the voice speaks but lacks much of the expertise and planning necessary to assure its existence in a more competitive marketplace, will the voice speak as strongly and be heeded as quickly?

Some publishers are hoping that some prominent information providers, such as AT&T, will carry Black newspapers along with them onto the information highway. At this writing, a group of Texas publishers is reported to be attempting to negotiate as much, aware that AT&T might want something in return. "But, hey," acknowledged one newspaper's general manager, "we as African American newspapers have to get up to speed. If you don't have the technology you can just drop by the wayside."

Absent such promising prospects, however, many Black newspapers will have to emulate their more successful kin, especially as it pertains to more effectively reaching the middle-class Black reader. Hope lies in the fact that African Americans reduce their use of media outlets that portray them negatively (Perry, 1996), so there is some control for Black newspapers as it pertains to content. But content won't matter if the product doesn't have adequate distribution. This is where taking advantage of such technologies as pagination and satellite transmission (electronic delivery) can make a difference.

Such technologically advanced newspapers will find their audiences more receptive to these overtures. The most technologically savvy newspaper in this study has recognized as much. "The future is how do you access the reader?" the publisher asked. "Those who have access will have power. Those who don't, won't." This visionary publisher added that getting a companion publication established in area high schools was important "because the schools are going to be the first place they're exposed to high technology. If we can get [the school district] to use [the newspaper] as a tool, then we've got our name in front."

This strategy (of using technology to target younger Black readers) may not sit well with some traditional owner-managers and their clientele, however, because, as one frustrated, youth-oriented editor said, "The African American elder generation thinks that if they let us go like White folks let their kids go, that we'll shoot them in the head." In short, the Black newspaper may find itself having to choose between a new—technologically advanced and less traditional—product and business as usual. The latter choice still appears a healthy one, given the fact that even some of the smaller cities have two or more Black newspapers (often the author discovered that many of the studied newspapers do not consider themselves "in competition"). However, a desire for significant growth and continued influence may complicate the choice.

The role of technology in this choice is clear. It is—and always will remain—a tool, nothing more or less. The ever-increasing choice potential posed by new, developing media, however, changes the notion of the media-audience relation as it regards selection. With so many choices, consumers—especially affluent African American consumers—will become even more elusive for African American newspapers. "You have to know the difference between circulation and readership," one publisher said in reference to the fact that many Black newspapers are freely distributed in order to pump up circulation figures. "Many Black newspapers don't."

Finally, such newspapers must ask themselves if they truly are serving the readers they claim when they do not take advantage of the available advanced technology. New media do not usually replace older ones but instead evolve to adjust to new usage patterns. Can traditional Black newspapers complete such an evolution? Can they use technology to adjust to new patterns and new readers? The evidence (in one of the newspapers studied) shows that such evolutionary adjustments are possible; their probability depends on the foresight of the manager-owners as well as their ability to command the necessary resources. But limited education and financial resources will always be a problem in gaining access to the information superhighway (Graber, 1995). Smaller firms, such as Black newspapers, must overcome the additional handicap of a lack of infrastructure—perhaps the AT&T partnership may be somewhat foretelling—that specialized publication in the electronic world will necessitate (Horowitz, 1995). Whether the Black newspaper industry will clear this hurdle remains to be seen.

REFERENCES

Bates, T. (1973). *Black Capitalism: A Quantitative Analysis*. New York: Praeger.

Bates, T. (1993). *Banking on Black Enterprise: The Potential of Emerging Firms for Revitalizing Urban Economies*. Washington, DC: Joint Center for Political and Economic Studies.

Bernstein, M. (1989, June). Pressing on. *Black Enterprise, 19* (11), 142-148.

Boyd, H. (1991). The Black press: A long history of service and advocacy. *Crisis, 98* (3), 10-13.

Bradford, W. D. (1990). *Wealth, Assets, and Income in Black Households*. Afro-American Studies Program, University of Maryland.

Brimmer, A. (1966). The Negro in the national economy. In J. David (Ed.), *American Negro Reference Book*. Englewood Cliffs, NJ: Prentice-Hall, (pp. 251-321).

Brimmer, A., & Terrell, H. (1971, Spring). The economic potential of Black capitalism. *Public Policy 19*, 289-308.

Brooks, B. S. (1997*). Journalism in the Information Age: A Guide to Computers for Reporters and Editors*. Boston: Allyn & Bacon.

Caspari, G. G. (1983). *The Impatient Press: Placing Black newspapers in the ideologies of Black progress*. Paper presented at Association for Education in Journalism and Mass Communication Convention, Corvallis, OR.

Chen, G. M. (1993). Minority business development: Where do we go from here? *Review of Black Political Economy, 22* (2), 5-10.

Cragg, P. B., & King, M. (1993). Small-firm computing: Motivators and inhibitors. *MIS Quarterly, 17* (1), 47-60.

Davidson, J. (1989, June). An agenda for the 1990's. *Black Enterprise, 19* (11), 152-158.

Durant, T. J., Jr., & Louden, J. S. (1986). The Black middle class in America: Historical and contemporary perspectives. *Phylon, 47* (4), 253-263.

Fitzgerald, M. (1986, August 30). Threatened with extinction? *Editor & Publisher,* 11-12.

Fitzgerald, M. (1990, July 14). Silver lining in ad gloom. *Editor & Publisher,* 26-27.

Gagnon, Y. C., & Toulouse, J. M. (1996). The behavior of business managers when adopting new technologies. *Technological Forecasting and Social Change, 52* (1), 59-74.

Gatignon, H., & Robertson, T. (1989). Technology diffusion: An empirical test of competitive effects. *Journal of Marketing, 53,* 35-49.

Graber, D. A. (1995). Potholes along America's public information superhighway. *Research in Political Sociology, 7,* 299-324.

Guzda, M. K. (1984, March 31). A battle for ad dollars. *Editor & Publisher,* 13-14.

Hatchett, D. (1991). The Black newspaper: Still serving the community. *Crisis, 98* (3), 14-17.

Holzinger, A. G. (1993). Small firms' usage patterns. *Nation's Business, 81* (8), 39-40.

Horowitz, I. L. (1995). The assured future of specialized publishers in the electronic world. *Logos, 6* (3), 158-161.

Hunte, C. N. (1984). *An assessment of Black farmers' adaptability to agricultural technology.* Paper presented to Southern Association of Agricultural Scientists.

Hunte, C. N. (1986). *An inventory of farm equipment on Black farms.* Paper presented to Rural Sociological Society.

Johnson, J. H. (1990). Recent African American migration trends in the United States. *Urban League Review, 14* (1), 39-55.

Joseph, W. F. (1985, July 25). Identity crisis hurts minority press. *Advertising Age,* 51-52.

Julien, A. P. (1995). New technologies and technological information in small businesses. *Journal of Business Venturing, 10* (6), 459-475.

Katzman, N. (1974). The impact of communication technology: Some theoretical premises and their implications. *Ekistics, 225,* 125-130.

LaBrie, H. G., III, & Zima, W. J. (1971). Directional quandaries of the Black press in the United States. *Journalism Quarterly, 48* (4), 640-644.

Lacy, S., & Ramsey, K. A. (1994). The advertising content of African American newspapers. *Journalism Quarterly, 71* (3), 521-530.

Lacy, S., Sohn, A. B., & Wicks, J. L. (1993). *Media Management: A Casebook Approach*. Hillsdale, NJ: Lawrence Erlbaum Associates.

Lacy, S., Stephens, J. M., & Soffin, S. (1991). The future of the African American press. *Newspaper Research Journal, 12* (3), 8-19.

Landry, B. (1987). *The New Black Middle Class*. Berkeley: University of California Press.

Lefebvre, L. A., Harvey, J., & Lefebvre, E. (1991). Technological experience and the technology adoption decisions in small manufacturing firms. *R & D Management, 21* (3), 241-249.

Logan, J. R., & Schneider, M. (1984). Racial segregation and racial change in American suburbs, 1970-1980. *American Journal of Sociology, 89*, 874-888.

MacPherson, A. D. (1994). Industrial innovation among small and medium-sized firms in a declining region. *Growth and Change, 25* (2), 145-163.

Markwalder, D. (1981). The potential for Black business. *The Review of Black Political Economy, 11* (4), 303-312.

Moore, G. (1991). *Crossing the Chasm*. New York: HarperBusiness.

Muhammad, T. K. (1996, May). Keeping pace with technology. *Black Enterprise, 26* (10), 42.

O'Hare, W. P. (1989). In the Black. *American Demographics, 11* (11), 24-28.

O'Hare, W. P., & Frey, W. H. (1992). Booming, suburban and Black. *American Demographics, 14* (9), 30-35.

Perry, E. L. (1996). Media use habits of African Americans in a small midwestern city. Paper presented at Association for Education in Journalism and Mass Communication Convention, Anaheim, CA.

Picard, R. G., & Brody, J. H. (1997). *The Newspaper Publishing Industry*. Boston: Allyn & Bacon.

Pierce, J. (1947). *Negro Business and Business Education*. New York: Harper & Brothers.

Rogers, E. M. (1983). *Diffusion of Innovations*. New York: Free Press.

Rose, H. M. (1976). *Black Suburbanization*. Cambridge, MA: Ballinger.

Schweitzer, J. C. (1992). Marketing research in the newspaper business: A study of researchers and publishers. In S. Lacy, A. B. Sohn, & R. H. Giles (Eds.), *Readings in Media Management*. Columbia, SC: Association for Education in Journalism and Mass Communication, pp. 153-180.

Smith, A. W., & Moore, J. V. (1985). East-West differences in Black economic development. *Journal of Black Studies 16* (2), 131-154.

Statistics Canada (1991). Indicators for Science and Technology 1989. Survey of Technology. Catalog 88-002. 1(4).

Stein, M. L. (1990, February 3). Black publishers' perspective: Newspaper execs meet to discuss the state of their business. *Editor & Publisher, 11*, 43.

Strader, J. (1992). Black on Black. *Washington Journalism Review, 14* (2), 33-36.

Suggs, R. (1986). Recent changes in Black-owned business. Paper produced for the Joint Center for Political Studies, Washington, DC.

Sylvie, G. (1995). Editors and pagination: A case study in management. *Journal of Mediated Communication, 10* (1), 1-20.

Taylor, J. R., Moore, E. G., & Amonsen, E. J. (1994). Profiling technology diffusion categories: Empirical test of two models. *Journal of Business Research, 31* (2-3), 155-162.

Thong, J., & Yap, C. S. (1995). CEO characteristics, organizational characteristics and information technology adoption in small businesses. *Omega-International Journal of Management Science, 23* (4), 429-442.

U.S. Department of Commerce (1988). *Current Industrial Reports: Manufacturing Technology 1988*. Washington, DC: Author.

Ward, F. B. (1973). The Black press in crisis. *Black Scholar, 5* (1), 34-36.

Williams, F. (1987). *Technology and Communication Behavior*. Belmont, CA: Wadsworth.

Winsberg, M. D. (1985). Flight from the ghetto: The migration of middle class and highly educated Blacks into White urban neighborhoods. *American Journal of Economics and Sociology, 44* (4), 411-421.

Wolseley, R. E. (1990). *The Black Press, U.S.A.* Ames: Iowa State University Press.

CHAPTER 5

FCC Policy and the Underdevelopment of Black Entrepreneurship

G. Thomas Wilson II

INTRODUCTION

The Federal Communications Commission (FCC) policies, combined with those of the U.S. Economic Development Administration (EDA), lending institutions, and advertisers, have had a cumulative, adverse effect on the sustained growth of telecommunications ownership in the Black community. FCC ownership policies emphasize serving the "public interest, convenience, and necessity" (PICN), with diversity being a major "pillar" of PICN. Although the Constitution, the First Amendment, the Communications Act of 1934, the Telecommunications Act of 1996 and their amendments were worded as inclusive documents, in implementation, application, and practice, they appear to be very exclusive.

This chapter examines, primarily, the relationship between the sustained growth of minority ownership of broadcast stations and the pertinent FCC policies, programs, and implementation practices. Additionally, it examines the relationship between pertinent EDA and federal Equal Credit Opportunity Act (ECOA) lending policies, lending institution (LI) practices, and minority ownership. This component is extremely important based on the fact that in a capitalist system, if a business does not have equitable access to capital for start-up, operation, and maintenance and/or expansion, it cannot exist in that system.

The First Amendment of the U.S. Constitution is based on great ideals and sound principles. The Communication Act of 1934 was similarly written in a language that purported to benefit **all** the people, but it also excluded groups including minorities and women. The media system of the United States is based on private ownership and operation. The Communications Act of 1934, however, authorized various types of licensing and regulation developed and implemented by FCC to serve the PICN.

FCC DIVERSITY POLICIES

From 1952 until 1984, due to the scarcity of spectrum frequencies on the radio and television (TV) dials, the FCC's multiple ownership rule allowed owners of broadcast properties to own only a maximum of seven AM radio stations, seven FM radio stations, and seven TV stations nationwide. This rule was known as the "7-7-7 Rule." The stated purpose of the rule was twofold: (1) to encourage diversity of ownership in order to foster the expression of varied viewpoints and programming and (2) to safeguard against undue concentration of economic power (better known as monopolies).

In 1978, to encourage further diversity of ownership and to foster even more expression of varied viewpoints and programming, the FCC enacted policies to encourage minority ownership of broadcast properties. This action was taken because minority groups observed, and the FCC concurred, that the 7-7-7 Rule had not adequately increased minority ownership. One policy included using a lottery system for determining which of the many applicants for broadcast frequencies and stations would be allowed to participate in the license-granting process. Minorities and ownership groups with significant numbers of minorities in their ownership/ management team were allowed "two balls" in the lottery process to increase their chances of being selected. Furthermore, when stations were sold in the normal transaction of business, if the current owner(s) sold the station to minorities or to a group with 51% minorities in it, capital gains tax certificates were granted by the commission allowing a lower/delayed tax liability. The required time for reinvestment of the profits was also extended. Additionally, those current owners who were scheduled for a hearing to have their licenses revoked for violating FCC regulations were allowed this same "tax certificate" privilege with one major stipulation—that they must transfer or assign their license(s) at a "distress sale" price to minority applicants.

Distress sale price meant that the owner(s) had to sell the station at 75% of its market value. However, with the tax certificate "loophole," the owner(s) still got the equivalent of market value by inflating or misrepresenting the station value by 25%. The practice of inflating or misrepresenting the value of a business, in general, was rampant during the late 1970s and throughout the 1980s. (U.S. Senate, 1989).

RESEARCH QUESTIONS

The three major issues that this chapter seeks to address are as follows:

1. What is the association between FCC regulatory policies and the sustained growth of minority ownership of broadcast stations; specifically, did FCC regulatory policies encourage or discourage sustained minority ownership growth?

2.   What is the association between EDA's regulatory policies and the sustained growth of minority ownership of broadcast stations? The main points to be examined are as follows:

   a.   Do EDA regulatory policies encourage or discourage sustained minority ownership growth?

   b.   Do LI practices encourage or discourage sustained minority ownership growth?

   c.   Do LI practices adhere to the spirit and/or the letter of the federal Equal Credit Opportunity Act (ECOA)?

3.   Do the combined regulatory policies and practices of the FCC, EDA, and lending institutions encourage or discourage the sustained growth of minority ownership of broadcast stations?

I contend that the combined regulatory policies and (nonenforcement) practices of the FCC, EDA, and lending institutions *discouraged* the *sustained growth* of minority ownership of broadcast stations.

Before I discuss these issues, I provide some background on the development and rationale of modern FCC ownership and diversity policies.

OWNERSHIP AND DIVERSITY

From 1952 until 1984 the broadcast industry abided by the FCC's 7-7-7 Rule. The stated purpose was to foster diversity and disallow the growth of monopolies. However, in 1984 the FCC deleted the 7-station rule and implemented the 14-14-14 station rule, which became known as the "12-12-12 Rule." At best, this is another code word for saying "you people" and, at worst, "you niggers" and other derogatory names for people of color. This rule of 14 allowed entities to own up to 12 each of AM, FM, and TV stations *without* including minorities or women as part of the ownership team. However, if owners wanted to own a 13th and 14th station in either or all categories, the ownership team had to include a substantial number of minorities and/or women. This is how the misnomer of 12-12-12 developed, because very few, if any, nonminority multiple owners included (or intended to include) minorities as part of their team. However, a substantial number of these owners used/misused nonminority women and/or the names of nonminority women (grandmothers, mothers, wives, daughters, secretaries, maids, friends, etc.) to qualify for, and acquire, stations 13 and 14. Therefore, in the mid- to late 1980s, the FCC removed "women" from the minority-and-women ownership rule. Whenever abuses of these policies were reported, these nonminority owners who profited and nonminority women were seldom, if ever, implicated, but Blacks were.

Some of the objections to increasing ownership limits from 7 to 14 were that the already prohibitive media prices would drastically increase, and become even more prohibitive, and the media groups and networks would buy more stations (Broadcasting, 1989). This action would encourage ownership concentration (monopolies) and limit the availability of stations and other telecommunications properties for other independent owners, including minorities. The commission's multiple ownership rule of 14 favored big corporations and increased ownership concentration. Further, this duopoly policy had the appearance of hurting potential owners who happened to be minorities. There were also changes made in the comparative hearing process.

The FCC, in a 1989 comparative hearing among seven minority applicants for a new FM station in Marco, Florida, permitted a company not among the original seven to come in and buy out the others. Therefore, this new policy permits a nonminority to enter the process and outbid minorities. The National Black Media Coalition (NBMC) asked the FCC to "restrict such outside party buyouts to those that will foster diversification of mass media ownership."

In March 1992 the commission adopted new radio station ownership rules. Previously, owners had been limited to 14 AM, FM, and television (TV) stations, but the new rules initially set the limits at 30 AM and 30 FM stations, with TV stations remaining at 14. Additionally, the minority ownership requirements were removed. After much opposition, protests, and threatened legal action by media and citizen activist groups and individuals, the FCC amended the rule in August 1992 ("Sikes Says," 1992; "FCC Amends," 1992). This amendment allowed owners up to 22 AM and 22 FM stations, with TV stations remaining at 14. The rule became known as the "18-18-12 Rule" because owners could purchase up to 18 AM and FM radio stations and 12 TV stations without including minorities in the ownership team. However, they could own up to 20 AM and FM stations if minorities were a minimum of 20% of the ownership team. Furthermore, they could own up to 23 AM, and 23 FM stations and 14 TV stations if they were "small business controlled or minority controlled" These increases/changes were, and still are, being opposed by media and citizen activist groups.

Concurrent with the "merger mania" and hostile takeovers of the 1990s, the FCC has been heavily lobbied to change the ownership limits for TV stations. FCC chairman William Kennard is studying how minorities can benefit if limits are lifted, that is, a return to some form of the "spin-off" aspect of the prior ownership rules.

LENDING POLICIES AND MINORITIES

For many years, minorities as groups and individuals have protested, complained, and filed grievances through the legislative, judicial, and executive branches of local, state and national government agencies about the marked inequities in the lending practices of lending institutions. A 1985/1986 study funded jointly by the U.S. Minority Business Development Agency (MBDA), the U.S. Economic Development Administration (EDA), and the U.S. Small Business Administration (SBA) provide major insight to minority business ownership, in general. The study is known as "the JACA study" (1985, 1986), as it was conducted by the JACA Corporation. This same information can also be applied to minority broadcasting ownership, specifically.

The JACA study states that one of the issues that arise in minority economic development is the availability and cost of capital to the minority-owned business relative to nonminority-owned business. Concerns have been voiced that both debt and equity capital are in short supply to the minority-owned business and that debt capital is more costly to the minority-owned firm when it is made available.

Equity capital has been said to be largely unavailable to minorities at business start-up on the grounds that minorities are believed to have accumulated very little net worth during their paid employment prior to business ownership due to low salaries. Hence, they have little money of their own to invest in their firms. To the extent that their friends and relatives are minorities as well, there is also said to be less equity capital from this source. Partly because minorities lack equity capital at start-up, their firms are believed to perform poorly even after they are established.

Debt-type capital is also said to be largely unavailable to minorities. The typical explanation is that there is discrimination against minorities in lending by commercial banks—by far the largest suppliers of debt-type capital to a firm, whatever the ethnicity of its owner. This discrimination is said to exist despite the Federal Equal Credit Opportunity Act (ECOA), which made discrimination based on a number of factors, including race, illegal beginning in the mid-1970s. An alternative explanation has nothing to do with discrimination: loans to minorities pose greater risks of default to banks; hence, loans are denied. The loan program of the U.S. SBA—while an important source of debt-type capital to minorities—is said to be unable to make up completely for the lack of bank credit.

Therefore, many, if not all, Blacks are forced to resort to venture capitalists (VCs) for financing. From my perspective, many VCs are the loan sharks/ pawnshops of the business world. They require from 51% to 90% partnership in the business and a very high interest rate on the business loan. This means that Black owners have to service this major debt, or the VC will take over the property and sell it back to White single- or multistation owners. The other option for Blacks wanting to become owners is to "partner" with major multistation owners and also settle for 5% to 20% ownership. Additionally, Blacks are put in the position of rationalizing to themselves that if they want to play the game to make a difference in negative media images or for fame and fortune, "5% of something is better than 100% of nothing."

Until the mid-1980s, there was no national database of business owners who provided information on these (and other) capital issues and who differed in their ethnicity. As a result, there was no way to evaluate these capital issues for the minority-owned business relative to the nonminority-owned business. Without an empirical evaluation of capital issues, no policy position could be taken.

Although there has not been a published study on lending practices to minority-owned broadcast businesses specifically, the FCC did hold an en banc hearing in February 1986. This occurred after actual and proposed legal action(s) by many media/citizen activist groups. The stated purpose of this hearing was to address the issues of financing broadcast acquisitions by minorities and increasing advertising placements at minority-owned radio and television stations. The commission posited that "discussion of these issues among minority entrepreneurs, financiers, and advertisers is another in a series of FCC efforts to remedy the problem of under-representation of minorities in broadcast station ownership."

The hearing amplifies the aforementioned JACA study findings with the added jeopardy of nonminority businesses withdrawing, reducing, and/or refusing advertisement with minority-owned stations. Advertising is the primary source of income (lifeblood) for *every* broadcast station. When advertisers in a Michigan multicollege area discovered the owner(s) of a rock station were African American, they withdrew advertising (even branches of the military). The same occurred with a country and western station in Nebraska. Many minority owners testified that even though their stations were number one or so in their market (based on Arbitron/Nielsen rating services), the advertisers refused to pay proportionate rates. Nonminority-owned stations that were rated much lower were paid at the highest rates. Many also testified that Arbitron/Nielsen refused to document the station's rating (new stations) or reduced the station's rating (existing stations) after they discovered the station was minority-owned. Additionally, these owners voiced their concerns that there were very few, if any, minority households used in either rating system.

More recently, *The Final Call* ("White Ad Agency Memo," 1998) reported that further proof of "old-fashioned racism" came to light. A 1997 memo circulated at Amcast, a division of Katz Media Group, argued that advertisers should not advertise on Black radio stations, because "advertisers should want prospects not suspects."

Combined with having to service major debts and being paid less per ad, even though they are number one in the market, Black-owned stations have to play more commercials per break—for radio and TV—and more infomercials for TV. This formula drastically reduces programming for community and public interest.

MINORITY AND MAJORITY OWNERSHIP

One could contend that the ownership levels were increased so the group- and multiplestation owners could absorb the failing stations of minorities and nonminorities. Additionally, one could conclude that the limit for inclusion of minorities in the ownership team was set so high to ensure that minority owners of these failed stations would not be considered for "mergers." Therefore, minority owners would not automatically be considered part of the stations' ownership or management, which also eliminates the probability of functional diversity.

Under the guise of the federal government's Paper Reduction Act of 1980, effective April 1, 1981, the FCC eliminated the requirement for stations to gather, report, and maintain the information that had been used as evidence to revoke station licenses, such as station logs, and community ascertainments. The FCC called this process the marketplace theory, which provided a basis for the deregulation of the radio and television broadcast industry, especially relative to program content. The commission's view was that market incentives will ensure the presentation of programming that responds to community needs and provide sufficient incentives for licensees to become and remain aware of the needs and problems of their communities.

From 1978 to November 1989 the FCC approved a total of 38 distress sales and issued 201 tax certificates in conjunction with the assignment or transfer of radio and TV stations. Based on these figures, especially in 1979-1983, one could surmise that a plethora of stations were caught breaking the law, that their licenses were being revoked, or that the rest of the industry "straightened up." The FCC version (policy) of the Paper Reduction Act helped eliminate an adequate "audit trail" that could lead to license revocation.

Table 5.1
The Number of Stations Owned from 1977 to 1982

	1977			1982		
Medium	Total	Minority	Black	Total	Minority	Black
TV	965	8	4	1,045	18	13
Radio	8,175	43	34	9,101	178	13

Source: National Association of Broadcasters. Minority Broadcasting Facts (1984, August and 1986, September). Washington, DC: Department of Minority and Special Services.

Prior to the minority ownership policies of 1978, minorities owned 0.8% of the TV stations (8 of 965); Blacks owned 0.5% (4 of 965). Minorities owned 0.5% of the radio stations (43 of 8,175); Blacks owned 0.4% (34 of 8,1750). From 1978 to 1982, *four years,* minority ownership of TV stations grew from 0.5% to 1.7% of the total market (18 of 1,045); Blacks owned 1.2% (13 of 1,045). Minority ownership of radio stations grew from 0.5% to 2.0% of the total market (178 of 9,101); Blacks owned 1.5% (134 of 9,101).

Table 5.2
The Number of Stations Owned as of August 1997

	1997		
Medium	Total	Minority	Black
TV	1,193	38	28
Radio	10,282	284	165

Source: U.S. Department of Commerce. Minority Commercial Broadcast Ownership in the United States: 1993-1998. Washington, DC: National Telecommunications and Information Administration.

From 1982 to 1997, *15 years*, minority ownership of TV stations grew from 1.7% to only 3.2% of the total market (38 of 1,193); Black ownership grew from 1.2% to 2.3% (28 of 1,193). Minority ownership of radio stations grew from 2.0% to only 2.8% (284 of 10,282); Black ownership grew from 1.5% to only 1.6% (165 of 10,282). This growth rate is extremely poor, stagnated, and retarded, considering the "economic boom this country claims to have occurred since 1992 and continues."

Table 5.3
The Number of Stations Owned as of August 1998

	1998		
Medium	Total	Minority	Black
TV	1,209	32	26
Radio	10,315	305	168

Source: U.S. Department of Commerce. Minority Commercial Broadcast Ownership in the United States: 1993-1998. Washington, DC: National Telecommunications and Information Administration.

Conversely, majority-owned stations continue to grow at a much greater rate. Mergers and takeovers grow daily, as evidenced by the September 1999 proposed purchase of CBS by Viacom for $37.3 billion. Other mega mergers are rumored to follow to take advantage of merging technologies for better distribution of programming, especially over the Internet and cable entities.

During 1981, in conjunction with the many other industries being deregulated, the FCC passed the Radio (TV) Deregulation Act of 1981. The full effect was not evident until late 1982 and beyond. These data partially support my research questions by demonstrating the relationships as stated earlier; that is, although the percent growth appears greater for minorities, this is due to the much smaller base number (i.e., if the base number is one, and one station is obtained, then 100% increase occurs).

Economics, access to capital, nonenforcement of equity laws and regulations, and the economy are the primary contributing factors to the overall difference between radio and TV ownership growth. These factors include the following: the capital requirements for TV ownership are two to ten times greater than those for radio, depending on the market the station is in; in the 1990s the media industry, like other industries, was still experiencing a recession (the minority community was experiencing a depression); and nonminority, independent owners experienced similar "hostile takeovers."

Under the guise of saving the taxpayers' dollars, the tax certificate policy was repealed to prevent Frank Washington (a U.S. citizen, Vietnam veteran, and African American) from purchasing Viacom. Yet, a few months later, the policy limiting foreign ownership of media was waived to allow Rupert Murdock (a foreigner) to retain   ownership   of   print   and   electronic   outlets   to   include   Fox network and the New York Post. This foreign ownership was allowed to continue after it was proven that Murdock falsified documents to acquire these entities.

Another major factor contributing to these data is the census timing, that is, the minority owner's starting the sale or bankruptcy process in the beginning or middle of the year. The *group owners* wait until the end of the year to complete the hostile takeover/purchase (*to get a lower price and for tax purposes*).

To determine the implications of these data in the context of my three specific research questions, other factors were examined to strengthen the relationship between these principal variables. The factors of FCC, the EDA, lending institutions, and advertisers do, in my opinion, have a substantial bearing on the primary relationship, in this case policy development, implementation, evaluation, and administration.

Deregulation means different things to different people. To the average person, it means that antiquated laws and regulations will be removed from "the books." To the regulation entrepreneurs, it means that the regulated industry will return to operating with less regard for public interest. To the regulation terminators, it means that the regulated industry will return to operating with less interference due to regular evaluations by regulators.

I contend that an even more devastating effect has, emerged and may continue to emerge. That effect is that Blacks and other minorities will never have equitable media ownership. Furthermore, I contend that the station ownership limits were increased from 7-7-7 to 23-23-14 to allow the group owners enough capacity to absorb "failed" minority-owned stations (without "mergers" with the minority owners) and to accommodate those minority- and nonminority-owned stations acquired through hostile takeover.

The results indicate that the issues explored in this study have been supported. In essence, this study suggests that the FCC policies, combined with EDA, LI, and advertisers' policies, are written to be inclusive and applied equally. However, the actual practice(s) and nonenforcement of these policies, in general, have *discouraged the sustained growth* of minority ownership of broadcast stations. This study further contends that, generally, wealth remains in the top 5% of the population (in the world, not just the United States). Therefore, in this case, the majority of the stations owned remain in the hands of a few, and with megamergers, even those hands are becoming fewer.

Additionally, *power*, like wealth, remains in the control of a very few. It appears to be sustained by both active and tacit influence (or conspiracy) based on the symbiotic relationship(s) between regulation and economics. Horwitz (1989) and power theories describe this relationship in the regulatory theories by Parenti (1978, 1983, 1986). These authors conclude that although public policies are designed to enhance safety, redistribute resources (share power), and so on, in many cases, they only appear to share power. Actually, power manipulates and controls access to power through this symbiotic relationship, with little or no way of determining direct culpability and responsibility. Therefore, it is imperative that evaluation of prospective change to the status quo be viewed through a "power prism" to determine the extent, longevity, and frequency of evaluation and modification.

Bagdikian (1981) was one of the first to inform us that a small number of companies owned most of the media. By 1996 ownership concentration (monopolies) drastically increased, especially with the advent of the Telecommunication Act of 1996, "merger mania," and the "information superhighway." These concepts merged cable and telephone companies, the movie and music industries, data/computer industries, and many other information-related industries. One year after the implementation of the Telecommunications Act of 1996 Hickey (1997) summarized its impact on the media landscape in this way:

It removed all limitations on the number of radio stations one company can own nationally, and allowed up to eight per company locally (instead of only four); relaxed the rules about how many TV stations one company can operate; ordered the FCC to consider easing the rule limiting the ownership to one TV station per market, as well as the bar to ownership of a Newspaper and a broadcast outlet in the same city; permitted common ownership of cable systems and broadcast networks; ended all rate regulation of smaller cable systems and promised the same for large ones later on; extended the license term of TV and radio stations to eight years from four; allowed TV networks to start and own another broadcast network if they choose. (pp 1-2).

The writer concluded that the legislation created unprecedented mergers, consolidations, buyouts partnerships, and joint ventures that have changed the very nature of mass media control in the nation.

In June 2000, the FCC granted conditioned approval to the merger of one of the largest telephone companies and one of the largest cable TV companies in the nation. The joining of AT&T and Media One would have given the new company the opportunity to provide service to nearly 42 per cent of all cable TV subscribers in the nation (FCC 2000, June 5a). FCC policy stated, however, that cable companies could serve no more than 30 per cent of cable service market. Therefore, the FCC ordered AT&T-MediaOne to comply with the FCC 30 per cent policy by May 2001. The company was given 3 alternatives for reducing their control of the cable TV market place (FCC 2000, June 5b):

1.   Divest MediaOne's 25.5 percent interest in Time Warner Entertainment, LP (TWE).

2.   Divest AT&T's programming interests in TWE.

3.   Divest ownership interests in other cable systems serving 11.8 percent of the cable TV market place.

At the time of the proposed deal, FCC Chairman William E. Kennard felt that once the new company complied with FCC policy, the merger would benefit telecommunications industry and its consumers (FCC 2000, June 5a). He stated: "In many ways, today's action represents the very goals of the 1996

Telecommunications Act – allowing new entrants into emerging markets without allowing big companies to have a stranglehold on their core markets."

IMPLICATIONS FOR THE BLACK COMMUNITY

This major merger between two communications giants is typical of the merger mania that is taking place in the contemporary media ownership environment in America. Under the Telecommunications Act of 1996 and FCC ownership policies, individual media giants are prevented from having a "strangle hold" on media markets. Nevertheless, since one company can own up to 30 per cent of the market place, 4 or 5 can legally control the entire market place. In the mean time there are hardly any provisions in the law that aid Blacks and other minorities in having a role in the media control and ownership environment of the new millennium. In this situation, the laws and policies of the government have put Blacks and other minorities in a position where it is virtually impossible for them to own and control major media entities.

FCC and other polices should address the problem of how to enhance minority ownership of broadcast properties, which increases the diversity in the control of the media and thus functional diversity, benefiting the public and serving the principle(s) of PICN and the First and Fourteenth Amendments. Additionally, minority ownership underdevelopment will decrease, and minority ownership will develop.

RECOMMENDATIONS

In 1988 Michael Starr suggested that the Communication Act of 1934 be rewritten "with the goal of comprehensive communication policy for *all the diverse elements* of the spectrum instead of piecemeal regulation." He further proposed that "a Cabinet-level Department of Communications be established, making communications a coordinated national priority and fund it adequately to employ experts and professional staff capable of designing and implementing long-term strategy in this world of evolving technology." The Communications Act of 1934 has been rewritten as the Telecommunications Act of 1996; however, it eliminated the "diverse elements" wording that had encouraged minority ownership, in general, and Black ownership, specifically.

In March 1998 Rev. Jesse Jackson (Electronic Media, 1998) suggested a 12-point program, that included (1) a full FCC hearing on competition and equal opportunity in the telecommunications field; (2) public hearings before the FCC on all media and telecommunications mergers worth more than $500 million; (3) restoring the minority tax certificate program; (4) creating a capital base to help fund minority ventures; and (5) increasing public-interest requirements for digital TV license holders.

In addition to the recommendations of Starr and Jackson, I feel certain other issues must be addressed. A sufficient number of personnel will have to be placed in the Compliance and Enforcement Division of whatever agency is designated that responsibility. With this increase of enforcement personnel, there will definitely be an increase in the number of court cases at many levels; therefore, more judges and related personnel will be required.

If the current telecommunication regulatory system is maintained, FCC commissioners should not be allowed to reenter the telecommunications industry for a minimum of three to five years. Currently, they can reenter after one year. Conceivably, many of the Department of Commerce and FCC decisions and/or nondecisions are based on potential personal earnings in the telecommunication industry.

If a cabinet-level department is established, it would probably be less political than the current system. The present commission stagnation can be traced, in part, to recurring vacancies on the FCC. Such vacancies tend to exist for extended periods of time. A secretary of communications appointed by the president would enable the policy-making and regulatory body to function at all times with key personnel.

This change would not alter any political realities. The party in power controls three out of five present commission spots. The secretary would be subject to Senate confirmation and would appear before congressional committees. There is no difference between a secretary of communications and a one-seat majority (commission chair) for the party in power. The gain caused by the change would be an increase in planning, coordination, efficiency, uniformity of law/rule/ regulation, implementation, application, and accountability.

CONCLUSION

The FCC's policies, combined with Economic Development Administration, lending institutions, and advertisers' policies and practices, have, in general, discouraged the sustained growth rate of Black and other minority ownership of broadcast stations. Generally, wealth remains in the top 5% of the population (in the world, not just the United States). Therefore, in this case, the majority of the stations owned remain in the hands of a few.

This nation has a First and Fourteenth Amendment right to receive, and/or have available for it to receive, printed and/or electronically transmitted information about its diversity as well as its commonality. Because of the meaning that the media (especially electronic) have for our nation and the world, they should be required to perform on a higher level of communication and principle. We have gone from an agrarian society, to an industrial society, to the current and projected "high-tech" and Information Society. Currently, radio and TV have a most profound effect upon us. According to Schwartz (1983), the media industry has godlike power, in that it is "everywhere." Therefore, it must accept godlike responsibility to the people who lend an ear and/or an eye. The media are the window to a changing world.

Through this window to the world, we witnessed Freedom Fighters (Dr. M. L. King and others) abolishing many forms of *American apartheid*; the assassination of some of those abolitionists, a president, and a former attorney general (and presidential candidate); our bicentennial; a president resigning; the Vietnam War (and invasions of Grenada, Libya, Panama, and Iraq); elections; and other local, national, and international meetings, partings, celebrations, and tragedies.

Broadcasting's reach and sensory immediacy—the form and nature of its engagement—render it an intrinsically powerful instrument for learning. The statistics are all too familiar. More than 70% of Americans rely on TV as their principal source of news (and information). The average high school graduate has spent over 50% more time in front of the TV set than in the classroom.

Therefore, general learning has occurred more rapidly than in previous generations, but not at the expense of print media. Since the early 1960s, there has been much discussion by Marshall McLuhan, Bagdikian, and others concerning whether or not contemporary society has moved or is moving from a predominantly "print" culture to a more "audiovisual" one.

The relationship between print and electronic media specifically and developing telecommunication technology in general is best described by Schwartz (1983). In essence, he observes that for most of us, learning to read was the first step toward learning to learn. Without that ability to read, one could not know about the world beyond the hill. Today, everything beyond the hill and the moon comes into our homes and minds, bypassing the school and library. Even before radio and TV, the telephone reduced the need to read and write as letter writing declined. Therefore, the relationship between the print and electronic media is no more antagonistic than that between the horse and automobile. The horse and automobile are not angry with each other. The equestrians and horse-related businesses got angry at the automobile, and print-oriented teachers and businesses get angry with TV, computers, and other electronic media when, in fact, a peaceful coexistence is possible.

Similarly, the broadcast stations are not keeping down the sustained growth of minority ownership. The institutional policies and practices perpetuate colonization of information, and economic, cultural, and intellectual tyranny adversely affects women and minorities in general and Africans and their descendants on the continent and throughout the diaspora, specifically.

Developing, enhancing, implementing, and enforcing policies and practices to increase minority ownership of broadcast stations will drastically reduce the aforementioned colonizing and tyrannical effect.

To paraphrase Fuller (1984), one could contend that: (1) those who have the ability and/or power to eliminate the station and telecommunication ownership inequity do not have the will to do so; (2) those who have the will do not have the ability and/or power to do so; (3) those who practice and/or perpetuate ownership inequity are smarter (more knowledgeable of the system) and more powerful than those who do not; and (4) those who do not practice and/or perpetuate ownership inequity and strive to reduce/eliminate it have proven that they are not as smart (knowledgeable) and powerful as those who do; otherwise, there would be no such thing as ownership inequity.

REFERENCES

Bagdikian, B. H. (1981). *Media Monopoly*. Boston: Beacon Press.

Bennett, Carolyne L. (1993, September). Diversity in media. About . . . time, epilogue, 40.

Broadcasting (1989, January 30). Lawmakers prepare more stringent EEO bill for broadcasting and cable. pp. 56-58.

Carnevale, M. L. (1992, May 15). Popularity of cable causes FCC to plan easing caps on TV station ownership. *Wall Street Journal*, p. B4.

Congressional Research Services (1988/98, June 29). *Minority Broadcast Station Ownership and Broadcast Programming: Is there a Nexus?* Library of Congress: Washington, DC: FCC Form 346, Section V, Preferences

Electronic Media, (1998, March 23). Debate on diversity. 1, 3

Federal Communications Commission (1981). *In the Matter of Deregulation of Radio, Notice of Proposes Rulemaking*. 46 Fed. Reg. 13888, 84 FCC2d 968, recon. granted in part, 87 FCC2d, 797 (1981), 49 RR2d 1, January 1981 (1986, February 2).

FCC amends radio ownership rules (1992, August 6). *The Norman Transcript*, 10.

FCC (1986, February 2). *Minority Ownership Financing and Advertising En Banc Hearing*. Washington, DC.

FCC News Release (2000, June 5a). *Statement of FCC Chairman William E. Kennard regarding conditioned approval of AT & T-MediaOne Merger*. Washington, DC: Federal Communications Commission. [On-line]. Available: http://www.fcc.gov/Speeches/Kennard/Statements/2000/stwek045.html

FCC News Release (2000, June 5b). *FCC grants conditioned approval of AT&T-MediaOne merger; divestitures ordered for compliance with FCC 30% subscriber cap*. [On-line]. Available: http://www.FCC.gov/Bureaus/Cable/News_Releases/2000/nrcb0015.html.

Fife, M. D. (1979). *The Effect of Minority Ownership on Broadcast News Content: A Multi-Market Study*. Washington, DC: National Association of Broadcasters.

Fife, M. D. (1986). *The Effect of Minority Ownership on Broadcast News Content: A Multi-Market Study*. Ann Arbor: Michigan State University Press.

Fuller, N., Jr. (1984). The United Independent Compensatory Code/System/ Concept. *Textbook for Victims of Racism (White Supremacy)*. Washington, DC: Auther.

Hickey, N. (1997, January/February). *So big. The Telecommunications Act at one year. Columbia Journalism Review*. pp. 1-9. [On-line]. Available: http://www. cjr.org/year/97/1/telecom.asp.

Hill unit says minority ownership generates more diverse programming (1988, August 1). *Broadcasting*, 56.

Horwitz, R. B. (1989). *The Irony of Regulatory Reform: The Deregulation of American Telecommunications*. New York: Oxford University Press.

JACA Corporation—Management Consultants & Engineers (1985, 1986). *Minority Economic Development: The Availability and Cost of Capital to Minority-Owned Business Relative to Non-Minority-Owned Business*. Washington, DC: U.S. Minority Business Development Agency, U.S. Economic Development Administration and the U.S. Small Business Administration.

Nakao, A. (1980, May 11). Rebellion against media stereotyping. *San Francisco Examiner*. 5.

National Association of Broadcasters. *Minority Ownership of Broadcast Stations in the United States: 1982-1992*. Washington, DC.

National Telecommunications and Information Administration. *Minority Commercial Broadcast Ownership in the United States: 1993-1998*. The Minority Telecommunications Development Program, U.S. Department of Commerce.

Parenti, Michael (1978). *Power and the Powerless*. New York: St. Martin's Press

Parenti, Michael (1983). *Democracy for the Few* (fourth ed.). New York: St. Martin's Press.

Parenti, Michael (1986). *Inventing Reality*. New York: St. Martin's Press.

Schwartz, T. (1983). *Media: The Second God*. New York: Anchor Press.

Sikes says change likely for new radio ownership rules (1992, July 7). *Broadcasting*, 6.

Starr, M. F. (1988, December 26). Monday memo. *Broadcasting*, 25.

Title 44—Public Printing and Documents, *Paperwork Reduction Act of 1980, Public Law 96-511, 94 Stat. 2812*, December 11, 1980, effective on April 1, 1981.

TV dereg: Turning the rules upside down. (1992, April 27). *Broadcasting*, 4, 15.

U.S. Senate (1989, September 15). *Minority Ownership of Broadcast Stations*. (S.Hrg.101-339). Washington, DC: U.S. Government Printing Office.

U.S. Small Business Administration (1997). *Report of the SBA Task Force on Venture and Equity Capital for Small Business*. Washington, DC: Author.

White ad agency memo draws fire from Black media outlets. (1998, June 2). *The Final Call*, 8.

CHAPTER 6

The New Model of Black Media Entrepreneurship: BET Holdings, Inc.

John T. Barber and Alice A. Tait

INTRODUCTION

It is a paradox that while the Black community is losing ground with ownership and control of the broadcast media in the information age, one Black media company is setting a new pace for media empowerment in this community and, in general, reaching new heights in the media world. While Black radio and television stations are being consumed in media merger mania, this company is creating a strong relationship with media power brokers, maintaining its own control and identity, and expanding into diverse, media-related areas.

BET Holdings, Inc. (BET), the parent company of Black Entertainment Television, represents a new model of Black media ownership and control in America today. Here, we explore this model by discussing the foundations of BET Holdings, Inc. and its early success, how it uses its ties to the African American community and Afrocentric culture to generate economic power to maintain its success, and the strategic expansion of this company, which is beginning to be a significant player in the media and entertainment industries. We also draw some conclusions about the contribution that BET is making to the Black community and the whole nation as the American Information Society continues to unfold.

THE FOUNDATIONS OF BET

The keys to BET's success are strong ties with influential media players, securing major advertising support, and expanding its subscription base. As the founder and chief executive officer (CEO) of the corporation, Robert L. Johnson has built BET into a major media player by forging strong relationships with powerful media brokers. BET's most powerful allies have been Telecommunications, Inc. (TCI), Time-Warner, Inc. (TWI), and others.

Starting in the early 1980s, Johnson arranged deals and formed ties with media companies that could guarantee success for his cable television network. One of his most insightful and rewarding moves was to form a financial alliance with John Malone of TCI. Early investments for his fledgling company came from TCI and Taft Broadcasting. In those days, Johnson persuaded the USA Network to provide his network with satellite time, and arranged for Warner Cable, American Telecommunications Corp., Teleprompter, TCI, and other national cable systems to carry his programming (Barchak, 1993). Johnson gave Time-Warner, Inc. part ownership of the network in exchange for airtime on its Home Box Office (HBO) satellite transponder. Likewise, at this time, TCI and Taft each owned 16% of the new network, but Johnson remained the majority shareholder and eventually purchased Time-Warner's shares of his company.

To establish economic stability in a highly competitive arena, BET used a strategy of combining advertising and subscriber revenues. Advertisers have been willing to advertise on the network because they can reach a wide African American audience and those who turn to BET for African American-oriented programming. Early on, Johnson convinced Proctor and Gamble (P&G), one of the largest media advertisers in the nation, that the BET network reached users and potential users of its products. P&G made a commitment to buy substantial time on the BET network, although it had a history of not spending much of its advertising budget with African American-owned media entities (Donaton, 1988).

Johnson was successful in gaining major advertisers by informing them that African Americans watch more television than any other group in the nation, that African Americans prefer programming that features African Americans, and that the BET network was the vehicle for African American consumers (Donaton, 1989). By the late 1980s key advertisers on the network included Amtrak, AT&T, Bristol-Myers, Campbell Soup Co., Coca-Cola Co., Ford Motor Co., General Foods, General Mills, General Motors Corp., Lever Bros., RJR/Nabisco, Polaroid Corp., Proctor and Gamble Co., Ralston Purina, Revlon, Inc., Time, Inc. United Airlines, and others. To bolster his advertising revenues, Johnson used program-length paid commercials on the network. One company paid the BET network as much as $500,000 per month to run various "infomercials" (Beck, 1989).

BET continued to gain advertising revenue as the number of African Americans whom advertisers seek to reach subscribed to the network in increasing numbers. A growing number of "crossover" consumers, non-African Americans who watch BET for Black entertainment programming, also became a significant part of the population that advertisers wanted to reach through the network (Beck, 1989; Jones, 1990). By 1993 the network had over 35 million subscribers (Jeffrey, 1993) with 90% of the nation's African American cable households subscribing to this cable channel (Katz, 1993). At the same time, however, 60% of the BET audience was non-African American.

Gaining strong support from powerful investors, garnering revenue from major advertisers, selling large quantities of "infomercial" time, and securing "crossover" subscriptions brought BET Holdings, Inc. financial success and made it a force to be reckoned with in the media world. In 1992 Johnson made his company the first African American-owned and -operated company to be listed on the New York Stock Exchange and offered 4.2 million shares of BET stock for sale. This move alone brought BET and its investors nearly $73 million in profits (Williams, 1992).

BET AND THE AFROCENTRICITY MODEL

BET maintains an Afrocentric approach to programming in all of its networks and operations. Afrocentricity involves a systematic exploration of relationships, social codes, cultural and commercial customs, mythoforms, oral traditions, and proverbs of the peoples of Africa and the African diaspora. Afrocentricity is the belief in the centrality of Africans in postmodern history (Asante, 1989). The real concern of Afrocentricity is whether or not the concern or issue is in the best interest of people of the African diaspora. *The Cosby Show*, although not explicating every avenue of African American life, represents the prototype Afrocentric television program, as the images produced in the show are consistently reflective of African American culture. The direction of the programming was African American-influenced. Conversely, the *Amos and Andy* show was the antithesis of Afrocentrism (Tait & Perry, 1994).

AFROCENTRIC MEDIA

Asante's Afrocentricity acts as an effective tool to develop a holistic understanding of the people of the African diaspora. Specifically, BET media programming, using Afrocentrism as a guide, can embrace, and has embraced, the major characteristics of Njia, the Afrocentric worldview, to further enhance its programming efforts and enlighten its viewers on issues facing African Americans.

Njia is composed of the following elements:

1. Honoring ancestors

2. Poetry and music creativity

3. Nommo or generative word power (Afrocentric discussions)

4. Affirmations

5. Teachings from Njia

6. Libation to posterity

Using all or some of these concepts, Afrocentric media are indeed the vehicle for expressing Njia. The major principles guiding Njia's concepts are discussing all concepts from a liberationist perspective and valuing collectivistic thought over individualism. This allows for the recognition that power rests in group solidarity and how this is pertinent to the African experience. Nommo is essentially the modality of Afrocentric television programming.

Three major categories are played out in Afrocentric news, public affairs, and entertainment programming. These are oral traditions; collectivistic political, social, and geographical orientations; and subjective analytical base. Oral traditions include discussions on activism (to change or improve conditions), liberation (from systematic and cultural oppression), unification (through educating Africans on collective empowerment), and inversion (certain terms must either be redefined or eliminated due to their inherent racist and derogatory nature, denial of individual ethnic identity based on a Eurocentric basis for identification, and disregard of a worldview in which persons of European descent (i.e., White) are actually a "minority". The collectivistic social, political, and geographical orientation includes recognition of the common heritage of activities that are practiced by collectivist's action of, and the intracultural responsibility of, people of African descent. Finally, the subjective analytical base is the discussion of methods for self-determination, self-definition, and specific or special needs of people of African descent.

Since 77% of BET's programming consists of music videos, an analysis of the relevance or irrelevance of these is necessary for BET's racially mixed audience. BET's audience breaks down as follows: 25% Anglo-American, 25% African American, and approximately 60% non-African American. Most of these viewers fall between 18 to 24 years of age (Barchak, 1993). While there is a tendency to dismiss music as superficial and inconsequential, a closer examination places it at the forefront of African and African American cultural traditions.

Much of African American music has derivatives of both African and European elements. Also, connections between early American jazz and West African musical styles have been traced. Oral traditions were the primary means of spiritual survival and dissemination throughout a largely illiterate (by European standards) slave and folk community. African American music is the primary historical link of generations and would not have survived without oral traditions (Lomax, 1968; Ottenheimer, 1993).

An analysis of the major African American music genres is necessary for complete understanding of the cultural significance of music to BET's audience.

RAP

.   Rap, similar to rhythm and blues (R&B) and jazz in their infancy, has been surrounded by controversy. Rap has earned what some feel to be an undeserved reputation. Gangsta rap, hitting upon issues of misogyny, racism, and homophobia, if it represents a real depiction of the African American community, has used this vehicle to express surprising and shocking phenomena to America. Some gangsta rappers call for the blame to be placed on the government and economic conditions for the current state of urban Black America (Kelley, 1992).

Rappers themselves range from former gang members to middle-class teens. Their topics range from street violence, brutality, and drug sales, to clean-cut, sanitized raps. Some songs do urge kids to stay in school, and avoid crime and drugs; however, most are concerned with nothing more than macho boasting.

Berry (1993) and Baker (1993) argue that cultural politics within hard core rap music is creating a powerful discourse concerning the African American experience in America from artists such as Public Enemy, NWA, Ice Cube, Ice T., and Sister Souljah. While seen as deviant and unacceptable to the mainstream, others, understanding these frustrations, see the presentation of this reality through the cultural and historical representation of knowledge and experience. Baker heralds rappers for their ingenious use of technology, techniques, strategies, and creativity. He further urges Black studies programs to provide a platform for its understanding and crystallization.

BLACK RELIGIOUS MUSIC

The Black religious tradition operates on two levels. First, psychologically and emotionally, it locates the people's sense of heritage. Second, it mobilizes and strengthens the resolve for struggle. Black sacred music is the primary reservoir of Black people's historical context and an important factor in the process of social change.

RHYTHM AND BLUES

Rhythm and blues (R&B), a term originated in the 1940s as a description of a synthesis of Black musical genres (gospel, blues, and swing), is musical and socioeconomic. Later called rock and roll to camouflage its Black roots, R&B parented the offspring's soul, funk, disco, rap, and so on. (George, 1988). The blues depicts "secular" Black life and sings of worldly issues of love and sex. The blues describes every aspect of a man's and woman's feelings toward one another. Through the blues, Black people express their views about infidelity and sex (Cone, 1972).

Contrary to popular opinion, the blues does not represent complete despair and utter hopelessness. However, hope of the blues is grounded in the historical reality of the Black experience and in the belief that things will change one day.

Black music is unifying and functional. It is unifying in that it confronts the individual with the truth of Black existence and that being Black is possible only in a communal context. It unites the joy and sorrow, the love and hate, and the hope and despair of Black people and moves the people toward liberation.

Black music is functional in that it tells us about the feeling and thinking of African people and the mental adjustments necessary in order to survive in an alien land. For example, work songs were used to heighten energy, as were slave ballads and spirituals (Cone, 1972).

BET is the only national network showcasing one of the great cultural traditions of African American music. That art form reflects African American history, struggle, and culture. Music reflects not only the African American community's political dispositions; but also it creativity in fashions, hairstyles, choreography, and composing. In these categories, the implications are endless. Music and cuisine appear to be the most effective cultural change agents. In that regard, BET's interracial viewers are exposed to the African American culture in a nonthreatening, palatable mode. BET's 18- to -24-year-old viewers will either change or maintain the social injustices. Perhaps videos will provide a platform for creating the collective consciousness necessary for their involvement.

In 1995 BET showcased several Afrocentric programs. *Lead Story* was a 30-minute news program with African American journalists discussing news from an African American perspective. *Our Voices* was a talk show exploring issues from an African American perspective. *BET News* was a 30-minute news program presenting issues from an African American perspective. *Screen Scene* reflected a clear entertainment focus with an emphasis on African Americans in movies and videos. *The Color of Money* aired on Saturdays and explored financial issues from an African American perspective. Situation comedies were aired early in the morning and late in the evening. The problem with situation comedies is their tendency to frame the African American community dilemma in humor. Infomercials occupy a great deal of BET's programming schedule. They advertise exercise machines, culinary equipment, psychic networks, perfect hair, and cosmetics appealing directly to African American females. Perfect Hair infomercials promote Eurocentric hair as the ideal hair.

BET's African American community images differ from, and replicate images found in mainstream media. Viewers see more African Americans on BET than they have ever seen on any major network at any time in the history of television or any other medium. Viewers see African Americans in diverse roles: newscasters, anchors, journalists, actors, comedians, professionals, dancers, criminals, and so on. Viewers cannot get this broad spectrum on few, if any, other television programs or any other medium. BET is undeniably Afrocentric. It embraces many of the characteristics of Afrocentricity. Music is the greatest Afrocentric expression. However, the public affairs programs also do a fairly good job of issue exploration. *Our Voices* was extremely effective in exploring issues to determine their impact on African Americans. The *Our Voices* set utilized an African motif, which can motifs can sporadically be seen in commercials and other programs. These programs achieved issue exploration by using African Americans as primary sources.

THE BET EXPANSION MODEL

Capitalizing on its ability to generate profits by providing Afrocentric programming, BET is not only enjoying economic prosperity in cable and other media but also expanding into new ventures. Bob Johnson always had a vision of BET's being more than just another cable business. Publishing was one of the first areas into which Johnson ventured in his effort to build a multifaceted Black entertainment empire.

Johnson announced plans in 1990 to launch a magazine aimed at Black teenagers (Webb, 1990). He wanted to reach this underserved media market and provide some positive influences for young African Americans. *YSB* (Young Sisters and Brothers) became the first national lifestyle magazine for Black youth. At the same time, BET bought Time-Warner, Inc.'s stake in *Emerge* magazine and took control of this monthly periodical aimed at the upscale African American market (Farhi, 1991). With publishing and cable under his belt, Johnson was moving toward his goal of making BET a company that advertisers could turn to for a well-defined group of Black consumers (Singeltary, 1993). Nevertheless, his publishing efforts were met with difficulty. *Emerge* was taken over when Mettersmedia bought 55% of the stock in the upscale magazine, and the publication of the magazine aimed at the hip-hop culture was suspended after a few years of publication (Iverem, 1996).

Despite setbacks in publishing, BET continued to enjoy much economic success. As one of the largest Black-owned businesses in the nation, BET offered stock to the public for the first time in 1991 (Potts, 1991). BET subsequently became the first African American company to be listed on the New York Stock Exchange, which valued the company at $475 million (Hinden, 1991). The sale of the stock was suspended by BET when traders became uncertain about the correct number of subscribers to the cable network (Sugawara, 1991). After this brief fall, BET stock gained in trading on the market and eventually provided the company with a profit (Burgess & Hinden, 1991).

After establishing himself as one of the leading businessmen in the nation's capital, Johnson in 1994 offered to use his own money to build a downtown sports arena for the financially strapped city (Leonhardt, 1994a). Johnson knew that if he owned a sports arena, it would give BET access to profitable sports contracts and offer broadcasting rights for sports events to his cable company. His effort to build such an arena was met with resistance.

When negotiations started, the owner of the city's basketball and hockey teams, Abe Pollin, also positioned himself to build the arena. Pollin wanted to build the arena using city funds. Since the D.C. government favored Pollin and his arena plan, Johnson vigorously challenged the idea that city funds should be used for the project when the city was having major financial difficulties. Johnson felt that his plan was superior because it relieved the citizens of Washington, D.C., of the burden for paying for the establishment (Hochberg, 1994). He accused the business group conducting the arena negotiations of catering to Pollin while neglecting the interests of the city (Leonhardt, 1994b). After a long battle with D.C. officials and Pollin, Johnson stated that he would concede if Pollin would build the arena with his own funds (Schneider, 1995). Pollin agreed to do so, and eventually, after some legal encounters, the two men agreed to consider becoming business partners in future endeavors (Miller & Solomon, 1996; Pyatt, 1996). Johnson was defeated in this effort to realize his vision of an empire of sports, cable, and entertainment on the Potomac.

Johnson was undaunted, however, and went on to extend BET into new media markets and related entertainment and financial arenas. In the media industry BET had acquired cable franchises, a $10 million studio for producing African American programming, a pay-per-view movie channel, and a jazz channel before it moved on to launch a movie channel and an on-line computer service for and about African Americans (Tait & Barber, 1996). Johnson understood that Blacks frequently attend movies and purchase more than their share of theater tickets (Farhi, 1996). At the same time, Black households subscribe to premium cable services more than many other American households. BET, therefore, struck a deal with Encore Media Corp. in 1996 to start a cable pay-channel for African American movies. Since Encore is owned by BET's old partner, TCI, Johnson moved to launch the new channel on TCI's vast network of cable systems (Stump, 1996). In this deal, BET and Encore would each hold 49% of the new channel, and a management group of BET and Encore executives would hold the rest. Part of BET's investment was to come from actor Denzel Washington and Johnson Publishing Co., publisher of *Ebony* magazine.

BET Movies/Starz 3 was packaged with Encore's Starz and Starz 2, which carry movies from Universal Pictures, New Line Cinema, Hollywood Pictures, Miramax, and Touchstone Films (Stump, 1996). Starz and Starz 2 reach over 5 million homes. BET Movies/Starz 3 was to show films from Encore's library of 6,000 films and original productions from upcoming Black filmmakers. Examples of films in the Encore library that would appear on the new channel because they were about, or directed by, Blacks or featured Black performers included *Seven, A Good Man in Africa, Pulp Fiction, Major Payne, Clockers, The Crying Game, Corinna, Corinna,* and older films such as *To Sir with Love, Cry Freedom, and The Autobiography of Miss Jane Pittman*.

The Black movie channel was launched in February (Black History Month) 1997 on six TCI systems in three states to about 300,000 TCI subscribers (Mitchell, 1997). In the long term, BET hoped to have the new channel carried in the more than 43 million households that currently carry Black Entertainment Television. Johnson believed that the new channel could attract the Black audience it needed because there are over 4 million Black pay-TV subscribers in the nation, and, when given the choice, Black people often prefer to watch Black performers.

During February 1997 BET also launched its first effort in cyberspace on the Microsoft Network at the Web site: http://www.msbet.com (Breznick, 1997c). Named MSBET, this Web site is the result of a joint venture between the world's leading software maker for personal computers and BET. Microsoft Corporation announced in a press release in 1996 that the two companies would work together to "produce a broad range of engaging content, including Internet on-line programming, interactive television, and CD-ROM titles. The goal is to create a premier brand for African American consumers on the information superhighway."

MSBET, while equally owned by Microsoft and BET, is run by BET and presently features programming and promotional information on BET's three cable networks and other properties (Breznick, 1997c). It also presents music, arts and entertainment, public affairs programming for teenagers, and home-shopping segments for Black consumers (Breznick, 1997b). The site tries to appeal to Blacks who are on-line. Since Blacks enjoy less personal computer (PC) ownership than Whites, Johnson feels that his on-line offerings (including Black Entertainment Television's home page) would help to increase the number of Black households that have PCs and use on-line services. (See Chapter 13 of two book for a discussion of BET.com, the latest Internet venture of BET).

The venture onto the information highway was only part of BET's expansion into areas outside cable television. In April 1997 BET teamed up with Chevy Chase Bank to offer a BET Visa credit card to African Americans nationwide (Singletary, 1997). In this partnership, the bank could pursue its goal of doing business with more African Americans, and BET could begin to build BET Financial Services, a new company that planned to offer mortgage and brokerage services, mutual funds, and home equity loans. To run the company, Johnson teamed with Alma Brown, the widow of the late secretary of commerce, Ronald H. Brown.

In this deal, BET demonstrated that it had the brand name that appeals to middle-class Black consumers whom bankers want to go after. While BET is the face that draws the Black consumer to this credit card, Chevy Chase Bank manages the credit card operations and financial services on behalf of BET Financial Services. Once again Johnson and BET had created a financially lucrative business arrangement with a powerful ally, and this one had more than $5 billion in assets (Singletary, 1997). Johnson had not only diversified his financial portfolio but, at the same time, successfully ventured into an industry where Blacks played little or no role in ownership.

During the same period of time that BET made entries into cyberspace, on one hand, and financial services, on the other, it also opened a chain of restaurants called BET SoundStage. Plans for the national entertainment-themed restaurant chain began as early as 1995, and the first was opened in Prince

George's County, Maryland, in January 1997 (Montgomery, 1995; Pierre, 1997). The 365-seat restaurant was designed to make customers feel as if they were part of a soundstage (Iverem, 1997). Three 70-foot video screens and 42 video monitors are scattered throughout the restaurant to help create the production studio atmosphere. During the day, the establishment airs music videos and programming from its cable stations, and at night SoundStage becomes interactive with live celebrity feeds via satellite and Internet chats with stars.

Since opening the premier restaurant, SoundStage has drawn overflow crowds to the Maryland location with soul music and southern cuisine that has "crossover" appeal (Pierre, 1997). BET is looking to build up to 25 SoundStage restaurants in such metropolises as Los Angeles, Detroit, Chicago, New York, Philadelphia, Atlanta, Charlotte, North Carolina, and other places where its cable network is well received.

To ensure the successful expansion of the SoundStage restaurant venture, Johnson has teamed up with another powerful partner in the entertainment world. In June 1998 BET, the restaurant, and Walt Disney World Resort opened a SoundStage Club at the Pleasure Island area of Downtown Disney in Orlando, Florida (MSBET, 1998). BET owns, and Walt Disney World manages, the SoundStage Club, which is Disney's first African American-themed location (Grant, 1997a).

The BET and Disney combination puts patrons on the cutting edge of state-of-the-art, multimedia, urban contemporary entertainment. Downtown Disney, where SoundStage is located, features unique restaurants, the world's largest Disney character store, a 24-screen movie theater, and an eclectic collection of clubs and stages featuring live shows (MSBET, 1998). The 5,000-square-foot waterfront SoundStage features live musical performances and programming from the BET SoundStage Network. When it opened, Johnson expressed his satisfaction with the venture: "The strong brand identity of BET, combined with the exciting venues of Walt Disney World will create a unique attraction for African American and urban consumers. We are pleased to be able to partner with the world leader in themed entertainment" (MSBET, 1998).

In 1998 Johnson also announced plans to launch an African American-owned movie studio before the end of the year (Waxman, 1998). In July of that year, Johnson established BET Pictures II, one of the nation's first owned movie studios designed to produce African American theatrical films. In March 1999, Johnson established BET Arabesque Films, a movie production company created to produce African American films for movies and television.

In yet another major venture, Johnson continued his expansion strategy: forming alliance with powerful partners, utilizing BET's appeal to the Black community and name recognition, and creating venues targeted at the African American consumer. To make this venture a reality, however, Johnson had to join with his old partner John Malone of Liberty Media Group and TCI to buy back all stock shares from BET stockholders (Farhi, 1997; Segal, 1997). Before the deal was done, however, BET and its stockholders engaged in a serious conflict over the value of the stock and the price at which it should be sold. BET stockholders challenged Johnson and Malone in a lawsuit that claimed that the original offer was too low and amounted to a freeze-out of minority shareholders (Breznick, 1997). BET's board was also criticized for naming a committee of one—National Public Radio president-CEO Delano Lewis—to review the offer of $48 per share at a time when BET profits were up, and its stock value was rising. At that time (1997) BET's revenue totaled $154.2 million, up 17% from the previous year (Neel, 1997). Lewis concluded that the offer was too low, and BET and Liberty Media subsequently offered to pay $378 million or $63 per share to the stockholders (Farhi, 1998; Knight, 1998a, 1998b). The BET board accepted this offer. Based on this offer, all of BET's stocks were worth about $1.2 billion (Neel, 1998). Johnson owned 64% of the new privately held company, BET Holdings II, Inc. (BET), and Malone's Liberty Media Group owned the remainder. Johnson stated that he and Malone wanted to buy the 6 million publicly traded shares to operate BET without the pressure to show rising profits and increasing stock prices each quarter (Neel, 1998).

As the sole owners of BET, Johnson and Malone wanted to build an African American-themed hotel and casino in Las Vegas. Earlier, Johnson had received the first gaming license issued to an African American. As a result, Johnson became a director of Hilton Hotels Corp and began plans to build a $200 million BET casino in Las Vegas targeted toward the 2 million African Americans who visit the city each year. To date the hotel has not been built but in September 1999, Johnson established the *Tre Jazz* restaurant in the *Paris* Las Vegas Casino Resort.

Recently, BET announced diverse ventures in clothing, publishing, and telecommunications that will continue the expansion of its media-entertainment empire. The company's Design Studio has launched a men's clothing line called EXSTO XXIV VII, which targets African American and urban consumers.

BET has made a couple of major moves in the publishing arena. With two magazines, *Emerge*, a Black news publication, and *BET Weekend*, a monthly lifestyle magazine, already under its roof, BET added *Heart and Soul* magazine to its family of magazines (Company Press Release, 1998a). This national health, fitness, and beauty magazine targeted toward African American women was purchased from Rodale Press, Inc. BET planned to use its brand strength and marketing expertise to enable the magazine to expand its circulation and advertising value. Moreover, BET Publishing Group established partnerships with leading African American professional health organizations like the National Medical Association and the National Dental Association in the hopes of delivering the latest health information to the Black community.

Magazines are not the only reading materials to be found in the BET publication collection. BET also purchased Arabesque, the only line of original African American romance novels distributed by a major publisher (Company Press Release, 1998c). BET purchased the book company from Kensington

Publishing Corporation, the leading American publisher of romance novels and the second largest publisher of such materials worldwide. The sale included the Arabesque publishing program of four new books each month, an extensive list of 150 titles, and the Arabesque Book Club, which was the fastest growing club in the Kensington group. Perhaps more importantly for the planned BET movie studio, BET also secured the dramatic right to Arabesque Books for possible television and film development. BET also planned to expand the Arabesque book line through BET media properties, which target Black consumers, including the cable network, the Internet, BET's magazines, and a planned show called *Buy the Book*.

In the field of telecommunications, BET joined with a company at the forefront of the new communication and information industries. With Bell Atlantic, BET planned to test-market packages of telecommunications services designed to meet the needs of African American consumers (Company Press Release, 1998b). The alliance is designed to help Bell Atlantic reach the African American community and extend BET's brand name into the telecommunications marketplace. Planned services to be a part of the tests included cellular, paging, voice mail, and Internet access. Under this arrangement, Bell Atlantic provided sales and management support, and, in return, the telecommunications firm used the BET brand name in its advertising and promotional activities and material.

Bell Atlantic has 41 million telephone access lines and 6.7 million wireless customers worldwide (Company Press Release, 1998b). Bell companies are premier providers of voice and data services, leaders in wireless services, and the world's largest publishers of directory information. Bell Atlantic has global telecommunications interests with operations and investments in 22 countries.

Bell Atlantic Retail Group president Bruce Gordan expressed the significance of this deal: "This is a good fit. It establishes a relationship alliance with one of the nation's premier African American businesses. We will be able to combine our knowledge and expertise about the African American market to meet its growing telecommunications needs" (Company Press Release, 1998b).

In his latest venture, Johnson is making flight plans (Phillips & Stern, 2000). He has created a company called DC Air that will take over most of the US Airways routes at Reagan National Airport near Washington, D.C. DC Air will serve 22 cities with over 100 daily departures. This opportunity came about as a result of a merger between United Airlines and US Airways. As a member of the Board of US Airways, Johnson was able to make the deal because United had to sell off a part of US Airways' routes to avoid dominating the airline business in the Washington region. When making the purchase, Johnson said: "as a long time citizen of Washington, D.C., I'm extraordinarily pleased to have the opportunity to help create the premier airline that this great metropolitan region deserves."

CONCLUSIONS

BET has demonstrated that providing information and entertainment to, for, and about African Americans is profitable business in the twenty first century and that Black individuals are capable of leading such a business to the highest levels of economic prosperity in the nation. Bob Johnson, the leader of BET, has accomplished this in an era when Black ownership in electronic media was at an all-time low. It seems, therefore, that Johnson has built a model to which African American media owners should pay attention. BET's success seems to be built on forming alliances with majority media owners and controllers, providing quality Afrocentric programming themes and products merging with major telecommunications entities outside the cable industry, and diversifying into new areas of entertainment and recreation. Future researchers should explore the complex relationships between the components of Johnson's media entertainment empire and attempt to explain their impact on the economic standing of the Black community as the Information Society continues to evolve.

REFERENCES

Asante, M.K. (1989). *Afrocentricity*. Trenton, NJ: Africa World Press.

Baker, H.A., Jr. (1993). *Black Studies, Rap and the Academy*. Chicago: University of Chicago Press.

Barchak, L. J. (1993). Black Entertainment Television. In R. G. Picard (Ed.), *The Cable Networks Handbook*. Riverside, CA: Carpelan, pp. 15-22.

Berry, V. (1993, August 24). *Hardcore rap and the revolution of cultural politics*. Paper presented at the AEJMC Conference, Kansas City, MO.

Beck, K. (1989, June). BET faces the music, comes up with talk. *Channels*, 58-60.

Black Entertainment Television, Inc. (1990, August). *Personnel Policy Manual: Welcome to BET*.

Breznick, A. (1996, February 12). BET, Microsoft jump on-line. Venture to target African Americans; some bold Internet predictions. *MediaCentral*. http://mediacentral.com/Magazines/CableWorld/News96/96qt1/1996021205.html.

Breznick, A. (1997a, February 3). BET, Microsoft aim to bring Blacks on-line with Web site. MediaCentral http://www.mediacentral.com/Magazines/md/OldArchives/199702/1997020306.html.

Breznick, A. (1997b, February 3). MSBET targeting African Americans. BET-Microsoft service aims to bring Blacks on-line; Road Runner in Calif. *Media Central* http://www.mediacentral.

Breznick, A. (1997c, September 22). BET faces shareholders lawsuit. *Media Central* http://www.mediacentral.com/Magazines/CableWorld/News97/1997092204.html.

Burgess, J., & Hinden, S. (1991, December 20). Stock of cable network ends free fall. BET gains nearly $3 following statement. *Washington Post* (Financial Section), p. B10.

Company Press Release (1998a, May 12). BET acquires Heart & Soul Magazine; BET adds health, fitness and beauty magazine to its family of magazines. *Business Wire* http://biz.yahoo.com/prnews/980512/dc_bet_hol_1.html.

Company Press Release (1998b, May 21). Bell Atlantic, BET to jointly market Telecommunications Services. Market test targets African American consumers. *Business Wire* http://biz.yahoo.com/bw/980521/bet_holdin_1.html.

Company Press Release (1998c, July 30). BET Holdings embraces romance. Nation's largest Black-owned and operated media-entertainment company purchases Arabesque, an African American line of romance novels. *Busine*/biz.yahoo.com/bw/980730/bet_holdin_3.html.

Cone, J. H. (1972). *The Spirituals and the Blues*. New York: Seabury.

Donaton, S. (1988, August). P and G boosts and buy on Black TV. *Advertising Age*, 3, 70.

Donaton, S. (1989, April). Johnson broadens the range for BET. *Advertising Age*, 531-532.

Farhi, P. (1991, May 24). Black cable channel to buy controlling stake in magazine. *Washington Post*, p. F1.

Farhi, P. (1994, August 20). BET magazine is saved by new investor: Mettersmedia will own 55% of *Emerge*. *Washington Post*, p. F1.

Farhi, P. (1995, November 3). BET Holdings to buy back stock from Time Warner unit. *Washington Post*, p. D2.

Farhi, P. (1996, September 25). BET senses a new niche. Network to start pay channel for African American movies. *Washington Post*, p. F1.

Farhi, P. (1997, September 12). A powerful partnership pays off. *Washington Post*, p. E1.

Farhi, P. (1998, March 17). Johnson increases bid for BET stock; founder's offer to take his company private grows to $378 million. *Washington Post*, p. C1.

George, N. (1988). *The death of rhythm and blues*. New York: Pantheon.

Grant, T. (1997a, May 12). A BET-Disney Production. *Washington Post*, p. F3.

Grant, T. (1997b, July 14). Dining at home. *Washington Post*, p. F3.

Hinden, S. (1991, November 1). Black cable network stock makes the big time. Start of NYSE trading values DC-based BET at $475 million. *Washington Post*, p. F1.

Hochberg, L. (1994, December 17). Johnson opposes Pollin plan. No public funds for downtown arena, says BET president. *Washington Post*, p. F1.

Iverem, E. (1996, October 23). Death of an ideal. YSB magazine wanted to lift young Blacks. Instead it sank under Hip Hops weight. *Washington Post*, p. D1.

Iverem, E. (1997, January 17). Robert Johnson's $6.5 million restaurant is all glitz in shades of Black. *Washington Post*, p. D1.

Jeffrey, D. (1993, March). Subscribers, ad revenue augment BET sales, profits. *Billboard*, 4.

Johnson, B. (1982, October). Making a BET on Black programming. *Broadcasting*, 87.

Jones, F. G. (1990). The Black audience and the BET channel. *Journal of Broadcasting and Electronic Media, 34*, 477-486.

Katz, R. (1993, June). Going beyond the hood. *Cablevision*, 12.

Kelley, R. D. G. (1992, June). Straight from the underground. *Nation*, pp. 793-796.

Knight, J. (1998a, February 2). For Lewis and shareholders, BETs buyout offer is too low. *Washington Post*, p. F7.

Knight, J. (1998b, March 23). Perseverance pays off for BET, Marriott shareholders. *Washington Post*, p. F7.

Leonhardt, D. (1994a, August 11). Arena group to consider proposal by TV executive. *Washington Post*, p. C1.

Leonhardt, D. (1994b, August 12). Arena talks denounced by executive. Group catering to Pollin, BETs Johnson alleges. *Washington Post*, p. B1.

Lomax, A. (1968). *Folk song style and culture*. Washington, DC: American Association for the Advancement of Science.

Microsoft Press Release (1996, February 1). Black Entertainment Television and Microsoft announce new alliance: Companies to form joint venture to produce multimedia content for the Internet and interactive television.

Miller, B., & Solomon, G. (1996, April 24). Pollin, Johnson make up. Agreement to end suit lets arena go forward. *Washington Post*, p. D1.

Mitchell, K. (1997, February 3). BET Movies launches to 300,000 TCI subscribers. *MediaCentral* http://www.mediacentral.com/Magazines/CableWorld/News97/1997020303.html.

Montgomery, D. (1995, October 27). Video age restaurant to cater to Black suburbs. *Washington Post*, p. B1.

MSBET (1998). BET SoundStage club brings new sound to downtown Disney Pleasure Island. *What's Hot* http://www.msbet.com/home.html.

Neel, K. C. (1997, October 16). Money manager: BET offer is inadequate. *Media Central* http://www.mediacentral.com/Magazines/md/OldArchives/1997101606.html.

Neel, K. C. (1998, March 23). Johnson, Liberty sweeten BET offer: Buyers offer to pay $63 a share: AT&T looking for looking for cable partners. *MediaCentral* http://www.mediacentral.com/Magazines/CableWorld/News98/1998032310.html.

Phillips, D. & Stern, C. (2000, May 24). BET Chief looks to new market. His DC Air would operate out of Reagan National. *Washington Post*. p.1.

Pierre, R. E. (1997, July 7). In Prince George's, the place to be: Upscale BET soundstage a big attraction for county. *Washington Post*, p. B1.

Potts, M. (1991, September 20). Black-owned TV firm to issue stock: BET plans offering of Class A shares. *Washington Post*, p. F1.

Pyatt, R. A., Jr. (1996, April 25). Johnson and Pollin call a truce that could lead to cutting a deal. *Washington Post*, p. D12.

Pyatt, R. A., Jr. (1997, April 10). BET-Chevy Chase alliance is a big deal in several ways. *Washington Post*, p. C3.

Schneider, H. (1995, January 5). Johnson applauds Pollin plan, bows out of arena talks. *Washington Post*, p. B.

Segal, D. (1997, September 12). Johnson, TCI make offer to buy all of BET holdings. Wa*shington Post*, p. E1.

Singletary, M. (1993, May). Picturing more than TV shows at BET. *Washington Post*, p. F11.

Singletary, M. (1997, April 1). BET entering the financial services market: Chevy Chase Bank to join effort to offer products to Blacks. *Washington Post*, p. C1.

Smith, D. (1993, July). BET making foray into direct marketing arena. *Billboard*, 10, 113.

Stump, M. (1996, September 30). BET, Encore Media map a new service. *MediaCentral*   http://www.mediacentral.com/Magazines/CableWorld/News96/1996092703.html.

Sturgis, I. (1993a, January). Johnson to buy Mile-Hi. *Black Enterprise*, 17.

Sturgis, I. (1993b, September). BET expands into pay-per view. *Black Enterprise*, 15.

Sugawara, S. (1991, December 19). Trading halted in Black cable network stock. Confusion over subscribers leads firm to stop sales. *Washington Post*, p. B10.

Tait, A. A., & Barber, J. T. (1996). Black Entertainment Television: Breaking new ground and accepting new responsibilities. In V. T. Berry & C. L. Manning-Miller (Eds.), Thousand Oaks, CA: Sage. *Mediated Messages and African American Culture*, pp. 184-196.

Tait, A. A., & Perry, R. L. (1994). African-Americans in the television media: An Afrocentric analysis. *Western Journal of Black Studies, 18*, 195-200.

Waxman, S. (1998, July 11). First Black film studio is planned; BET's Johnson to head effort. *Washington Post*, p. A1.

Williams, T. (1992, January). Taking stock of the BET IPO. *Black Enterprise*, 11.

Webb, M. K. (1990, December 24). A magazine devoted to Black youth. BET president cites need to explore tough issues. *Washington Post*, p. F6.

CHAPTER 7

A New Spectrum of Business: African Americans and Wireless Telephony

John T. Barber

As the Information Society emerges in the United States, African American businesses are on the rise. According to the Bureau of the Census (1996), Black-owned firms grew 46% between 1987 and 1992. During this time, the number of Black businesses increased (from 424,165, to 620,912) at a faster rate than U.S. businesses as a whole. Black businesses are concentrated, however; in particular business sectors; few of them are establishments that profit mainly from production, processing, and distribution of information. In 1992, according to the Census Bureau, the majority of Black-owned businesses were concentrated in the service industries. These industries accounted for 54% of all Black-owned firms and 34% of gross receipts. Sixty-eight percent of the receipts generated by Black-owned firms were concentrated in services, retail trade, finance, insurance, and real estate. Little more than 3,000 firms had sales of $1 million or more, while over half of the businesses had receipts under $10,000. The vast majority of Black firms were operated as individual proprietorships. So, while Black businesses are increasing, they are still small and not concentrated in the new wave of information enterprises.

In the meantime, the era of the information infrastructures has ushered in new business opportunities in high-tech communication industries. Former chairman of the Federal Communications Commission (FCC), Reed Hundt, summed up the contemporary communications business environment at the Women in Wireless Conference in November 1994. "Today we stand at the brink of enormous change and opportunity in communications," he said. "All women and minorities can be at the forefront of this change. Wireless communications is the world's most exciting industry and there is opportunity for everyone to participate in this new market" (FCC News Release, 1994).

Personal communications services (PCS) will form a major component in the platform of wireless communications businesses of the future. Businesspersons who access and use the airwaves for cellular phones, car phones, pagers, and the transmission of voice, data, and video will operate these businesses. Blacks are making tremendous strides in the business arena, but will they be able to participate and succeed in this new spectrum of business as Chairman Hundt predicted?

This chapter looks at the efforts of Blacks to obtain some PCS so that they can operate the lucrative businesses that will emerge during the information revolution. This discussion describes the PCS technology and the FCC auctions that granted licenses to winning companies to provide communication services throughout the nation by using the electromagnetic spectrum. An analysis is made of one of the PCS auctions to illustrate how Blacks fared in this competition for the opportunity to operate the spectrum-based, wireless communications businesses of the future. Specifically, the chapter deals with congressional and FCC policies that affected the success of Blacks in this process, the outcome of efforts of Blacks to bid for, and win, licenses, the impact of the results of the auctions on the Black community, recommendations for future research on Blacks and wireless technology, and an assessment of where Blacks stand in this arena.

THE AIRWAVES BELONG TO THE HIGHEST BIDDER

The airwaves that are used for communications business are a segment of an array of electromagnetic radiation called the electromagnetic spectrum. This spectrum includes gamma rays, X-rays, ultraviolet rays, visible light, infrared rays, microwaves, and radio waves. The radio portion of the spectrum is used in a number of different ways to serve the daily needs of citizens of this nation. These uses include broadcasting radio and television, satellite direct broadcasts, police and fire communications, and all forms of mobile communications systems used by business, industry, and the general public. Moreover, a large amount of the spectrum is used for carrying voice, data, and video signals over long distances using microwave relay and satellite systems.

The radio spectrum is generally thought of as an unusual common good or natural resource because it cannot be destroyed by use. It is treated as a scarce resource, however, because only one user can use a particular portion of it at a time. Various governmental bodies regulate the radio spectrum to ensure that users' transmissions do not interfere with each other. Use of the spectrum in the United States is managed using a dual system in which the National Telecommunications and Information Administration (NTIA) manages the federal government's use of the spectrum, and the Federal Communications Commission (FCC) regulates all other uses.

Until recently, the FCC issued licenses to use the spectrum using comparative hearings or lotteries. In a comparative hearing, two parties interested in gaining spectrum usage would argue before an administrative law judge who would award a license to the applicant whom the judge determined to be best able to serve the public interest. Lotteries involved giving each applicant a number for a license and then picking the winner through random selection. Hearings and lotteries often took more than a year to complete and were criticized for being slow, cumbersome, and ineffective in serving the public's needs.

In 1993 the Congress decided that all future licenses would be sold to offset the federal deficit. By passing the Emerging Telecommunications Act, the U.S. legislature allowed the FCC to reallocate the radio spectrum through auctions. Government revenue was to be gained from this process under the following constraints: (1) the allocation had to be designed in a way that encouraged competition and avoided the emergence of a monopoly in the future, (2) the government could not restrict spectrum space in an effort to increase profits, and (3) the government had to establish a level playing field so that underrepresented groups such as small businesses, minorities, and women would have an incentive to bid and actually win licenses.

To fulfill the third mandate of the Congress, the FCC established procedures that would allow Blacks to be viable bidders for spectrum space in the auctions. Then chairman of the FCC Reed Hundt expressed the optimism of the commission at the beginning of the auction process. "This means that our licensing of the spectrum should not only include big established companies, but also small businesses, including those owned by minorities and women," he said. "By encouraging such participation, all U.S. citizens will benefit from the imagination, competition, and spirit that these entrepreneurs will bring to this industry and to this country." This optimism reflected the government's affirmative action position, which supported the development and formation of Black-owned businesses as a remedy to the racism and other barriers that have stifled minority business in the past.

AUCTIONING THE AIRWAVES

To ensure that Blacks would be included in the information revolution that would take place as the airwaves were auctioned off, the FCC proposed that Blacks and other "preference groups," such as small businesses and women, be given discounts on the prices they bid for available spectrum space. These groups were named "designated entities" and were required to pay a sum equal to the bid in an auction minus the discount. In developing rules for the auction, the FCC sought to make awards to bidders who would highly, value, their licenses and rapidly introduce valuable, new services to the public.

The FCC sought to adopt a type of auction that, unlike lotteries and comparative hearings, could be carried out in a rapid manner. The agency adopted a simultaneous, multiple-round auction design in which all competitors bid for as many licenses as they wanted and used computers or telephones to bid from their offices or other remote locations.

Each applicant that was accepted to participate in an auction remitted an up-front payment in order to be eligible to bid at the auction. If a bidder won a license, the up-front payment was retained as part of a down payment on the license. If a bidder did not win, the up-front payment was refunded, provided the bidder had not incurred any bid withdrawal or default penalties. After each auction, the winning bidders were supposed to submit a down payment on the license within five business days. If the FCC accepted the winners' application, and no petitions to deny were filed against the applicant, the FCC granted the license on the condition that the payment of the remainder of the winning bid was made. These were the rules the FCC sought to follow in granting PCS and other licenses to all parties, including Blacks and other designated entities.

THE *ADARAND* DECISION

The positive approach of including and making special provisions for Blacks and other preference groups in the auction process encountered a major setback with the Supreme Court ruling in the *Adarand v. Pena* case. In this case, Adarand Constructors, Inc., a White company, lost a bid to install guardrails on a federal project in Colorado, although it put in the lowest bid. A minority-owned, disadvantaged business won the bid because of its preference group status. Adarand brought a suit against the secretary of transportation claiming that the preferential treatment violated the equal protection clause of the Constitution. The Supreme Court ruled that preferential treatment of groups in granting government contracts must meet "strict scrutiny" standards, must serve a compelling government interest, and must be narrowly tailored to further that interest (*Adarand v. Pena*, 1995). President Bill Clinton subsequently directed all federal agencies to review existing programs for evidence of quotas, preferences of unqualified individuals, reverse discrimination, or the continuation of programs after their purpose had been achieved.

In 1996 the FCC modified its rules applicable to its PCS auctions in order to reduce legal uncertainties and prevent delay of the auctions as a result of the Supreme Court's decision in the *Adarand* case. In a report and order released on June 24, 1996, the FCC stated that it had insufficient evidence in its record to support racial preference groups under the strict scrutiny required by the *Adarand* decision. "We have tentatively concluded that although we have some general evidence of discrimination against certain racial groups, the evidence in the record to date does not appear adequate to satisfy the strict scrutiny standard of review," the FCC said (FCC Tenth Report & Order, 1996). Thereafter, it made its rules for auctions "race- and gender-neutral" until such time that it could collect documentation that met the high court's requirement. The commission determined that it could still meet the congressional mandate of providing increased opportunities for Blacks, other minorities, and women by giving them preferences if they owned small businesses. After all, nothing in the *Adarand* decision called FCC small business provisions into question.

THE NEW COMMUNICATIONS PARADIGM

If Blacks are going to reap profits from the communications revolution, the PCS auctions may be a significant point of entry. Rezai and Bell (1996) have described PCS as the technology that will alter the way we deal with communications in the future: "More broadly, the advent of PCS marks an overall shift in the 'Communications paradigm.' . . . Specifically, the prospects for 1) mass-market adoption of wireless services and 2) the convergence of wired and wireless services from both voice and data perspectives will dramatically change conventional wireless distinctions and thinking over the next decade, (p. 5). The FCC has described PCS as a family of mobile or portable radio services, that can be used to provide services to the public. PCS has two-category narrowband and broadband. Broadband systems will be capable of interfacing with personal digital assistants that allow subscribers to send or receive data and video without being connected to a wire. Both allow the public to use paging and cellular phones over regional and national areas of the country. Owners of either type of PCS license will profit by selling time on the spectrum they have acquired by winning a license.

RESULTS OF THE PCS AUCTIONS

The FCC held its first spectrum auction July 25-29, 1994, and was the first to use simultaneous, multiple-round bidding (FCC-Wireless Telecommunications Bureau Auctions Fact Sheet, 1996). Twenty-nine qualified bidders submitted up-front payments of $350,000 in advance of the auction (see Table 7.1). The auction closed after 47 rounds, with bids for the licenses totaling $617,006,674. Ten licenses were auctioned, and six bidders were winners.

Table 7.1
License Winners

Auction Number	Service	# of Licenses	# of Winners
1	Nationwide Narrowband PCS	10	6
3	Regional Narrowband PCS	30	9
4	Broadband PCS A & B Block	99	18
5	Broadband PCS C- Block	493	89
10	Broadband PCS C-Block Reauction	18	7
11	Broadband PCS D, E, and F Block	1472	125
	Totals	2716	432

Source: FCC Wireless Telecommunications Bureau.

From October 26 through November 8, 1994, the FCC auctioned 30 regional narrowband PCS licenses, including six licenses in each of the five regions of the nation. This auction was the first to use a computerized system that allowed bidders to bid from remote locations or at FCC headquarters. This auction closed after 104 rounds of bidding and provided special opportunities for Blacks, other minorities, and women in the form of bidding credits and installment financing. Minorities and women won 11 of the 30 licenses won by small businesses. The total revenue from this auction was $394, 835, 784.

The FCC conducted the first auction of broadband PCS from December 5, 1995, to March 13, 1995. Broadband PCS encompasses mobile and/or portable radio, multifunction portable phones, portable fax machines, and other advanced devices that are expected to compete with existing cellular, paging, and other land mobile services. This auction offered license winners the opportunity to offer services in the 51 major trading areas (MTA) covering the entire nation and its territories. Coming after the *Adarand* decision, this auction did not include special provisions for Blacks, other minorities, and women. The MTA broadband PCS auction generated more than $7.7 billion, and 18 bidders won licenses.

The C band auction ran from December to May 1996 and raised $10,216,506,324 after 184 rounds of bidding (FCC News Release, 1996). This auction was limited to entrepreneurs who had less than $125 million in gross revenues and less than $500 million in total assets. Small businesses with less than $40 million in gross revenues were given special provisions such as bidding credits and installment payments. Eighteen bidders and more companies claiming minority ownership won 31% of the licenses.

The D, E, and F band auctions were completed in January 1997, with 1,479 licenses granted to provide broadband PCS service to 493 basic trading areas (BTA) in the nation (FCC Public Notice, 1997). There were 125 winning bidders, and $2,517,439,565 was raised for the U.S. government. Over 40% of the licenses were won by small businesses, and minority-owned entities won 4.8%. Although eligibility for the F block was limited to entrepreneurs, entrepreneurs also won 15% of the D and E block licenses.

A SPECIAL CASE: THE C BLOCK AUCTION

Section 309(j) of the Telecommunications Act of 1996 required that PCS licenses be disseminated among a wide variety of auction applicants. The C block auction was very special because it tested the theories set forth by the Congress and the FCC—that they would foster diversity in ownership and control of new communications technologies. This auction was called the entrepreneur's auction, and the FCC auctioned off 493 BTA licenses to provide PCS service in the 2 GHz band of the spectrum. This was the commission's fifth spectrum auction since the Congress authorized the FCC to award licenses by auction in 1993. The August 1995 auction was the first to ensure that small businesses, women, minorities, and rural telephone companies have the opportunity to participate in the provisions of PCS services (see Table 7.1). Since the *Adarand* decision, the FCC gathered information on this auction to assess its race- and gender-neutral policies and found that 36% of the winners were minority- and women-owned firms (FCC Report & Order, 1996).

The applicants for these licenses were allowed to pay for their licenses by means of a 10% down payment, 5% of which was to be paid at the close of the auction, and installment payments (FCC Public Notice, November 1, 1996). To be granted the license, each applicant was required to pay the remaining 5% on November 8, 1996. Applicants who did not submit the payment within the deadline were deemed in default and subject to license cancellation and default payments. Payment of the remainder of the amount due on each license would be made in quarterly installments. The agency felt that this would mean that the licensing of the spectrum would include big, established companies as well as small companies owned by minorities and women.

Some winners in the C block auction did not pay their down payments on time, and were deemed by the FCC to be in default, and their licenses were scheduled to be reauctioned on July 3, 1996 (FCC Public Notice May 30, 1996b). Two companies, BDPCS, Inc. and National Telecom PCS, Inc., defaulted on 18 license payments. The auction of these licenses was completed by July 16, 1996, and raised a total of $904, 607, 467 for the U.S. Treasury.

AFRICAN AMERICAN WINNERS

Since the C band auction was a special auction for entrepreneurs and had special provisions for minorities and women, it was chosen for analysis as a case in point of the capability of Blacks to prosper in the new communications technology businesses. Determining the number of African Americans who won PCS licenses was a very difficult task because the FCC does not track the race of licensees. Therefore, this writer used a variety of methods to ferret out who the Black winners were. Telephone inquiries to FCC officials revealed that the FCC took the position that it was not necessary to determine which racial groups applicants belonged to and that it was sufficient that they simply indicate that they were owned by members of a minority group or groups on the PCS license application. The FCC indicated that challenges to minority status could be handled in the court system if necessary.

The FCC did, however, provide access to license applications for the C band auction. The C band auction was therefore analyzed by the author as a case of the performance of Blacks in PCS auctions. Using the computer system that was provided to the public at FCC headquarters in Washington, DC, all of the license applications for this auction were reviewed to determine which applicants indicated that they belonged to a minority group. The applications of all license winners were then reviewed to determine the minorities that won licenses. An inspection of licenses of minority winners revealed that some winners indicated in the application which racial groups they belonged to, and some did not. A telephone and mail survey was conducted to determine the race of the minority winners who did not indicate their race in the applications. The four winning minority applicants whose race could not be determined by their writers included Cellutech, Loralen, Longstreet Communication International, and TWS, LLC. CH - PCS, Inc. indicated that they are Black- and Asian-owned, and POLYCELL Communications, Inc. and RLV - PCS I Partnership stated that they are Black- and American Indian-owned. The following results are based on this investigation.

Table 7.2
PCS Licenses Won by Blacks in the C band Auction

Company Name	Market	Amount of Winning Bid
CH PCS, Inc	El Centro-Calexico, CA	5,362,500
	Flagstaff, AZ	3,506,250
	Kahului-Wailuku-Lahaina, Hi	7,752,000
	Nogales, AZ	1,240,500
	Prescott, AZ	4,575,000
	Sierra Vista-Douglas, AZ	2,242,500
	Sierra Yuma, AZ	5,437,500
		Total 30,116,250
Chase Telecommunications L.P.	Chattanooga, TN	15,966,000
	Clarksville, TN-Hopkinsville, KY	4,177,768
	Cookeville, TN	1,306,554
	Dyersburg-Union City, TN	1,238,475
	Florence, AL	2,997,148
	Jackson, TN	2,882,442
	Kingsport-Johnston City, TN-Bristol, VA/TN	8,524,848
	Knoxville, TN	23,865,315
	Memphis, TN	52,327,500
	Middlesboro-Harlan, KY	1,681,514
	Nashville, TN	60,122,953
		Total 175,090,517

Table 7.2 (Continued)
PCS Licenses Won by Blacks in the C band Auction

Company Name	Market	Amount of Winning Bid
National Telecom PCS, Incs	American Samoa	411,000
Polycell Communications, Inc.	Billings, MT	3,210,833
	Clarksburg-Elkins, WV	788,250
	Clinton, IA-Sterling, IL	863,333
	Coos Bay-North Bend, OR	334,500
	Klamath Falls, OR	459,000
	Sioux City, IA	4,989,166
		Total 10,645,082
R & S PCS, Inc.	Benton Harbor, MI	4,206,000
	Canton-New Philadelphia, OH	8,987,250
	Columbus, GA	5,265,000
	Elkhart, IN	6,620,250
	Erie, PA	6,870,750
	Mansfield, OH	5,541,000
	Peoria, IL	13,511,250
	Youngstown-Warren, OH	12,059,250
		Total 63,060,750
RLV-PCS I Partnership	Duluth, MN	4,032,750
	St. Joseph, MO	2,749,999
		Total 6,782,749
Roberts-Roberts & Associates, LLC	Cape Girardeau-Sikeston, MO	2,502,750
	Jefferson City, MO	2,122,500
	Quincy, IL-Hannibal, MO	1,531,500
	Rolla, MO	804,750
	Sedalia, MO	445,500
	West Plains, MO	262,500
		Total 8,175,750

Table 7.2 (Continued)
PCS Licenses Won by Blacks in the C band Auction

Company Name	Market	Amount of Winning Bid
Roberts-Roberts & Associates, LLC	Cape Girardeau-Sikeston, MO	2,502,750
		2,122,500
	Jefferson City, MO	1,531,500
	Quincy, IL-Hannibal, MO	804,750
	Rolla, MO	445,500
	Sedalia, MO	262,500
	West Plains, MO	Total 8,175,750
Southern Communications Systems, Inc.	Cleveland, TN	506,250
Urban Communicators PCS Limited Partnership	Burlington, NC	1,669,500
	Fayetteville-Lumberton, NC	9,845,250
		1,819,500
	Goldsboro-Kinston, NC	1,925,250
	Greenville-Washington, NC	2,288,250
	Jacksonville, NC	2,182,500
	New Bern, NC	46,949,250
	Raleigh-Durham, NC	642,000
	Roanoke Rapids, NC	1,644,000
	Rocky Mount-Wilson, NC	5,657,250
	Wilmington, NC	Total 74,622,750
		Grand Total 1,041,011,098

Eight Black-owned firms were among the 89 winners of PCS licenses in this auction. These African American firms won 40 of the 493 licenses that were granted. Black-owned firms made up 8% of the winners of licenses, and they won about 8% of the licenses that were granted. It should be noted that CH PCS, Inc. won one of its eight licenses in the C block reauction.

Black-owned firms bid over $1 billion to gain access to new business opportunities (see Table 7.2) in major markets around the nation and in American Samoa. Three firms were among the top 20 bidders by dollar value of high bids. Chase Telecommunications L. P. had 11 winning bids totaling more than $175 million, Urban Communicators PCS Limited Partnership had 10 winning bids totaling over $74 million, and R & S PCS had 8 winning bids totaling over $67 million.

CH PCS, with seven winning bids before the reauction, was in the top 25 high bidders with bids totaling more than $30 million. In the reauction, however, CH PCS put in a winning bid of more than $200 million for the license to provide PCS service to Phoenix, Arizona.

Non-African American firms, however, won over 90% of the licenses in this auction and, of course, made the highest bids. The eight Black winners collectively bid $1 billion. The top three non-Black bidders, however, bid over $1 billion each and won 113 of the 493 licenses. NextWave Personal Communications, Inc. bid over $4.2 billion for 56 licenses, DCR PCS, Inc. bid more than $1.4 billion for 43 licenses, and GWI PCS, Inc. bid about $1 billion for 14 licenses.

Strategic alliance seemed to be a key for successful Black bidders for licenses. The fact that several of the companies formed limited partnerships or other kinds of unions becomes obvious when one simply observes their company names (see Table 7.2). The companies that established partnerships between Blacks and another minority were very successful in this competition. CH PCS, Inc, a Black and Asian firm, and POLYCELL Communications, Inc. and RLV - PCS I Partnership, two Black and American Indian firms, won 16 licenses and bid over $261 million to gain these permits. Perhaps this partnering strategy will continue to be meaningful in the future.

A well-known Black broadcaster and a trailblazing Black cablecaster used their financial prowess and communications acumen to become successful bidders in this auction. Urban Communicators PCS Limited Partnership, which is partially controlled by Inner City Broadcasting's Percy Sutton, was one of the largest winners among African Americans, with ten licenses and over $74 million in bids. R and S PCS, Inc., owned by Robert Johnson of BET Holdings, Inc., won eight licenses, for which it bid more than $63 million. Successful Black communicators seem to be finding PCS an area in which they can diversify and expand their financial portfolios.

AFTERMATH OF THE C BAND AUCTION

The effort to allow as many people as possible to obtain PCS licenses has proven to be a worthwhile ideal but one that is not easy to achieve. On March 31, 1997, several C band licensees filed a joint request with the FCC to modify their existing installment payment obligations. Many of these companies found themselves unable to pay and even went bankrupt trying to do so. On March 31, 1997, the FCC suspended its requirement for payment and indicated that interest would continue to accrue on all unpaid installment payments until further notice.

On September 25, 1997, after receiving public comment on the issue of installment payments, the FCC ordered that installment payment requirements be reinstated and required that the payments begin on March 31, 1998. It also provided four options for repayment:

Option 1: Existing Note Obligations. Licensees may elect to continue making payments under their original installment plan. Licensees using this option will pay over eight equal payments and all interest that has accrued and was unpaid during the period of payment suspension.

Option 2: Disaggregation. On or before January 15, 1998, any C band licensee may elect to desegregate one-half of its spectrum in any or all of its licenses and return such spectrum to the FCC for reauction. In return, the licensee will be forgiven for half of its debt. Fifty percent of the down payment will be applied toward the debt for the retained spectrum, and the licensee will forfeit the other 50% of its deposit. The licensee will be prohibited from rebidding on the spectrum or otherwise from acquiring it for two years from the date of the reauction. Accrued interest will be paid in the same fashion as in the preceding option.

Option 3: Amnesty. On or before January 15, 1998, any C band licensee may return all of its licenses and in return will have its outstanding C band debt forgiven. The down payment and any payment made on or before March 31 will not be returned. The licensee, however, could bid on any of its returned licenses or any other licenses in the reauction.

Option 4: Prepayment. On or before January 15, 1998, any C band licensee may purchase any of its licenses at face value as a bid at the prior C band auction. A licensee must purchase all BTA licenses it now owns within any single MTA. The licensee may use 70% of its down payment and any additional moneys that it is able to raise in order to buy out as many of its licenses as it desires. Licenses that are not prepaid in accordance with this option must be surrendered to the FCC for reauction, in exchange for FCC's forgiveness of corresponding debt. A licensee may not rebid at the reauction for any of the licenses that the licensee relinquishes and may not otherwise acquire any such license in the secondary market for two years.

This writer was unable to ascertain from the FCC which, if any, African American companies requested bid modifications or which options, if any, they could use to make payments. The agency is prohibited from publishing, even under the Freedom of Information Act, any information that might be deleterious to companies that bid for licenses.

Reed Hundt, then FCC chairman did, however, make these comments in the Second Report and Order: "A half dozen holders of the C Block licenses for about two-thirds of the country by population are in financial distress and apparently unable to pay monies promised to the government by these licensees in a fair auction of the C Block licenses . . . A handful of large C Block licensees have been unable to attract sufficient financing to create viable businesses. These are Nextwave, Pocket, GWI, ChaseTel and ClearComm." None of these are African American companies.

ENTERING NEW MARKETS AND ENCOUNTERING OLD OBSTACLES

The results of the C block PCS auction seem to indicate that Blacks are moving in the right direction with cutting-edge communications technologies but lack the economic power to be significant players in the new communications technology game. On the positive side of things, African Americans gained more ownership in the PCS arena than they currently enjoy in the broadcast arena. Black ownership is on the decline in commercial broadcasting. Black Americans own less than 2% of the radio stations and less than 1% of the television stations in America. In this PCS auction, Blacks, however, gained 8% of the licenses for wireless services. Wireless communications may be an area in which Blacks can gain empowerment in the communications revolution.

Blacks make up 12% of the U.S. population but won only 8% of the C band PCS licenses. One could argue that Blacks still are not adequately represented in the communications business arena. Nevertheless, Blacks are performing better in the PCS marketplace than they are in the broadcast arena, where they own less than 2% of radio and television stations. This may be an indicator that Blacks are getting in on the ground level of a communications technology that will allow them to be minor players in the communications revolution of the future.

Blacks may have performed better if the FCC policies and promises that were in place at the beginning had been in place throughout the auction. The FCC's efforts bear some special criticism in light of the *Adarand* decision. Three days before the C band PCS auction, the Supreme Court decided the *Adarand* case. This decision essentially required that racial preferences could not be used unless they were given a high level of scrutiny.

The FCC chose to eliminate all of its racial preferences and regulations that would apply to the C band auction. The agency and minority applicants felt that this was a way to avoid litigation, which would delay the auction. The commission then announced that it would conduct a comprehensive study to determine if preferences were necessary to help Blacks enter the ownership ranks in PCS. This study would be used to meet the strict scrutiny requirement of the *Adarand* decision.

The FCC has recognized for more than 50 years that Blacks and others in American society encounter numerous barriers to entering the telecommunications industry. How the FCC can now claim that there is no record to substantiate that Blacks have been discriminated against in entry to the telecommunications industries is a bit of sophisticated double talk. Cases too numerous to mention here bear this out. For example, testimony before Congress has been presented showing the lack of Black ownership of telecommunications licenses; the Congress has also established that, nationally, minorities lack equal access to capital that is clearly needed to be a player in the telecommunications businesses (Bush & Martin, 1997). Furthermore, the commission for decades granted radio and television licenses using methods that favored non-Blacks. The Supreme Court's decision that all racially based preferences should meet compelling governmental interest should have been easy for the FCC to comply with since the FCC has long been trying to increase minority participation in ownership of telecommunications. The commission stated in its own 1997 report on proceedings to identify and eliminate market-entry barriers for Blacks, other minorities, and women: "There is a long history of recognition by this agency, as well as by the courts, Congress, and the public that minorities and women have experienced serious obstacles in attempting to participate in the telecommunications industry and that their greater participation would enhance the public interest," (p. 129). The main obstacle that Black businesses and other small enterprises have faced in participating in the telecommunications industry is gaining the capital necessary to conduct business. Congress recognized this and, through the Telecommunications Act of 1996, created a special fund to promote access to small communications businesses and stimulate economic growth, innovation, and technological growth (FCC News, 1997). The Telecommunications Development Fund (TDF) is capitalized by the interest earned from the up-front payments that businesses submit to participate in the FCC's spectrum auctions, returns from its loans, and investments and charitable contributions (FCC, 1998). In the early part of 1997, TDF had $20.2 million to fund loans, equity investments, and assistance to small communications businesses; TDF earns additional interest from FCC auctions as they occur.

The chairman of the FCC has been given the authority to appoint the directors of the TDF. A seven-member board of directors runs TDF. Four directors are from the private sector, while three are from the FCC, the U.S. Small Business Administration, and the U.S. Department of Treasury. At the time of this writing, TDF investment and loan applications were not available, a chairman was being appointed to head the fund, and the board of directors was studying market needs and models to determine effectively how to fulfill its statutory mandates and finalize the organization structure, loan and investment criteria, and application process.

IMPACT ON THE BLACK COMMUNITY

What happened in this case of the FCC and the struggle of Blacks to achieve parity with Whites in the "information revolution" brought about by auctioning of the airwaves may be a sign of what is to come in the Information Society with regard to Black Americans in the communications industry.

1. New communications technologies require expensive, complex infrastructures to support profit-making businesses. Too often these infrastructures, including the purchase of spectrum licenses, will be too expensive for minorities to afford.

2. Ineffective policies and/or preferential policies that would help Blacks will be useless because of challenges from the majority community.

3. Few, if any, Black companies will be able to participate in this higher end of the Information Society as it advances.

4. Efforts like the TDF will have to continue and be expanded so that Black businesses can realize the capital needed to participate in the Information Society of the twenty first century.

5. Blacks must mobilize political and economic forces that will bring about favorable conditions for themselves in the new communications environment.

RECOMMENDATIONS FOR FUTURE RESEARCH

Communication studies on Blacks have mainly concentrated on images in the media and control and ownership of broadcast facilities. Until now, most communications investigations have stayed away from telephony. However, this seems to be a fertile ground for those who study the new wave of communications. Several approaches to research seem to be evident in view of the foregoing analysis:

1. Analysis of congressional and FCC policies on racial preferences in the aftermath of the *Adarand* decision.

2. Racial makeup of owners and controllers of wireless systems that provide voice, data, and video service to the public.

3. Strategic alliances of Blacks and other minorities to gain power in the telecommunications industry.

4. Analysis of telecommunications services to Black communities by Black-owned firms.

CONCLUSION

Whites and other non-African Americans are constructing the groundwork for the wireless marketplace, while Blacks are making a huge investment to remain marginal participants. Gaining 8% of the PCS licenses has allowed

Blacks to make inroads into new communications technologies arenas. Whites and other groups, however, rallied together and forced the FCC to change the rules and created a situation in which they would have more time to cover bids that they knew were outlandish in the first place. It appears that, for the most part, Blacks paid the going rate under the prescribed requirements. Bidders who have since claimed that they could not pay without special restructuring may have driven up these rates. In short, the few Blacks who had the capital to play this game in the first place probably paid too much for what they got in comparison to some non-Black bidders.

If Blacks are going to gain parity with others in the telecommunications industry, the FCC must stand firmly behind its race-based policies when faced with challenges from the majority community. The new spectrum of business should offer the opportunity for all sectors of society to participate in ownership. If this does not take place, Blacks will find themselves in the same position as in the past with regard to the broadcast industry: major consumers and minor owners.

The FCC should stop engaging in bureaucratic double talk. It proclaims, on one hand, that it recognizes that discrimination exists when Blacks and other minorities attempt to enter the telecommunications marketplace as owners, yet it must conduct studies to show that this is a reality. The following recommendations seem appropriate:

1. The FCC must create policies that allow Blacks to gain parity with Whites in the telecommunications industry.

2. The FCC must avoid creating barriers to Blacks entering the telecommunications field by reneging on promises and acquiescing in the face of legal challenges.

3. The FCC must rethink its ownership policies and promulgate new ones that will foster diversity of ownership in new communications businesses.

4. The FCC must complete its various studies and set up programs so that they can be tracked properly to create the database of information that would provide strong evidence to withstand a challenge on the basis of race.

To conclude with a popular metaphor, while Blacks are entering the information superhighway at a relatively slow rate, policies need to be in place that will help them overcome financial roadblocks. Their destination should be the control and ownership of more of the highway system's toll roads. Profits from such enterprises should lead to the construction of more and improved Black communities in the Information Society.

REFERENCES

Adarand Constructors, Inc. v. Pena (1995). Syllabus. No. 93-1841, U.S. Supreme Court.

Bureau of the Census (1996). *Black Owned Businesses: Strongest in Services. A Statistical Brief Issued by the Bureau of Census.* SB/96-3. Washington, DC: U.S. Department of Commerce.

Bush, A. C., & Martin, M. S. (1997). *The FCC's Minority Ownership Policies from Broadcasting to PCS.* [On-Line]. Available: http://www.law.indianna.edu/fclj/v48/no3/bush.html.

FCC (1993). *Fact Sheet on Interactive Video and Data Services.* Washington, DC: Author.

FCC (1998, February 5). *The Telecommunications Development Fund Fact Sheet.* Washington, DC: Author.

FCC (1996, January). *Wireless Telecommunications Bureau Auctions Fact Sheet.* Washington, DC: Author.

FCC Fifth Memorandum Opinion and Order (1994, November 23). *Implementation of 309 (j) of the Communications Act Competitive-Bidding.* (FCC 94-285). Washington, DC: Author.

FCC News Release (1994, November 4). *Chairman Hundt Reiterates FCC Commitment to Female and Minority Participation in Communications Businesses at First Women of Wireless Conference.* Washington, DC: Author.

FCC News Release (1996, May 6). *Broadband Personal Communications Services C block auction Closes Historic Auction Designed Solely for Entrepreneurs.* Washington, DC: Author.

FCC News Release (1997, July 23). *Chairman Hundt Announces Appointment of W. Don Cornwell as Chairman of the Telecommunications Development Fund.* Washington, DC: Author.

FCC Public Notice (1996a, May 8). *Entrepreneurs C Block Auction Closes. FCC Announces Winning Bidders in the Auction of 493 Licenses to Provide Broadband PCS in Basic Trading Areas.* (No. 5. DA 96-716). Washington, DC: Author.

FCC Public Notice (1996b, May 30). 18 *Defaulted Licenses to Be Re-auctioned. Re-auction to Begin July 3rd.* (DA 96-87). Washington, DC: Author.

FCC Public Notice (1996c, July 17). *Entrepreneurs C Block Re-auction Closes FCC Announces Winning Bidders in the Re-auction of 18 Licenses to Provide Broadband PCS in Basic Trading Areas.* Auction Event No. 10. (DA 96-1153). Washington, DC: Author.

FCC Public Notice (1996d, November 1). *FCC Announces Grant of Broadband Personal Communications Services Entrepreneurs C Block BTA Licenses. Final Down Payment Due November 8, 1996.* (DA 96-1795).

FCC Public Notice (1997, January 15). *D, E, and F Block Auction Closes Winning Bidders in the Auction of 1,479 Licenses to Provide Broadband PCS in Basic Trading Areas.* (DA 97-81). Washington, DC: Author.

FCC Report (1994, April 20). *FCC Adopts Spectrum Auction Procedures for Interactive Video and Data Service.* (No. DC-2591). Washington, DC: Author.

FCC Report (1997, May 8). *Section 257 Proceeding to Identify and Eliminate Market Entry Barriers for Small Businesses.* (FCC 97-164). Washington, DC: Author.

FCC Report & Order (1996, June 24). *Amendment of Parts 20 and 24 of the Commission's Rules—Broadband PCS Competitive Bidding and the Commercial Mobile Radio Service Spectrum Cap.* (FCC 96-278). Washington, DC: Author..

FCC Tenth Report & Order (1996, November 21). *Implementation of Section 309(j) of the Communications Act.* (FCC 96-447). Washington, DC: Author.

Gilder, G. (1995). *Auctioning the Airwaves.* [On-line] Available: http://www.seas.upenn.edu/~gaj1/auctngg.htm.

McAfee, R. P., & McMillan, J. (1996). Analyzing the airwaves auction. *Journal of Economic Perspectives, 10,* (1), 159-175.

National Telecommunications and Information Administration (1995, April). *Capital Formation and Investment in Minority Business Enterprises in the Telecommunications Industries.* Washington, DC: U.S. Department of Commence.

Rezai, J. J., & Bell, C. (1996). *PCS: A New Paradigm for Communications.* A Special Report. Pryor, McClendon, Counts.

U.S. Supreme Court (1995). *Adarand Constructors, Inc. v. Pena,* Syllabus. (No. 93-1841). Washington, DC: Author

PART III

The Occupational Dimension

It is critical that Blacks not only own and run profitable information businesses and companies in the Information Society but also gain employment in information jobs. Unemployment is a continuing problem in the Black community, and many analysts have pointed out that advances in technology, along with racism, employment discrimination, and other factors, have kept Blacks out of the job market.

Only a portion of the Black community, however, encounters this plight. Most African Americans hold jobs and are employed in a variety of occupations. The question here is to what extent Black Americans are pursuing employment that might be classified as information jobs, that is, jobs that have as their main function the processing, production, and dissemination of information.

Information work is skilled labor, and persons who perform such work must be properly trained. Getting such training has typically been a problem for members of the Black community. In Chapter 8, John T. Barber uses data from the U.S. Bureau of Labor Statistics and information labor classifications to demonstrate that Blacks are poorly represented in high-tech information jobs but are concentrated in occupations that deal with the processing and distribution of information. In Chapter 9, Gloria P. James expresses the need for collaboration between information corporations and historically Black colleges to prepare the new generation of information professionals. She discusses the recent collaboration between Clark Atlanta University and Atlanta Olympic Broadcasting as an example of how this can be accomplished.

CHAPTER 8

Information Labor and African Americans

John T. Barber

For several decades researchers have been forecasting the coming of a time when the American workforce would witness a decline in industrial workers and an increase in the number of people performing jobs that create knowledge or have information as an input or as a final product (Machlup, 1962; Bell, 1976; Rubin & Huber, 1986). In his warning of the decline of the global workforce as the result of advanced technologies being introduced into the workplace, Rifkin (1995) described the impact of this trend on the Black community: "Today millions of African Americans find themselves hopelessly trapped in a permanent underclass. Unskilled and unneeded, the commodity value of their labor has been rendered virtually useless by the automated technologies that have come to displace them in the new high-tech global economy," (p. 80).

While Rifkin's statement is true for many African Americans who have been unable to adjust to the information age job market, the majority of Blacks do not fit into this category. This chapter, therefore, looks at Blacks who are employed and asks the question, To what degree are Blacks performing in occupations that create knowledge or have information as an input or as a final product? To answer this question, overviews of employment trends in the American workforce in general and in the African American community in particular are presented. Next, the term "information labor" is defined, and classification schemes for determining which jobs are information jobs are outlined. Then the Current Population Survey (CPS) of the Bureau of Labor Statistics is described as a tool for analyzing African Americans' employment in various occupations. Finally, Machlup's (1962) scheme for classifying information jobs is combined with CPS data to provide a picture of the kinds of information jobs that African Americans held during the first half of the 1990s.

AMERICA DEVELOPS AN INFORMATION WORKFORCE

One of the indicators that a nation is an Information Society is its shift to creating information industries, rather than industrial ones. There is much evidence that there are a worldwide shift to information work and an emergence of an information sector in the workforce (Katz, 1988), although some argue that this shift varies from nation to nation (Castells & Aoyama, 1994). Information industries have the creation of knowledge as their output. Measuring the amount of information work that is carried out in a society is a way of evaluating the extent to which an Information Society is progressing. The more a nation shifts from doing industrial or some other type of work, to performing information work, the more it can be considered an Information Society. An increase in information work is, in fact, essential to the emergence of an Information Society.

The U.S. Bureau of Labor Statistics projects that from 1994 to 2005 employment in America will increase by 14%, or 17.7 million jobs. During this period, it is expected that service-producing industries will account for most of the new jobs and that the goods-producing sector will decline. Employment in professional specialty occupations is projected to increase at a faster rate than that of any other occupational group. The fastest growing occupations reflect growth in computer technology and health services. Technological change and declining industry employment will cause a decline in such areas as farming, garment sewing machine operation, and private household cleaning. Office automation and the increased use of word processors, for example, may cause a decline in the employment of typists. Education and training will affect job opportunities such that jobs requiring the most education and training will grow faster than jobs with lower education and training requirements. Jobs requiring the most education and training will be both the fastest growing and the highest paying. All these projected trends seem to jibe with analysts' predictions that an emerging Information Society will witness an increased number of people performing jobs that create knowledge or have information as an input or a final product. Furthermore, the trend of knowledge workers' outpacing industrial workers is projected to continue in the twenty first century.

AFRICAN AMERICANS AND THE AMERICAN LABOR FORCE

Since information work is clearly central to success in the twenty first century's Information Society workforce, we need to understand the extent to which the Black community within the American Information Society is participating in the shift from industrial work to information work.

To understand the occupational position of the Black community in the American Information Society, a bit of background information on this group is required. The Black population in America was 31.4 million in 1992, 14% of the country's total (U.S. Department of Commerce, Bureau of the Census, 1993). In this same year, 81% of Blacks 25 years and over had completed at least four years of high school. The proportion aged 25 and over who were college graduates was 12%. In 1991 the real median income of Black families rose to $33,310. Nevertheless, in 1991, 30% of Black families were in poverty, down from 34% in 1967.

In the meantime, the shift to work that relies on the creation, processing, storage, manipulation, and distribution of information is causing jobs to be located outside the central cities. This shift tends to have a deleterious impact on the Black community, especially among young Black men between the ages of 18 and 24, 22% of whom are unemployed (Skinner, 1995). William Julius Wilson (1996), in his landmark work on the world of poor urban Blacks, addresses this issue: "The decline of the mass production system, the decreasing availability of lower-skilled blue-collar jobs, and the growing importance of training and education in the higher-growth industries adversely affected the employment rates and earnings of low-skilled Black workers, many of whom are concentrated in inner city ghettos. The growing suburbanization of jobs has aggravated the employment woes of poor inner city workers," (p. 54).

Consequently, many Blacks face continuing unemployment in the Information Society due to a mismatch between their skills and education and the new way of working and because their distance from work is difficult to overcome with their transportation resources (Cohn & Fossett, 1996; Wilson 1996). This condition is exacerbated by immigration of other racial groups to take menial service jobs that some unemployed Blacks may have pursued (Aponte, 1996; Matloff, 1996).

Even when they are not at the urban poverty level, Blacks continue to lag behind Whites in nearly every measure of labor market success, according to the Bureau of Labor Statistics (U.S. Department of Labor, 1996). Blacks earned less than their White counterparts regardless of educational attainment in 1995. In the same year, only 14.8 million of the 23 million Black persons of working age (16 years and over) were in the labor force. In 1995 the unemployment rate for Black workers was 10.4%, compared to 4.9% for Whites. In 1995 the unemployment rates for Black men and women were 8.8% and 8.6%, respectively. In the same year the average duration of unemployment for Blacks was 19.6 weeks. Blacks were more likely in 1995 to be employed as operators, fabricators, and laborers than in managerial or professional positions.

The employment picture for Blacks, however, is not completely negative. Overall, more Blacks are employed today than ever before. Labor force projections indicate that there will be some changes in the future American labor force that favor Blacks. In 1990 there were 125 million Americans in the civilian labor force, with Blacks representing 10% of that group (Fullerton, 1993b). The Bureau of Labor Statistics projects that between 1990 and 2005 Blacks will add 7.3 million workers to the labor force, or 13% of all entrants. Blacks will thereby, increase both their numbers in the workforce and their share of the labor market. To what extent will Blacks be occupied in jobs that can be classified as information work?

The question today is not just whether Blacks are employed or unemployed but also whether or not they have viable employment in an Information Society where there is an increased emphasis on high-tech careers. More than 20 years ago, Bell (1976) pointed out that Blacks were moving in small increments toward information jobs. Marable (1983) stated later that Blacks were concentrated in just the jobs that were not viable in the coming Information Society. To unravel this problem, one needs to answer several questions. First, what types of jobs can be considered information jobs? Second, to what extent are Blacks concentrated in those occupations? Third, are Blacks are not already employed there moving into information work?

CLASSIFICATIONS OF INFORMATION LABOR

Expansion of information jobs in the workforce is a key feature of Information Societies, but how do we distinguish between jobs that involve information work and those that do not? Mainly in an effort to measure the extent to which economies were shifting from an industrial base to a knowledge or information base, several authors have attempted to create classifications of information work. Machlup (1962) was one of the earliest analysts to tackle this task and defined the information industry as consisting of education, research, publishing, and broadcasting. He estimated that 31% of the American workforce was engaged in knowledge work in 1958. Bell (1973) felt that Machlup's categories were too broad and that a classification of information work should include only workers who produce information and not those who transmit it. In this way, Bell concluded that the main contributors to the expansion of the Information Society were those engaged in professional and technical occupations that constituted 12.2% of the total civilian employment at the time of his work.

Porat (1975) asserted that information workers are those who are engaged in creating and processing information. Initially, he concluded that there were three types of information workers: those whose final product is information, those whose main activity is informational in nature, and those who operate information technologies. This information sector included those engaged in the production and distribution of knowledge as well as those who used information as an input for their final production. Porat's classification scheme is useful here and has been used by many researchers to measure the shift toward information work in Information Societies. Porat's work in 1977 refined his earlier definitions and provided a scheme based on data collected by a U.S. government agency. He classified 188 of the 422 occupations used by the Bureau of Labor Statistics of the U.S. Department of Commerce for compiling data on occupations by industry. They were classified in five functional categories: knowledge producers, knowledge distributors, market search and coordination specialists, information processors, and information machine workers.

MACHLUP'S CLASSIFICATIONS

Machlup's (1962) work has proven to be the most useful to analysts, and his classifications have been used in the more recent studies of the Organization for Economic Cooperation and Development (OECD, 1981), Rubin and Huber (1986), Katz (1988), Dordick and Wang (1993), and others to determine the extent to which Information Societies are developing in America and around the world. One of the reasons that Machlup's work is useful is that it presents five broad categories into which all knowledge industries can be placed. Each of those categories requires some explanation, since they will be used here to classify information work that is carried out by African Americans.

His first category is education. In this category, Machlup (1962) placed various types of knowledge that is produced through education. He included not only formal education carried out by teachers and professors but education in the home, school, and church, as well as training on the job and training in the armed forces.

Research and development, his second category, includes basic and applied research. Those engaged in basic research included researchers in the humanities and social sciences and those in applied research, including scientists and engineers.

The third category deals with the media of communication and workers who engaged in conveying knowledge from person to person or to the masses. Workers in this knowledge industry would include those engaged in the production of various printed materials, such as newspapers and books, those on the stage and in cinema, and those in radio and television, telephony, and the postal service.

Another of Machlup's (1962) categories, information machines, includes computers, information machines in the media of communication, office machines, and other instruments that measure and control. Workers in this category operate such machines and instruments.

Information services, the writer's final category, include legal, engineering, accounting and auditing, and medical services. Machlup felt that these were the professional services industries that specialize in producing and selling information and advice.

Machlup (1962) also discussed knowledge production and occupational structure. He regrouped 11 categories of workers published by the U.S. Bureau of the Census into three groups: white-collar workers, manual and service workers, and farmworkers. His occupational groups were further broken down into those that were knowledge-producing and those that were not. In this way, he concluded that more people were moving into knowledge industries and jobs than were moving into manual labor. Machlup (1962) and his followers, however, never addressed race in any of their classifications. To gain an understanding of how Blacks fit into information industries and jobs, Machlup's five broad categories of knowledge industries are used here, but we must turn elsewhere to develop a scheme of detailed occupations by race.

RACIAL STATISTICS FROM THE CENSUS AND LABOR BUREAUS

The CPS, conducted monthly by the Bureau of the Census for the Bureau of Labor Statistics (BLS) of the U.S. Department of Commerce, provides a comprehensive body of information on the employment and unemployment of the nation's population by race and a variety of other classifications. The CPS uses a scientifically selected sample designed to represent the civilian noninstitutional population 16 years of age and older.

The noninstitutional population means persons residing in the 50 states and the District of Columbia who are not inmates of institutions such as mental or penal facilities and the like. Respondents are interviewed to obtain information about the employment status of each member of the household.

This analysis is concerned with the data from the CPS surveys covering 1990 through 1996. The 1990 census-based sample design included about 66,000 housing units per month located in 792 selected geographic areas called primary sampling units, and the 1996 sample included about 59,000 households from 754 sample areas (BLS, 1997d). Each month, about 59,000 households are assigned for data collection. Using the estimating methods used in the CPS, all of the results for a given month become available simultaneously and are based on returns from the entire panel of respondents (BLS, 1997c). The estimation procedure involves weighting the data from each sample person by the inverse of the probability of the person's being in the sample. This gives a rough measure of the number of actual persons that the sample represents.

At the end of each year, the average employment figures for each occupation category are reported in *BLS' Employment and Earnings* publication. This summary is the annual averages of employed civilians by detailed occupation, race, and other characteristics. Some 300 detailed occupations are broken down into some 32 categories from managerial and professional specialty, to farming, forestry, and fishing. These categories of occupations are not classified as information or noninformation jobs. Using Machlup's five categories of information industries, the 300 detailed occupations were examined and either placed into one of the categories or not used (see Tables 8.1-8.5). The annual average summaries for 1990 through 1996 are utilized and show the extent to which Blacks are represented in jobs that may be classified as information jobs. By using data for the 1990s, we can observe whether Blacks are expanding their position in the Information Society of America as it is continuing to develop.

AFRICAN AMERICANS IN THE INFORMATION LABOR FORCE

Combining Machlup's information industry classifications and BLS' detailed occupation categories reveals the extent to which Blacks in America are occupying positions in information jobs (see Tables 8.1 to 8.5).

Table 8.1
Percentage of Blacks in Education 1990 to 1995

	1990	1991	1992	1993	1994	1995
Occupations						
Administrators, education and related fields	9.5	8.5	9.8	13.0	12.2	11.2
Teachers college and university	4.5	4.8	4.7	4.8	5.0	6.2
Teachers, except college and university	8.7	8.6	9.3	8.6	8.9	6.3
Prekindergarten and kindergarten	10.7	12.4	12.7	11.7	11.0	13.9
Elementary school	9.7	8.9	10.4	9.3	10.2	10.1
Secondary education	7.1	7.3	7.6	6.9	7.6	7.5
Special education	11.8	9.5	10.0	10.1	6.9	9.3
Librarians	5.5	6.1	5.8	7.0	10.5	7.6
Library clerks	9.1	8.8	10.1	11.6	10.8	13.7

Blacks are underrepresented in the education field in six out of nine areas, including teachers in higher and secondary education (see Table 8.1). The only area where Blacks seem to be progressing in education is in the areas of prekindergarten and kindergarten. There is a steady increase in library clerks, with the greatest percentage in 1995. Black education administrators reached a peak in 1993 and declined in the remaining years. Teachers, except in colleges and universities, hit a peak in 1992 and declined thereafter. They were at a lower point in 1995 than they were in 1990.

Table 8.2

Percentage of Blacks in Research and Development 1990 to 1995

	1990	1991	1992	1993	1994	1995
Engineers	3.6	3.6	3.9	3.7	3.7	4.7
Aerospace	4.8	1.9	3.3	2.1	.9	1.5
Chemical	1.7	3.2	.7	2.5	1.8	8.5
Civil	4.0	4.0	3.4	4.7	2.8	4.9
Electrical and electronic	3.8	4.9	5.2	4.5	4.2	5.8
Industrial	4.4	4.3	4.7	3.4	5.9	6.0
Mechanical	3.5	3.4	3.7	4.4	3.1	3.8
Mathematical and computer scientists	6.5	6.3	6.8	6.0	6.5	7.2
Computer systems analysts and scientists	7.0	5.8	5.9	5.8	7.2	6.1
Operations systems researchers and analysts	5.2	8.2	9.3	6.3	3.9	10.1
Natural scientists	7.2	3.3	3.0	3.8	3.6	3.9
Chemists, except biochemists	4.6	5.2	2.8	4.3	4.5	4.6
Geologists and geodesists	.6	.7	.3	1.0	.9	.5
Biological and life scientists	2.7	5.2	2.8	3.9	4.5	5.2
Medical scientists	*	*	4.1	5.8	1.1	4.1
Social scientists and urban planners	5.4	6.7	6.7	5.9	7.0	8.8
Economists	4.0	5.1	7.9	4.8	3.8	5.0
Psychologists	6.6	7.8	6.2	7.1	8.3	10.2

Blacks are grossly underrepresented in all areas of research and development (see Table 8.2). The number of engineers and mathematical and computer scientists rose slightly from 1990 to 1995. The number of natural scientists, however, declined from 7.2% to 3.9% during this time.

Table 8.3
Percentage of Blacks in the Media of Communication 1990 to 1995

	1990	1991	1992	1993	1994	1995
Writers, artists, and entertainers	4.5	5.0	4.9	5.3	5.3	6.2
Authors	2.3	1.4	2.7	2.4	2.8	3.2
Technical writers	1.6	5.3	3.8	2.7	4.0	3.0
Designers	2.6	2.9	3.0	3.7	3.4	4.2
Musicians and composers	9.6	7.6	11.2	8.8	10.2	10.0
Actors and directors	5.9	10.5	6.6	10.4	3.8	9.8
Painters, craft artists, and artist printmakers	2.8	2.7	2.8	3.5	4.6	4.2
Photographers	2.9	7.7	6.4	6.5	4.6	6.5
Editors and reporters	3.8	4.5	4.4	5.0	5.4	4.7
Public relations specialists	7.7	8.3	5.5	7.0	5.0	8.3
Announcers	6/9	6.2	6.8	*	*	*
Mail and message distributing occupations	20.0	21.1	19.0	19.0	18.5	20.4
Postal clerks, except carriers	25.1	27.7	26.6	26.8	28.2	29.3
Mail carriers, postal service	14.4	17.1	14.5	12.6	11.6	13.8
Mail clerks, except postal service	23.8	20.6	21.3	22.5	24.2	26.2
Messengers	17.9	18.3	13.3	14.2	8.1	12.0

In the media of communication, Black representation shows a distinct dichotomy (see Table 8.3). Blacks are grossly underrepresented in the information production categories of writers, artists, and entertainers and overrepresented in the mail and message distribution occupations. Black writers and others did have a slight increase over the time period from 4.5% in 1990 to 6.2% in 1995. During the same time period, Black employment in mail and message distribution remained near 20%, with postal clerks having the highest number of persons employed.

Table 8.4
Percentage of Blacks Operating Information Machines 1990 to 1995

	1990	1991	1992	1993	1994	1995
Computer equipment operators	13.1	13.9	13.1	13.7	14.2	15.7
Duplicating, mail, and other office machine operators	19.3	14.2	19.5	19.2	17.2	11.2
Communications equipment operators	19.9	19.1	19.5	20.9	20.8	25.6
Telephone operators	19.7	19.5	18.9	21.0	21.7	26.0
Printing machine operators	7.5	8.2	6.8	6.0	10.1	11.5
Printing press operators	*	*	6.3	6.9	11.	12.2
Typesetters and compositors	4.8	6.3	4.7	1.5	*	*
Photographic process machine operators	6.4	7.9	7.8	8.7	11.6	13.2
Billing, posting, and calculating machine operators	0	*	12.7	12.0	8.4	10.4

There is also a noticeable dichotomy in the number of Blacks employed in the information machines operation area (see Table 8.4). Black information machine operators outside the printing industry are overrepresented, while those in the printing industry are underrepresented. For example, Blacks are well represented among computer equipment operators and show a steady increase over the time period studied. Communications and telephone operators are areas where Blacks have good representation. In the printing occupations such as press operators and photographic process machine operators, typesetters, and compositors, however, Black representation is generally low.

In information services, Blacks are grossly underrepresented among lawyers, physicians, and accountants and auditors. They are, however, well represented in the records processing occupations, except for financial records processing.

Table 8.5
Percentage of Blacks in Information Services 1990 to 1995

	1990	1991	1992	1993	1994	1995
Lawyers	3.2	2.6	2.7	2.7	3.3	3.6
Physicians	3.0	3.2	3.3	3.7	4.2	4.9
Accountants and auditors	7.4	7.6	5.8	7.0	9.0	8.4
Information clerks	9.5	9.0	8.3	9.3	10.6	10.0
Interviewers	11.5	11.4	12.9	10.3	13.1	12.4
Records processing occupations, except financial	14.1	14.9	15.4	14.9	15.6	5.4
Order clerks	15.1	17.1	16.8	17.1	18.5	16.0
Personnel clerks, except payroll and timekeeping	21.7	18.1	12.2	15.2	17.3	12.9
File clerks	14.0	16.3	17.9	15.0	16.8	17.0
Records clerks	14.7	13.1	15.9	14.3	13.4	14.1
Financial records processing	6.2	6.2	5.3	5.4	6.0	6.1
Bookkeeping, accounting, and auditing clerks	5.2	5.0	4.3	4.9	4.9	4.9
Payroll and timekeeping clerks	11.5	9.0	7.1	5.2	9.5	10.5
Billing clerks	8.7	11.8	10.3	6.6	11.9	11.8

CONCLUSION

The Information Society in this nation is now moving into high gear. Blacks are making strides in all of the information jobs examined here. They constitute 10% of the American workforce and have made the shift from agricultural and industrial jobs to information occupations. But a particular pattern emerges when we investigate their presence in the information workforce. Blacks are concentrated in certain types of information jobs and are barely present in others. Blacks are well established in such information jobs as prekindergarten and kindergarten teaching, mailing and message distribution, computer and communications equipment operations, and clerical work and records processing. But they are hardly noticeable in such information jobs as higher education teaching, engineering, natural and social sciences, writing, art and printing, medicine, and law.

In the Information Society Black people need to move from the mailroom to the computer room and from the post office to the laboratory. They are more often the processors and handlers of information than they are the creators and producers of information. Time seems to be having little impact on this situation for Blacks.

This flies in the face of Information Society proponents who say that the emerging Information Society is an egalitarian one. If the shift to information work is an indicator of how well a community can perform in the Information Society, the Black community in America is in need of some preparation to fully participate.

Since Blacks are in the information workforce, perhaps upward mobility programs through communications technology training are needed to get Blacks out of the mailroom and into the computer room. Special programs at the elementary school level would prepare Blacks to pursue information-producing jobs in the future. Finding a way to close the gap between Blacks in the inner city and information jobs in the nonurban parts of the country should be the goal. Longitudinal studies are needed to determine if the number of Blacks is shifting to information jobs as the country's shift continues in an information-based economy.

REFERENCES

Angell, I. (1996). Winners and losers in the Information Age. *Society, 34,* 81-86.

Aponte, R. (1996). Urban employment and the mismatch dilemma: Accounting for the immigration exception. *Social Problem, 43,* 268-284.

Bell, D. (1973). *The Coming of Post-Industrial Society; A Venture in Social Forecasting.* New York: Basic Books.

Bell, D. (1976). *The Coming of Post-Industrial Society: A Venture in Social Forecasting.* New York: Basic Books.

BLS (1995). Tomorrow's jobs in the Occupational Outlook Handbook. [On-line]. Available: http://stats.bls.gov/oco/oco2003.htm.

BLS (1997a). Labor force statistics from the Current Population Survey Overview. [On-line]. Available: http://stats.bls.gov/cps over.htm.

BLS (1997b). Labor force statistics from the Current Population Survey. Technical notes: Collection and concepts. [On-line]. Available: http://stats.bls.gov/cpstn1.htm.

BLS (1997c). Labor force statistics from the Current Population Survey. Technical notes: Estimating Methods. [On-line]. Available: http://stats.bls.gov/cpstn4.htm.

BLS (1997d). Labor force statistics from the Current Population Survey. Technical notes: Sampling. [On-line]. Available: http://stats.bls.gov/cpstn3.htm.

Castells, M., & Aoyama, Y. (1994). Paths toward the Informational Society: Employment structure in G-7 countries, 1920 to 1990. *International Labour Review, 133*, 5-34.

Cohn, S., & Fossett, M. (1996). What spatial mismatch? The proximity of Blacks to employment in Boston and Houston. *Social Forces, 75*, 557-574.

Dordick, H. S., & Wang, G. (1993). *The Information Society: A Retrospective View*. Newbury Park, CA: Sage Publications.

Editor and Publisher (1995). Minorities in the newsroom. 39, 128.

Ellul, J. (1967). *The Technological Society*. New York: Alfred A Knopf.

Farley, R. (1984). *Blacks and Whites Narrowing the Gap?* Cambridge: Harvard University Press.

Fullerton, H., Jr. (1993a). The American work force, 1992-2005: Another look at the labor force. *Monthly Labor Review*, 31-40.

Fullerton, H., Jr. (1993b). Labor-force change exaggerated, one-third of new workers will still be White men. *Population Today, 9*, 6-7.

Fullerton, H., Jr. (1995). The 2005 labor force: Growing but slowly. *Monthly Labor Review*, 29-44.

Gibson, S., & Callaway, E. (1997). Colorblind? *PC Week, 97*, 97-100.

Hirsch, B. T. (1992). Labor earnings, discrimination, and the racial composition of jobs. *Journal of Human Resources, 27*, 602-628.

Holzer, H. J., & Ihlanfeldt, K. R. (1996). Spatial factors and the employment of Blacks at the firm level. *New England Economic Review*, 65-73.

Jet, (1995). Education gap closes significantly, yet Blacks still trail Whites in wages and jobs. *60*, 88.

Katz, R. L. (1988). *The Information Society: An International Perspective*. New York: Praeger.

Leonard, J. S. (1990). The impact of affirmative action regulation and equal employment law on Black employment. *Journal of Economic Perspectives, 4*, 47-63.

Lord, M. (1995). Cyberjobs. *U.S. News and World Report, 119*, 76-82.

Machlup, F. (1962). *The Production and Distribution of Knowledge in the United States*. Princeton: Princeton University Press.

Marable, M (1983). *How Capitalism Underdeveloped Black America*. Boston: South End Press.

Matloff, N. (1996). How immigration harms minorities. *The Public Interest*, 124, 61-72.

Organization for Economic Cooperation and Development (1981*). Information activities, electronics and telecommunications technologies*. Paris: Author.

Porat, M. U. (1977). *The Information Economy*. (U. S. Department of Commerce, Office of Telecommunications. OT Special Publication; 77-12. Washington, DC: U.S. Government Printing Office.

Rifkin, J. (1994). Laid off! Computer technologies and the re-engineered workplace. *The Ecologist, 24*, 182-189.

Rifkin, J. (1995). *The End of Work. The Decline of the Global Labor Force and the Dawn of the Post-Market Era*. New York: G. P. Putnam's Sons.

Rivkin, S. G. Black/White differences in schooling and employment. *Journal of Human Resources, 30*, 826-853.

Rubenstein, E. (1996). Right data. *National Review, 14*, 48.

Rubin, M. R., & Huber, M. T. (1986). *The Knowledge Industry in the United States 1960-1980*. Princeton: Princeton University Press.

Sigelman, L., & Welch, S. (1991). *Black Americans' Views of Racial Inequality*. New York: Cambridge University Press.

Silvestri, G. T. (1995). Occupational employment to 2002. *Monthly Labor Review*, 60-84.

Simms, M. C. (1995). More of us are working: But gains are threatened by courts and anti-affirmative action initiatives. *Black Enterprise, 26*, 25.

Skinner, C. (1995). Urban labor markets and young Black men: A literature review. *Journal of Economic Issues, 29*, 47-66.

Tidwell, B. J. (1989*). Stalling Out: The Relative Progress of African Americans*. Washington, DC: National Urban League.

U.S. Department of Commerce, Bureau of Census. (1992). *Blacks in America—1992*. (SB-94-12). Washington, DC: Author.

U.S. Department of Commerce, Bureau of the Census. (1993). *Black Americans: A Profile* (SB-93-2). Washington, DC: Author.

U.S. Department of Labor, Bureau of Labor Statistics. (1994). *Fact Sheet on Black and Hispanic Workers*. Washington, DC: Author.

U.S. Department of Labor, Bureau of Labor Statistics. (1996). *Fact Sheet on Black and Hispanic Workers*. Washington, DC: Author.

Wilson, W. J. (1996). *When Work Disappears: The World of the New Urban Poor*. New York: Alfred A. Knopf.

CHAPTER 9

Telecommunications Training: An Academic Perspective

Gloria P. James

During the past few years, the field of telecommunications has made monumental advances. As a consequence of these advances, the telecommunications industry has found itself in a state of constant flux. Subsequently, it has become virtually impossible for institutions of higher education to keep abreast of these new technologies. Most of the major institutions in the country have accepted the reality that properly maintaining their telecommunications programs will continue to demand an extraordinary amount of the operational moneys raised by the institution. The major institutions that have committed themselves to this area of study have likewise reaffirmed their commitment to expose their faculty and technicians to additional training courses. They have also developed networking relationships with local media for the purpose of exposing students and faculty to state-of-the-art equipment that ordinarily could not be purchased by the institution.

Historically Black colleges and universities (HBCUs) are most often not in a position to finance a telecommunications program competitive with that of a major institution. In most instances, the financial structure of the private institution prohibits the filtering of its limited funds into a program that requires constant maintaining and upgrading. The state-supported HBCUs may experience the same problem of limited funding, but not to the same degree. HBCUs, private or public, will probably experience problems reaching a funding level competitive with that in major institutions. Therefore, it has become increasingly critical that HBCUs set in place a Communications, Marketing, and Fundraising Office whose primary goal is to establish and maintain ongoing relationships with potential funding sources (industry, corporate, government agencies, foundations, etc.). This crucial role not only includes a moral commitment that must be met by HBCUs, but also encompasses a pragmatic dimension by which HBCUs must define their role in the area of telecommunications.

The programming efforts of the commercial media are totally nonrepresentative of our holistic society. The majority of the programs depict nonmainstream individuals in a biased and unredemptive manner. HBCUs should give more consideration to educating and training their communications majors in understanding the importance of the "image" that has been negatively portrayed in media and the impact this "image" can have on the economic survival of a people. Subsequently, it is hoped that these enlightened "media experts," trained by HBCUs, will participate not only in mainstream media but also in minority media ownership establishments. Furthermore, it is believed that increased participation will begin to reflect positive changes in media imagery, therefore fostering a greater moral commitment of the HBCUs.

HBCUs have another critical role to play in the area of telecommunications. It is incumbent upon all of these institutions to begin to educate and train professional managers for entrance into the communications industry. Again, emphasis must be placed on the need for HBCU students to attain more decision-making positions in mainstream media. More importantly, HBCUs must continue to build the types of networks that will support media ownership for minorities. HBCUs are, without a doubt, one such viable network.

As a unit, HBCUs have collaborated on many projects. Most of these projects have been geared toward the development of communications skills programs, videotape libraries, and so on. It is now time for HBCUs to become more political in their approach to the communications industry. Ownership and control should be the cornerstone to the building of a network designed to address the challenge of the telecommunications industry. Coordinating organizations that work closely with the HBCUs are in a unique position to coordinate a network interested in telecommunications. Therefore, HBCUs must closely research these existing possibilities in the industry and make a decision concerning the level of involvement that appears feasible for these institutions.

The first step to participation in communications technology may lie in conducting a needs assessment to address the problems that HBCUs are experiencing with the transmission of information from institution to institution. With this in mind, we should "link up" the HBCUs through a transmission system (e.g., teleconferences and Internet access) that would afford them the opportunity of sharing human resources and information. There would be, of course, some main, centralized center for coordination, implementation, and control.

HBCUs not only must begin to network among themselves but must also form long-overdue alliances with other minority organizations that are committed to the goal of creating a well-informed society. Through working relationships with organizations that are interested in establishing and nurturing an informed African American society, HBCUs would realistically develop mechanisms through which all of their communications and information needs could be met. These alliances are desirable because the capital expenditure necessary for the initiation and implementation of a viable communications system might prove cost-prohibitive if the HBCUs were to act alone.

THE ACADEMIC PROGRAM

Historically Black colleges and universities have traditionally been teaching institutions that have emphasized a broad-based liberal arts curriculum. These colleges have provided a much-needed service by educating, training, and graduating young African Americans. The area of telecommunications was one such technology-driven educational program that found its way into the curriculum of these institutions.

Communications programs as they appeared in the early 1970s were basic in design. There could be found, however, varying levels of programmatic sophistication. Most of the new communications offerings consisted of three or four print journalism courses and/or one or two television or film courses.

Research on these new programs in communications disclosed that, in most instances, the English Department or the Speech Department housed the newly designed communications curriculum. In a few institutions Mass Communications Departments were developed with a separate faculty and staff. However, in almost all cases, the operating expenses of these programs proved to be exorbitant from the onset.

Some of the larger historically Black colleges and universities that decided to embark upon these nontraditional training programs received grant moneys from media organizations or foundations to design, staff, and implement the new communications programs. These externally funded programs were able to avert some of the initial problems that plagued their less fortunate counterparts. They were privy, in most instances, to expert technical assistance from professionals working in the media. Therefore, curriculum and staffing criteria were planned with input from persons who worked in the area for which the students were being trained. Media professionals taught courses on a part-time basis, because full-time staffing was a problem that was difficult to address.

In almost all of the communications programs housed at HBCUs, attracting highly qualified media professionals as full-time faculty/staff persons proved to be difficult. Most of these professionals could not afford to accept full-time positions because of the institutions' low salary structure. In most cases, the experienced media professionals who chose to work with the students at these institutions had been trailblazers in a profession that had not been objective toward African American media consumers or African American media professionals. Consequently, their professional and personal experience added a wealth of knowledge to the training program in which they were teaching.

Having the option of concentrating in the area of communications appealed to many of the students attending these institutions. Since the beginning of the implementation of these programs, the number of students majoring in communications has steadily increased. Many of these students chose a communications major because they viewed it as a "glamorous" field of work. Because these young college students grew up with television, most of these majors aspired to becoming "on-camera talent." When asked what they wanted to do with their media training after graduation, the answer most commonly heard was, "I want to be an anchorperson on television." Another large number of these students declared an interest in becoming camerapersons or television reporters. Rarely would students express an interest in print journalism, research, media management, sales, and so on. This lack of knowledge of, and/or interest in, these career specialties can be traced to the fact that there were not a sufficient or visible number of African American role models in the early 1970s who could influence the career choices of students. Subsequently, these ambitious young people were most comfortable relating to the role models who were more visible and who served as living proof that African Americans could be successful in the media profession. The conceptualization and the implementation of communications programs served a twofold purpose. First, they opened up a new career option to students attending HBCUs; second, these programs filled a void in the profession by educating and training African Americans for a career in an area that had been historically a White, male-dominated profession. Through the initial success of these programs, society in general and African Americans in particular began to appreciate the contribution that these aspiring media professionals could make in the dissemination and/or interpretation of information.

Today, as in the embryonic stages of these communication programs, one can identify differences in programmatic thrusts. Most programs supported by grant moneys from both the public and private sector have become strong industry-oriented media degree programs. Consequently, some of the instructors working in these programs are usually trained media practitioners who have had professional experience and who hold appropriate academic credentials. Also, many of the HBCUs with communications programs are inheriting professionals who were graduates of early programs and who realized the advantage of attaining advanced training in their area of expertise. In most cases, this training was acquired with the hopes of receiving advancement within the communications profession. Some reached the professional level to which they aspired but decided to bring their skills and experience to the classroom; however, others experienced roadblocks in their careers and decided to use their skills in a different professional environment. Whatever the reasons, the institutions that acquired their skills have greatly benefited.

Because of the financial structure of most HBCUs, it has become increasingly critical that they develop new strategies, including cooperative alliances, to ensure continued viability for their highly technical programs. Only through these alliances will many of these institutions acquire the infrastructure to initiate and maintain external funding contacts. Institutions, that receive adequate external funding are most often those that have acquired a great deal of visibility. This visibility usually manifests itself in unique academic programs and active participation by the college and university leadership in national organizations. In short, the institutions that receive funding have earned positive exposure in the communications industry and are expected to provide the industry with competent media trainees.

Since attaining adequate funding is a major concern for Black colleges and universities, the importance of establishing well-designed programs that deliver well-trained graduates cannot be stressed enough. Funding agencies will not invest moneys in the programs that do not produce employable students. It is important for these programs to stress the liberal arts thrust of their institutions in addition to exposing their students to courses in business, economics, political science, and so on. This broad range of academic courses helps to ensure the development of graduates who can view the world from a holistic vantage point. Programs must prepare their students to function in the "real world of work." The manner in which minorities are portrayed in the media must be changed also. HBCUs can be instrumental in training their students to function as "change agents" once they enter the industry. The responsibility for effecting this change lies with individuals and with organizations that are concerned with this problem. HBCUs need to contribute to the solution by preparing media practitioners who develop alternative modes of character presentation. Additionally, these institutions must develop partnerships with media professionals in order to provide their graduates with access to decision-making positions.

"Access" to job opportunities in the communications industry is one of the most important concerns. These programs must begin to develop and nurture professional relationships with the industry in order to keep abreast of the employment criteria and training demands of this ever-changing industry. HBCUs must continue to prepare competent persons who have an understanding of the "total media" concept. These persons should be trained to appreciate the industry from the technical, aesthetic vantage point in addition to having a comprehensive understanding of the industry's business side. Graduates of these programs should have the ability to function as a leader or team member on any management team that has the decision-making responsibility for the organization. HBCUs must continue to emphasize training and education of their students to compete for positions on all levels.

In order to provide students with a wide range of industry exposure, the leadership of the communications program must provide vehicles through which the students majoring in communications can acquire cocurricular experiences. It is not sufficient to have a qualified faculty and expensive equipment in place. Students in these programs must be exposed to as many professional, media-related experiences as possible. Several HBCUs are addressing this issue through the following types of activities:

Annual Communications Conference. Several HBCUs sponsor annual conferences to which students from across the country come to be informed about the new trends in communications. As a part of these conferences, there is usually some information or activity, that addresses job opportunities in the media.

Professionals-in-Residence Programs. Students are exposed to seminars designed to simulate a professional work environment. The professional teaching the course assigns projects under deadline pressure and requires finished products that may be included in a preprofessional portfolio.

Internship Programs. Students receive short-term experience working as part-time employees during the semester or as full-time employees during the summer. Particular emphasis is placed on production skills and management training.

Cooperative Education Programs. These assignments are long-term (one semester to one year) experiences for mature students. As a result of the assignment, students receive 12 to 16 hours of credit for each semester's work.

These activities address the need for aspiring media professionals to have exposure to state-of-the-art information in the ever-changing communications industry.

With the advent of satellite systems, microwave, fiber, Internet, television (TV), and so on, the acquisition, utilization, and retrieval of information have been revolutionized. New career opportunities for communications majors are constantly being identified. In order to prepare students for the job market, the curricula of the existing programs are being reviewed and modified to ensure that there will exist a pool of qualified, highly trained persons capable of performing in the industry. Some of these programs have established an advisory board of local media managers for the purpose of offering guidance and advice in defining programmatic thrusts.

When reviewing the curricula of the more advanced programs, one will note an emphasis on courses in business management, marketing, financing, sales, computer technology, advertising, public relations, and psychology. Conversations with successful media managers have disclosed that students who have been exposed to these courses have an advantage when applying for entry-level positions. Through these courses, coupled with the specialized communications courses, the student acquires understanding of the total media and how they operate.

FUTURE TRENDS IN ACADEMIC PROGRAMMING

Traditional support for higher education from all sources has substantially declined over the past few years. The federal government, addressing the importance of the continued existence of historically Black colleges and universities, has issued executive orders. These executive orders have charged all cabinet officers to continue the implementation of federal programs to include participation of HBCUs in all federally sponsored programs.

Private sector businesses and institutions have been urged to assist in the strengthening of Black colleges and universities in a variety of areas, including management, financial structure, and research. The goal of the initial executive order in 1981 was "to advance the development of human potential, to strengthen the capacity of the Historically Black Colleges and Universities to provide quality education and to overcome the effects of discriminatory treatment."

In spite of these executive orders and subsequent legislation, an increase in financial assistance cannot be expected from the federal government. Additionally, corporate philanthropy has been substantially reduced. Even with the bleak economic picture, HBCUs, that have committed themselves to these communications programs must continue to identify and acquire the resources needed to compete in the training of prospective media practitioners.

The concept of "networking" has proven effective for many organizations that have a common purpose and goal. HBCUs should continue to build a strong networking system among themselves and should include other institutions and organizations interested in exploring both programmatic and ownership opportunities in the telecommunications industry.

Several HBCUs are embarking upon entrepreneurial activities designed to generate income for the institution while serving as a viable investment. The establishment of consortia of institutions interested in exploring media ownership is recommended, so that the benefits of a more effective communications system between institutions could be explored.

The field of communications in general and telecommunications in particular may serve as a force to promote cohesiveness and a team spirit for HBCUs. Recently, a great deal of legislation has been passed that serves as a crippling force to the very existence of them. As previously stated, funds have been drastically cut in all areas of higher education. HBCUs have received the brunt of these cutbacks. To protect them from further attempts to eradicate these African American institutions of higher education, HBCUs must begin to concentrate their training efforts in areas in which African Americans and other minorities are underrepresented. At the same time, they must continue to build and offer strong liberal arts programs. In other words, it is necessary to explore the new technologies that are destined to influence and control the economic pattern of society while maintaining traditional means of operating other liberal arts programs.

It should not be a difficult task for Black colleges and universities to produce media experts who are capable of establishing, implementing, and controlling communications systems. Fifteen years ago, research sponsored by the National Advisory Committee on Black Higher Education and Black Colleges and Universities documented that "Black colleges have produced 50% of Black business executives, 50% of Black engineers, 75% of Black military officers,

80% of Black federal judges, 85% of Black physicians." These statistics attest to the fact that HBCUs have succeeded in producing qualified professionals in areas where Black representation has been almost nonexistent. If it were not for the HBCUs, most of the businesses in our country would not be able to claim being an equal opportunity employer. Without the perseverance of HBCUs, there would not exist a pool of qualified minority professionals in various fields from which to choose.

A PROTOTYPE FOR COLLABORATION

Against the background of severe underrepresentation of minorities in the telecommunications industry, Clark Atlanta University (CAU) in Atlanta, Georgia, in cooperation with the Atlanta Olympic Broadcasting (AOB), the televising unit of the Atlanta Committee for the Olympic Games (ACOG), accepted the challenge in 1993 to train minority students for broadcasting internships. This challenge evolved into the Host Broadcast Training Program (HBTP). The primary purpose of this program was to give minority students an opportunity to work in the national and international professional media industry in televising the 1996 Centennial Olympic Games. Although housed at Clark University, the HBTP staff aggressively recruited students from HBCUs, local Georgia schools, and other colleges and universities. Students completed an intense training curriculum, and approximately 700 worked as peers with international professional broadcast technicians during the televising of the 1996 Olympics.

Program activities centered on training/assessments, academic advisement, placing/monitoring students during internships, and hiring students to work in the 1996 Centennial Games. The success of this effort allowed CAU and participating affiliate institutions to be part of a heritage that made deep international imprints.

Student participation in the program required meeting rigorous criteria. Qualified students:

- Were sophomores or juniors;

- Had a grade point average (GPA) of 2.5 or better;

- Met the Atlanta Committee for the Olympic Games hiring criteria;

- Had the ability to participate in a demanding, intense technical training program that required two semesters of course work and practical training (extended class periods were necessary; therefore, students had to be able to commit the time to this effort);

- Had the ability to complete successfully the interview/screening process (interviews were conducted by a panel).

To compete for AOB positions, students had to successfully complete all phases of the program:

- Phase 1—media core requirements

- Phase 2—specialized directed studies and specialized courses

- Phase 3—co-op/internship

- Phase 4—hands-on experiences in the outside broadcast vehicle

Each participating institution identified a liaison representative who served on the HBTP Liaison Committee. This committee had the responsibility of monitoring the ongoing effectiveness of the affiliate institution's plan of operation. Affiliate participation was on three levels: (1) encouraging students to participate in HBTP, (2) providing specialized courses, and (3) offering instructional services.

Many faculty and staff at affiliate institutions were hired as part of the Clark Atlanta University adjunct training staff. Faculty and staff engaged in train-the-trainer and staff/faculty development activities. In order to ensure quality of instruction, HBTP faculty and staff were evaluated during and at the end of each class. The results of these evaluations were used to improve teaching and learning during the instructional period. Evaluation of all phases of the HBTP was ongoing and intensive.

ACADEMIC SERVICES

The primary responsibility of the HBTP staff was to ensure that students had the support needed to succeed academically. Therefore, the HBTP placed emphasis on advisement and curricular enhancement.

Advising. Academic advisers served as program consultants to all HBTP students. The consultants, however, were not substitutes for departmental advisers. Students were expected to maintain regularly scheduled advisory sessions with their departmental advisers. The function of the HBTP advisers was to expedite the registration process for Clark Atlanta University students and students matriculating from affiliate institutions. Ways in which they performed these services included:

- Maintaining a matrix of course offerings and sites to aid students in determining when and where to take the courses needed.

- Establishing liaison relationships with appropriate academic officers and faculty members at affiliate institutions.

- Collecting and disseminating instructions and other information necessary for cross-registration or special course offerings.

- Helping students determine and select courses to satisfy their degree requirements while preparing for positions with the host and network broadcasters.

- Serving as on-site advisers for HBTP students from other institutions while enrolled at CAU.

- Arranging and interpreting the results of proficiency examinations.

Technological Curriculum. In most instances, students participating in the program were either sophomores or juniors. All HBTP students had to complete a media core of six to eight courses in broadcast operations and management.

In addition to core courses, HBTP students had to take directed studies and internships. This practical experience gave students opportunities to work in activities related to the video and audio staging of Olympic Games competitions.

It must be emphasized that students were not to think of themselves as "majoring" in host broadcast training. Instead, they were pursuing majors in media arts, foreign languages, art, computer science, and library science, to name a few, and were required to make steady progress toward their degree fulfillment while enrolled in the HBTP. In this regard, it was particularly important for students to receive adequate advising so they did not find themselves spending extra time in college because of their pursuit of short-term Olympic Games employment.

EMPLOYMENT SERVICES

The hiring process for positions was highly structured and was implemented by AOB, in 1996. The HBTP training office facilitated the hiring process by:

- Developing a recruitment strategy for attracting academically qualified applicants to the HBTP.

- Generating, in collaboration with the AOB training programs, manager, recruitment, and application materials for available positions.

- Preparing and periodically distributing to students bulletins and tips regarding professional work habits and other employment issues.

- Conducting regularly scheduled work ethic and professional development seminars for required attendance by HBTP students.

- Supervising a series of interview seminars for students in the weeks leading up to the AOB screening interviews.

- Coordinating student interviews for positions with the rights-holding broadcasters.

- Constructing, in collaboration with university counsel, contractual agreements to be executed between students and hiring entities.

- Informing students of application procedures and deadlines.

HOST BROADCAST POSITIONS

AOB, in 1996 hired over 700 students in ten positions. While each HBTP student worked toward competence in the standard curriculum, the order in which students moved through the curriculum and the courses they chose varied according to interests in the following positions available during the Olympics:

Archivist. Worked with the production department in maintaining an ongoing tape summary of the games by logging and filing each day's incoming feeds. Speed and accuracy were paramount, as taped information was used as highlights for the rights-holding broadcasters.

Audio Assistant. Under the direction of the senior audio operator at each venue, checked the functioning and operation of all audio equipment, including the various microphones and audio boards. Was also responsible for assisting the audio planning technicians at each venue, as well as general troubleshooting. Required good understanding of audio testing equipment.

Camera Operator. Operated the camera during the transmission of the international signal, under the guidance of the director and following the AOB production plan. Was responsible for setup, general maintenance, and teardown of the camera and its component parts before, during, and after competition. Required strong technical background.

Commentary Systems Operator. Worked at the venues and at the Commentary Distribution Center as assigned by the director of commentary systems. Functions included testing commentary equipment, dressing cable, placing microphones, setting up and dismantling systems booths, and managing audio circuits. Multilingual skills were preferred.

Graphics Assistant. Under the direction of the producer and director, operated character generator, prepared graphics from discs and manuals that were integrated with video images. Required good working knowledge of personal computers.

Liaison Officer. Worked with rights-holding broadcasters to ensure that all their information and production requirements were taken care of at the venues.

Logger. Kept ongoing written tape summary on the 1996 Olympic Games. Information had to be logged quickly and accurately. Loggers had to have strong writing skills and an understanding of the editing process.

Spotter. Informed and advised the production crew of any important activity in the field of play or other areas of the venue that may not have been immediately evident. Informed the production crew of activity occurring in the field of play, such as identity of next injured competitors, unexplained official calls, and unusual activity in the stands that was not immediately evident to the camera angles.

Video Operator Assistant. Technically optimized the quality of the pictures of international signals originated at the venue; ascertained that cameras were properly adjusted, and maintained and contained all necessary components for the smooth operation of the telecast.

Videotape Operator. Operated tape machines, including setting video and audio levels and providing a reference recording of the international signal.

The Clark Atlanta University's Host Broadcast Training Program was a unique, once-in-a-lifetime opportunity for college students to receive technical and hands-on experience on state-of-the-art digital broadcast equipment. The skills acquired as a result of this first-rate academic/training program qualified students to work as professionals in the 1996 Summer Olympics.

Over 900 students from local and affiliate institutions participated in the program, nearly 700 of whom successfully completed it. Because of the uniqueness of this collaborative effort, more than 38 institutions of higher learning received local and national publicity from all types of media outlets. This program exemplified the possibilities and opportunities that institutions with different strengths and foci can accomplish if they work cooperatively to enhance the education and training of prospective media professionals.

A MANAGER'S VIEW OF CHANGE IN ACADEMIC TELECOMMUNICATIONS

The field of communications, especially electronic media, is undergoing a dynamic, revolutionary change. This change is occurring less in the area of entertainment and more in the area of information dissemination and continuing education. Media—television, radio, and computers—are becoming increasingly sophisticated, complicated, and interactive. Their goal is to provide instantaneous service to every citizen and consumer for the maximum amount of economic, political, and cultural gain.

In order to discuss the role of HBCUs in the field of communications, a brief examination of various media is necessary:

Cable/Pay-Television (TV). These systems are being installed in American homes at record rates. Homes will receive cable over television sets capable of receiving an large number of programs on some 60 channels. Over the next decade, there will be some cable video services designed to meet specific needs such as health, economics, culture, ethnicity, and various professional ongoing educational courses.

Print. This medium is undergoing a major change through a proliferation of magazines and newspapers designed for every taste and every segment of the population, leading one to believe that with such an explosion employment opportunities would increase. However, this is not the case since print media are merging and utilizing higher technology, that is, computers, satellite transmission, digital photography, so as not to be labor-intensive.

Radio. Some 30 years ago, media analysts predicated the death of radio; however, radio, both AM and FM, is alive and well. Radio, like print media, is now available for every segment of the population and is a true demographic medium. Again, the drive is to make radio more automated, so as to use less labor.

Television. There are two television media, one being the networks (ABC, NBC, and CBS) and the second encompassing all of the rest. These networks will continue to dominate the market in terms of entertainment, news, and possibly sports. Independent stations will become more similar to their counterparts in radio and will pick up the lost network viewership by specifically gearing its programming to every taste and segment of the population.

Movies. Here is another industry that was marked for extinction some 30 years ago with the advent of television. However, it has survived. Movies will continue but will primarily be seen on pay-TV and cable television, videodiscs, and cassettes.

Satellites, Computers, Video Disc-Cassettes. All forms of media are becoming very integrated, with the emphasis on quick delivery of "software" programs at the lowest possible price. Satellites present the opportunity to deliver cost-effectively and broadly and have opened up untold opportunities for all aspects of media.

Multimedia Technology. This is in the forefront of new telecommunication technologies. Multimedia technology allows fully integrated text, graphic, animation, audio, image, color, and fullmotion video presentations to be created, edited, and displayed on a single personal computer.

Teleconferencing. This medium uses electronic channels to facilitate real-time, face-to-face communications among groups of people at two or more locations. It enables these individuals to exchange audio, audio/graphic, and video information.

Computerization is doing for all media what the typewriter did for offices. Practically, computers will affect all businesses. Not only does computerization provide for instant delivery, but it also contributes to savings related to the cost of labor. Videodiscs and videocassettes are mechanisms to deliver "software." As their per unit cost declines, these systems have become industry standards.

Experts in telecommunications are forecasting that as a result of combining media and publishing and the telecommunications and computer industries into a single industry, by the year 2000 the telecommunications industry will be in a position to produce over $3.5 trillion in revenues worldwide. The rapid change of telecommunications from analog to digital technology will make this significant increase in revenue possible.

If HBCUs are to play a critical role in increasing the number of minorities working in the industry, it is absolutely essential that they continue to help their students understand and, in some cases, train them to work in this pervasive industry.

HBCUs should have courses within their curricula that pertain to the new telecommunications technologies. The curricula should also contain courses related to the history, development, and present status of the media's industries. The overall objective of this type of education should be to help students understand the effect that this industry has on the world and to provide a framework in which they learn how to cope with the industry and effect positive change. This is by no means an easy task, but one of overriding importance since African Americans, especially children, watch more television, on the average, than any other ethnic group.

The media industry will need more competent people to address this and other important issues, but the job requirements are becoming more sophisticated and demanding. HBCUs can be a major provider for this industry if they are willing to meet certain requirements.

CONCLUSIONS AND RECOMMENDATIONS

On the practical side, only a few institutions should be in the training business. Media are intensive users of hardware and are constantly updating their equipment. Thus, if an institution cannot provide "hands-on" interaction with the best equipment, it is shortchanging its students. Since federal dollars are not available, and private dollars have become scarce, very few schools can afford to make a heavy investment in media hardware. Media equipment is also becoming more complicated and diverse. While HBCUs should develop training programs, it should be noted that a considerable amount of money must be spent if one is to be a formidable competitor in the media training game.

Telecommunications instruction is dynamic and interactive. It is, more than most businesses, dependent on "hands-on" experiences. Institutions must provide an environment that is very similar to "live" conditions. This helps students to become flexible and able to easily fit into the work world.

"On-the-job-training" such as internships or cooperative education placement is definitely required for telecommunications majors. An old adage explains this need: "If you don't have experience, you can't get a job, and if you have a job, you can't get experience." Institutions must have the resources to establish a successful, ongoing training program. These programs should be set up so both the trainers and trainees gain from the experience. After all, few employers will keep a program going if they perceive that students are not "carrying their load," and students will complain if they sense that they are not learning enough to obtain employment.

If institutions are to train students for the communications industry, people who know the business both from a hands-on point of view as well as from a theoretical point of view must teach them. It is critical that institutions bring in media professionals to help teach specific courses. However, full-time administrators and faculty must guide the direction and implementation of an excellent telecommunications training program. Unfortunately, for some institutions, these professionals are often expensive. *Yet, students will not and should not expect any less.*

If one can successfully predict where the media industries are going, institutions that train should be developing courses and opportunities in at least one of the following areas: (1) management, (2) technical, and (3) ancillary (management, computer science, engineering, etc.).

As previously stated, media are sophisticated and complicated. Thus, there is a continuing use for employees who are flexible enough to serve as today's managers, as well as visionaries for tomorrow. HBCUs can perform a valuable service by preparing those interested in telecommunications to become managers. Again, this requires the unique blend of good teaching and on-the-job training.

Since the telecommunications field is a "hardware" -intensive business, there is a great demand for engineers and technically oriented people to run, maintain, and further develop it. The industry is beginning to create a need for careers that did not exist in such great numbers a few years ago. Some of these jobs are in law, union management, computer programming, telecommunications policy, business management, sales, and copyrighting. Many of the job opportunities will occur as the industry further understands what the consumer wants in terms of media services. Therefore, academic training must transmit to the student that media are becoming more and more integrated. Future professionals must have the knowledge and flexibility to adapt to this dynamic, changing industry.

In summary, the role of HBCUs in the field of telecommunications is simply an extension of what their role has been in society throughout the years. It is recommended that the HBCUs provide leadership by ensuring that:

1. Students are trained in communications so that they may influence the manner in which African Americans are depicted by mainstream media.

2. Minorities are trained for decision-making positions in mainstream media.

3. Minorities are educated to understand the politics and the economics that will lead them to the ownership of media concerns.

4. Consortia agreements and internship programs are offered to provide students training in telecommunications exposure to the new technologies of the industry.

5. Faculty members and technicians have internships designed to update their already existing skills.

6. A network is formed between HBCUs to develop an in-house system for the dissemination of information between institutions.

7. Networks are established between HBCUs and other predominantly African American organizations for the purpose of developing, implementing, and controlling at least one form of telecommunications through which the communication and information needs of all of these organizations can be met.

8. Working relationships with the current media managers are established to influence the type of training students receive in preparation for the job market.

HBCUs must serve as vehicles through which an understanding of the media and how they affect society is transmitted. These institutions must emphasize the importance of becoming both effective media professionals and discriminating media consumers. Finally, HBCUs will, as they have in the past, continue to act as the driving force dedicated to creatively supplying mainstream America with new perspectives on traditional concepts. They will also tackle the new technologies of the telecommunications industry by contributing to the pragmatic business side of the industry and the programming efforts of the industry.

PART IV

The Spatial Dimension

No group has overcome greater constraints than African Americans have in their efforts to participate in public space and public institutions. In a paper presented at the Aspen Institute Conference in 1996, Jorge Schement pointed out, however, that information technology has shifted the locus of communication and participation from the public sphere to the private sphere. He stated: "Now a generation after [the late] George Wallace stood on the steps of the Alabama state capital and shrieked, 'Segregation now! Segregation tomorrow! Segregation forever!' the ability of minorities to participate in the public sphere has been transformed."

Cyberspace is rapidly becoming the place to conduct one's affairs in the Information Society. This probably became more apparent than ever before when the House Judiciary Committee released the Kenneth Starr report on the activities of President William Clinton to the Internet. In response, America Online, the nation's leading computer on-line service, provided a service for its subscribers to E-mail their congressional representatives and tell them how they felt about the investigation and possible impeachment of the president. Individuals who had personal computers (PCs), modems, and on-line subscriptions could instantaneously participate in this political process, and those who did not were left to less rapid methods such as "snail mail."

Joseph P. McCormick II and Taft H. Broome point out in Chapter 10 that having the ability to be active in cyberspace in the future may be essential to participating in American democracy, since major political activities will take place there. Using national studies of computer and modem use, they argue that African Americans may be at a political disadvantage if they do not have the needed software and hardware to reach cyberspace.

In Chapter 11, Jabari Simama points to a need for African Americans to ensure that political, economic, educational, and other systems in the Information Society work to the benefit of the Black community. He calls for Blacks to change their focus from civil rights to cyber-rights. He presents several case studies of African Americans' using computer networks at the local level to deal with housing, education, health, and other socioeconomic conditions in the Black community.

CHAPTER 10

Race and the Information Superhighway: Implications for Participatory Democracy in the Twenty-First Century

Joseph P. McCormick II and Taft H. Broome

This chapter attempts to answer two questions that are currently important: (1) what are the implications for participatory democracy in the twenty first century given the present demographic profile of computer use and access in American society and the increased likelihood that "cyberspace" will become increasingly important as an arena in which critical societal issues will be discussed and debated? and (2) to what extent will this expanding technology exacerbate existing forms of race- and class-based inequality, thereby giving new meaning to the terms "attentive public" and "participatory democracy"? These questions are answered, in part, through an examination of census data on selected demographics of computer use in the United States over the course of an 11-year period (1984 to 1994). This chapter concludes with a brief discussion on civic responsibility in the information age.

In a recent article in the *Washington Post*, political consultant Doug Bailey penned a futuristic scenario memo (dated January 28, 2008) to a fictional candidate for the U.S. Senate in which he advises him on the intricacies of using twenty first century e-campaign technology. The opening line in this memo reads, "Because you know how to run a computer campaign sooner and better than anyone else, the enormous political potential of the Internet got you to the House [Bailey's client was elected three times to the House: 2002, 2004, and 2006 as an Independent]. Now it's going to get you to the Senate" (Bailey, 1996). With each passing day this kind of scenario becomes more and more plausible.

In the 1996 presidential election, most of the Republican presidential candidates had home pages that one could readily find on the Internet. A number of the members of the House and the Senate in the 104th Congress were similarly situated. The current Speaker of the House, Newt Gingrich (R-GA) is a futurist who over ten years ago proposed legislation—the "Family Opportunity Act"—that would offer tax credits to any family that bought a home computer to use for work or education (Toffler, 1982, p. 32). Computer technology and the Internet are increasingly becoming a vital part of civic discourse and the political process. Each day citizens look to the Internet as a means of gathering information on issues, past and present elections, and the public policy process.

A cursory examination of the usage statistics from the Library of Congress' information resource Thomas (named after President Thomas Jefferson; see: http://thomas.loc.gov/) reveals that in the first five weeks of 1996, over 2 million files were transmitted from this multifaceted database (e.g., text of the *Congressional Record*; text of pending and recently enacted legislation; hypertext links to other branches of the federal government) to various users in the United States and abroad. Approximately 600 million bytes of data are transferred from this source to users each day.[1] It is reasonable to assume that the expansion (no explosion) of Web sites on the Internet is taking place as this chapter is being written (of course, on a computer). Thomas is but one of many Web sites that computer users who have an interest in public affairs and politics can visit on a daily basis.

In the months and years ahead, Web sites will expand, and people who have access to hard-wired and/or modem-aided computers will be in position to get information and communicate with others about a wide range of issues. We are in an era when access to information and the use of information essentially give those who possess such information the power to define significant issues of the day and to pivotally affect how such issues will be addressed in the arena of public policy, if at all.

More specifically, the Bailey memo scenario suggests that the expansion of computer technology will have a major impact on the way in which political campaigns and the election of public officials will be conducted in the future. With the use of mail ballots in the Oregon campaign to fill the seat of Senator Bob Packwood, for example, where 65% of the registered voters went to the polls, it seems reasonable to assume that in future elections we will see more and more voters expressing one of the most important connections with the democratic process from afar. For many, the voting booth of the future may not be in the neighborhood community center, school, or armory but in cyberspace. It is in cyberspace where future political campaigns are likely to be conducted and where participatory democracy may take on new meaning.

It is interesting to note that in Bailey's futuristic memo, its author speaks of the introduction of on-line voting as an innovation that would come in the early twenty first century. In this regard, he writes to his fictional client: "You are well-positioned to capitalize on next year's introduction of on-line voting. What a change! Using electronic registration code, you can vote from home, the office, or anywhere. Absentee voting will have no meaning anymore." He goes on to say, "It used to be that a higher proportion of older folks voted. But on-line has become a larger part of the life of each new generation, so the tables are now turned." After praising the merits of e-campaign technology, Bailey points to the one notable exception to the ranks of the proposed electronic outreach: "Unlike your suburban [House] district, the state has pockets of lower-income voters who aren't on-line and won't be e-voting. The living room e-center began as an expensive appliance conspicuously consumed by the haves; while costs have come down, it's still not affordable to everyone. You will need," he goes on to write, "an old-fashioned campaign to reach voters in places such as Chicago's inner city and some of the downstate towns" (Bailey, 1996).

As we point out in the next section of this chapter, an examination of the demographic profile of current computer use in the United States suggests that unless there are radical changes that would lower the cost and expand the public availability of computers, the proportion of the American electorate that is likely to vote could become more narrowly skewed by race, income, education, and geographical location. Doug Bailey's futuristic scenario could be one in which the American electorate would be divided into those who are fully enfranchised and those who are potentially electronically disfranchised. America could be moving toward a new political order where its citizens fall into two camps: a computer-literate, Internet-familiar techno-elite and a techno-peasantry that is either computer-illiterate and/or lacks access to computer technology and thus to the information that it provides. This former group operates as a fully participatory "attentive public" (Devine, 1970) that possesses the capacity and resources to interact with authoritative decision makers, while the latter group finds itself at the far periphery of key issues and information related to those issues. This latter group has been characterized in a report recently released by the National Telecommunications and Information Administration (NTIA) as the "information disadvantaged" (U.S. Department of Commerce, 1995). In a future scenario of cyberspace-politics, the techno-peasantry could conceivably be ignored by authoritative decision makers, at the peril of organized and civil society as we now know it.

THE DATA

Four surveys conducted by the U.S. Census Bureau between 1984 and 1994 permit us to develop a demographic profile of computer access and use in the United States and thus draw some inferences on what has been referred to as a techno-elite and a techno-peasantry. Between October 1984 and October 1993 the bureau conducted three surveys on computer use in the United States for the National Center for Educational Statistics. More specifically, the data from each of these surveys are taken from a special supplement to the Current Population Survey (CPS), a monthly, nationally representative household survey of the civilian noninstitutional population administered by the U.S. Census Bureau. In each of these surveys, questions concerning the availability of computers at home and the use of computers when one was present at home, work, or school were asked. Our attention in this chapter is focused primarily on the 1984 survey, the 1993 survey, and the changes that took place over the course of this ten-year period.[2]

Various demographic characteristics of the responding household and the adult who responded on behalf of each household that was surveyed were also included in each of the three CPS surveys. This type of information includes the householder type (e.g., married; female householder, no spouse present; male householder; no spouse present); the income of the household; household size (i.e., number of persons); the educational attainment of the adult respondent; the occupation of the adult respondent; the employment status of the respondent; the gender of the respondent; the race or whether the respondent was of Hispanic origin; and region of the country in which the household lived at the time of the survey. For purposes of the analysis done here, analytical attention was restricted to the race of the respondent, the age of the respondent (clustered in two groups 3 to 17 years and 18 years and over), access to a computer at home, whether a home computer was used, whether a computer was used at school (by both children and adults), and, in the case of adults, whether a computer was used at work. Households with children between the ages of 3 and 17 will henceforth be referred to as "households with children," while those with young adults 18 and over will be referred to as "adult households."

In an attempt to preserve the confidentiality of household-specific information, none of the aforementioned CPS surveys included a geographic identifier. Nor did any of the three surveys attempt to ascertain if the households surveyed had a telephone in the home. Additionally, while the 1989 and 1993 surveys asked the respondent whether a home computer, if there was one present, had a modem, the 1984 survey did not. The net result is that while these three surveys provide very useful baseline information on computer access and use, they did not enable us to determine how telephone access and access with a computer with modem vary by geographical location. In this regard, as the July 1995 NTIA report, on which this chapter relies, so aptly points out: "While a standard telephone line can be an individual's pathway to riches of the Information Age, a personal computer and modem are rapidly becoming the keys to the vault" (U.S. Department of Commerce, 1995, p. 3). The NTIA report is based on a November 1994 survey, also conducted by the U.S. Bureau of the Census. This is one of the most detailed surveys to date on computer access and use. Largely because of the inclusion of the geographical identifier, however, one can draw only limited comparisons with the previously described CPS surveys.[3] We rely on the data from the November 1994 survey to construct a demographic profile of those households most likely and those least likely to have a telephone, computer, and computer with modem in the home.

ANALYSES OF THE DATA

Computer Use at Home

While computer technology has tended to influence every aspect of our lives, it has significantly affected the educational spectrum from elementary through graduate, professional, and trade schools. Over the course of the ten-year survey between 1984 and 1993, households with children were more likely to have a computer in the home than those without children (see Table 10.1).

Table 10.1
Access and Use of Computers at Home and School: 1984 and 1993 by Race and Age (in Percent)

Characteristic	1984	1993	Change in Percentage Points '84 to '93
All Races			
Age 3-17			
Access to a Home Computer	15.3%	31.9%	+16.6
Uses a Home Computer*	74.2	74.7	0.3
Uses Computer at School	28.0	60.6	+32.6
Blacks			
Age 3-17			
Access to a Home Computer	6.1	13.0	6.9
Uses a Home Computer*	75.9	67.3	- 8.6
Uses Computer at School	15.9	50.9	+35.0
Whites			
Age 3-17			
Access to a Home Computer	17.1	35.8	+18.7
Uses a Home Computer*	74.0	75.3	1.3
Uses Computer at School	30.3	62.7	+32.4

*As a percentage of persons with access to a computer in the home

Source: U.S. Department o Commerce, Bureau of the Census, Current Population Reports, Series P-23, No. 155, *Computer Use in the United States: 1984* (Washington, DC: U.S. Government. Printing Office, 1988); and data collected in October 1993 in the Current Population Survey. The 1993 data were downloaded from the U.S. Bureau of the Census Web site: http;//www.census/gov./.

In 1984 about 15% of all households with school-age children had a computer in the home. Given the use of the computer as a "teaching machine," so readily connected with the educational process in elementary and secondary school, it is not at all surprising that one would be more likely to find this form of technology in the homes of school-age children than in those homes where there were no children who fell in this age range. This tendency for households containing children between the ages of 3 and 17 to have a computer held for both Black and White households over time, though in both 1984 and 1993 White households were almost three times as likely as their Black counterparts to have a computer in the home.

Over the course of ten years, the proportion of White households containing school-age children that had access to a home computer almost doubled (from approximately 17% in 1984, to 36% in 1993), while the proportion of Black households with school-age children that had a computer in the home expanded by a much slower rate, by almost seven percentage points. The data indicate that the rate of increase of a computer in the home for White households containing school-age children was more than 2½ times that of similar Black households where there were school-age children present.

As can be seen in Figure 10.1, White households with children made the most dramatic increase in computer acquisition over the ten-year survey period. This figure demonstrates two rather important findings:

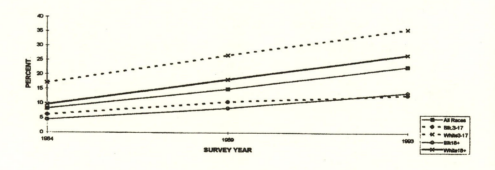

Figure 10.1
Access to a Home Computer by Race and Age, 1984, 1989, 1993

(1) as seen by the slope of the top two lines, White households with and without children showed a larger increase over the period than Black households (especially those with children), and (2) past trends show very little sign of similarly situated Black households closing this gap. From this age cohort the decision makers, information consumers, and voters of the twenty first century will come.

COMPUTER USE IN THE SCHOOLS

The importance of computer technology in the educational process leads us to next examine the access of school-age children to a computer in school. Here, the data reveal that school-age children were more likely to have access to a computer at school than to have access to such technology at home. This finding holds across the ten-year spectrum. Over the ten-year period, the proportion of respondents who indicated that their children had access to a computer at school more than tripled (from 28% in 1984, to almost 61% in 1993; see Table 10.1). While the rate of increase of use of a computer at school was slightly greater for Black children than for White children (about 35% versus 32%), White children were still more likely to have access to a computer in the schools at the end of this ten-year period. As Figure 10.2 suggests that it is in the schools where the greatest likelihood of the present interracial computer access gap being narrowed exists.

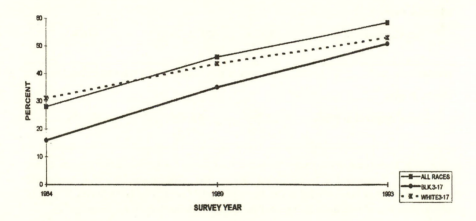

Figure 10.2
Use of a Computer at School by Race, 1984, 1989, 1993

COMPUTER USE IN THE WORKPLACE

The other arena where there has been a major expansion in computer use over the past decade is in the workplace. The number of adults who reported using a computer on the job more than doubled between the 1984 and 1993 surveys (an increase of 111%; see Table 10.2).

Table 10.2
Use of Computers at Work 1984 and 1993 by Race and Age (18 years +)

Characteristic	1984	1993	Change 1984 to 1993
All Races	(Numbers in Thousands)		(in percent)
18 yrs. & over			
Uses Computer at Work	24,172	51,106	111%
Blacks	(Numbers in Thousands & Percentage That Uses)		
18 yrs. & over			
Uses Computer at Work	1,724 (18.3)	4,072 (36.1)	136%
Whites	(Numbers in Thousands & PercentageThat Uses)		
18 yrs. & over			
Uses Computer at Work	21,795 (25.3)	45,326 (47.1)	107.9%

Source: U.S. Department of Commerce, Bureau of the Census, Current Population Reports, Series P-23, No. 155, *Computer Use in the United States: 1984*, (Washington, DC: U.S. Goverment Printing Office, 1988); data collected in October 1993 in the Current Population Survey. The 1993 data were downloaded from the U.S. Bureau of the Census Web site: http://www.census/gov./.

About 18% of Blacks surveyed in 1984 reported using a computer in the workplace, compared to about 25% of Whites; by 1993 these numbers had increased to about 36% for Blacks and about 47% for Whites. Despite the greater rate of increase for Blacks who used computers at work compared to Whites, an interracial computer use gap persisted over the course of the survey period. While the rate of increase in computer use in the workplace suggests that this is the second arena, following schools, where the greatest potential of narrowing the interracial computer use gap exists, Figure 10.3 leaves us less optimistic. Notwithstanding the past rates of increase in computer use in the workplace, if the past trend continues unaltered, there is little reason to believe that the interracial computer gap in the workplace will narrow in the foreseeable future.

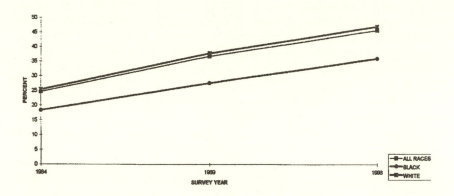

Figure 10.3
Persons 18 Years of Age and Older Who Use Computers at Work

This is especially true when one considers that the probability of using a computer in the workplace is associated with the type of job that one has. For example, the 1993 survey data indicate that managers and professionals were 4.5 times more likely to use a computer at work than operators, laborers, or fabricators (67.7% versus 14.9%). These data take on a racial character, however, when we take into consideration that Whites were twice as likely as Blacks to hold managerial or professional jobs, while Blacks were 1.6 times more likely than Whites to hold jobs as operators, laborers, or fabricators.[4]

To repeat, the interracial computer gap that we see in the workplace is significantly shaped by the type. of job that one has, and unless the distribution of the types of jobs currently held by Blacks and Whites is radically altered, there is little reason to believe that this interracial computer gap will change in the foreseeable future.

While the 1984 and 1993 CPS surveys enable us to get some sense of who has access to a computer in the home, school, and workplace, these surveys do not readily permit us to say very much about who possesses the capacity to access the much-touted information superhighway. As previously indicated, access to a hardwired computer (frequently found in the workplace) or to one that has a modem connected to a telephone is absolutely essential to access the multifaceted information superhighway, as we now know it. In this regard, the data from the November 1994 Census/NTIA survey are instructive. Released in July 1995 (U.S. Department of Commerce) the National Telecommunications and Information Administration appropriately entitled its report, *Falling through the Net: A Survey of the "Have-Nots" in Rural and Urban America.* Beginning with the proposition that at the core of U.S. telecommunications policy is the goal of "universal service" (i.e., the idea that all Americans should have access to affordable telephone service), the data from the NTIA survey reveal a pattern of computer access and use suggested by the 1984 and 1993 data previously described. By providing a more detailed rendition of the data with a focus on ethnicity and geographical location—variables not given this sort of attention in the 1984, 1989, and 1993 CPS surveys—the November 1994 Census/NTIA report allows researchers to gain a fuller understanding of who the "information disadvantaged" are, as this report labels them.

The data indicate that access to a telephone, a computer, and a computer with a modem tends to divide along an electronic fault line characterized by race, geographical location, income, age, and education (see Table 10.3). The general pattern that emerges from the 1994 data is one of lower-income, non-Whites (Native Americans, Aleuts, Eskimos, Blacks, Asians, or Pacific Islanders) who have less than a high school education and live in rural America on one side of this hypothetical electronic fault line and upper-income, college-educated Whites who live in urban and central city areas on the other. Certainly, these data indicate that the nature of the computer dichotomy of "haves" versus "have-nots" seen in the 1984 and 1993 CPS data goes beyond the Black/White schism. While the so-called racial divide can be seen in these data, the added dimensions of socioeconomic status and geographical location complicate this divide.

CONCLUSIONS

As one early twentieth-century thinker who was concerned with the socioeconomic order of his day once asked, "What is to be done?" Given the fact that the relevant hardware and software are commodities and not, at present, rights or entitlements, one's ability to access and use this package of resources will be governed in the near future by one's access to hard currency and/or to an elastic line of credit. Income and/or wealth is obviously a major determinant in shaping one's level of economic standard of living and in determining one's access and use of computer technology. The available survey data unequivocally indicate a positive covariation between reported income and the likelihood that one has access to a computer in one's home. Again, the data indicate that the

Table 10.3
Demographic Profile of Those Most Likely and Least Likely to Have Access to a Telephone, Home Computer, and/or Computer with Modem (November 1994) (in percent)

	Most Likely	Least Likely
To Have a:		
Telephone		
	Urban, White-non Hispanic (96.2)	Rural American Indian, Aleut, Eskimo (75.5)
	Rural, $75,000 + (99.2)	Central City, <$10K (79.8)
	Rural, 55 yrs. + (96.4)	Rural, <25 yrs. (77.2)
	Rural, College 4 yrs. + (98.7)	Central City, HS, 1-3 yrs. (83.7)
	Rural, NE Region (96.9)	Central City, NE Region (89.5)
Home Computer		
	Urban, White-non-Hispanic (30.3)	Rural, Black., non-Hispanic (6.4)
	Urban, $75,000 + (64.4)	Rural, <$10K (4.5)
	Urban, 45-54 yrs. (36.8)	Rural, 55 yrs. + (11.9)
	Rural, College 4 yrs. + (51.2)	Rural, & Central City, 0-8 yrs. (2.6)
	Urban, West (32.8)	Central City, NE Region (16.4)
Home Computer w/Modem		
	Central City, White, non-Hispanic (49.7)	Rural, Asian or Pacific Islander (26.7)
	Urban, $75,000 + (58.1)	Rural, <$10K (23.6)
	Urban, 25-34 yrs. (52.3)	Rural, <25 yrs. (27.4)
	Central City, College, 4 yrs. + (53.9)	Rural, HS, 1-3 yrs. (22.4)
	Urban, South (48.7)	Rural, West (35.3)

Source: U.S. Deptment of Commerce, National. Telecommunications and Information Administration *(1995) Falling through the Net: A Survey of the "Have-Nots" in Rural and Urban America*, selected tables. Downloaded from the Web site: http://www.ntia.doc.gov./.

school and the American home follows the highest recorded rates of computer use and access, with the workplace bringing up the rear. Certainly, the individual who uses and has access to computer technology in all three arenas is in the best possible position of accessing information that can be crucial in making important decisions about oneself and about others. If this society moves toward an electronic ballot box in cyberspace in the twenty first century, as the opening scenario to this chapter speculatively points out, and if past trends continue without any significant change, our analysis of the data suggests that the present demographic schisms seen in computer use and access are likely to be seen in the composition of the electorate in the twenty-first century.

The data we have examined indicate that it is in the schools attended by children between 3 and 17 years of age where the greatest prospects of exposure to computer technology exist. In elementary, middle, and high schools the rudiments of a more inclusive participatory democracy could be realized. If this nation is to avoid the sort of scenario described at the outset of this chapter, where the electorate may become divided between a techno-elite and a techno-peasantry, between the information haves and the information have-nots, between the citizens of the information age and those who could be electronically disfranchised, then all of us have the civil responsibility (1) to raise the level of computer literacy of all of those with whom we come into contact, particularly those who fit the demographic profile of the "information disadvantaged" and (2) to work to expand the access and use of computer technology in those presently woefully underserved parts of this nation.

Publicly accessible arenas are the most logical places where the sort of work that needs to be done should be done. This will require the commitment, input, and, yes, sacrifice of those in this society who possess the material resources to provide the computer technology. As the 1995 NTIA report points out, "There is a pivotal role to be assumed in the new electronic age by the traditional providers of information access for the general public—the public schools and libraries. These and other community access centers can provide, at least during an interim period, a means for electronic access to all those who might not otherwise have such access" (U.S. Department of Commerce, 1995, p. 7).

America can ill afford to close itself off from parts of itself. Ironically, because of this expanding technology we, as scholars, find ourselves in the position to know and therefore to do something about this coming crisis brought on by the expansion of computer technology. There is much work to be done; the struggle continues.

NOTES

1. These statistics are derived from usage data that can be examined via hypertext link on the Thomas home page (see: http://thomas.loc.gov/usage statistics).

2. At the time that this chapter was written (February 1996), the Census Bureau had published data from the 1984 and 1989 surveys as items in its series of current population reports. A third survey was conducted in October 1993, where questions similar to those asked in the 1989 survey were asked. While the Census Bureau has not yet published the 1993 data, they are available from a Web site maintained by that federal agency (see: http://www.census/gov.). See U.S. Department of Commerce, Bureau of the Census, 1988, and U.S. Department of Commerce, Bureau of the Census, 1991.

3. In the November 1994 CPS Survey, respondents were asked a set of questions that are referred to herein as "geographical identifiers." This term refers to the region of the United States in which the respondent lived at the time of the interview, whether the respondent lived in an urban or a rural area, and whether the respondent lived in a central-city area. The reader should be advised that there is no relation between data for central city and data for urban versus rural.

4. As of March 1994, 27.5% of Whites held managerial or professional jobs compared to 14.7% of Blacks. On the other hand, 30.7% of Blacks were employed as operators, fabricators, or laborers compared to only 19.3% of Whites (see Bennett, 1995, Table 2, p. 33).

REFERENCES

Bailey, D. (1996, January 28). The making of the cyberpol: A peek at the political future. *Washington Post*, p. C3.

Bennett, Claudia E. (1995). *The Black Population in the United States*: March 1993 & March 1994; Current Population Reports, Population Characteristics, P20-480, U.S. Bureau of the Census. Washington, DC: U.S. Government Printing Office.

Devine, Donald (1970). *The Attentive Public*. Chicago: Rand-McNally.

Toffler, Alvin (1982). Civil rights in the third wave. Perspectives, *The Civil Rights Quarterly*, 32-38.

U.S. Department of Commerce, Bureau of the Census (1988). Current Population Reports, Series P-23, No. 155, *Computer Use in the United States: 1984*. Washington, DC: U.S. Government Printing Office.

U.S. Department of Commerce, Bureau of the Census (1991). Current Population Reports, Series P-23, No. 171, *Computer Use in the United States: 1989*. Washington, DC: U.S. Government Printing Office.

U.S. Department of Commerce, National Telecommunications and Information Administration (1995). *Falling through the Net: A Survey of the 'Have-Nots' in Rural and Urban America*. Washington, DC: National Telecommunications and Information Administration. http://ntia.doc.gov/.

CHAPTER 11

Race, Politics, and Pedagogy of New Media: From Civil Rights to Cyber Rights

Jabari Simama

In 1980 educators and media activists met in Atlanta, Georgia, at a conference on Minorities in Cable, wherein they warned that cable—which had evolved into a significant part of the information revolution—was the last frontier for minorities in the Information Society. If minorities, particularly African Americans, didn't get on board with cable in areas of public access, ownership, and meaningful employment, they exhorted, racial minorities would be left behind in the new age of information. Little did they know that some 17 years later a major technological innovation—the Internet—which existed even at the time of the conference, would force them to raise anew some of the same hard questions like, How can communication technologies be used to combat racism and stimulate multicultural and international awareness? How can the community keep information technologies accessible to the largest number of citizens, so as to avoid creating another societal divide comprising the information-rich and information-poor? How does one prevent what is referred to today as the *digital divide*?

The purpose of this chapter is to analyze and discuss the impact of the Internet, new media, and computer technology on racial and ethnic communities in the United States. Several case studies from Atlanta are discussed to illustrate how the Black community is using computer technology and the Internet as a tool for empowerment. These examples hold relevance for the entire country because they focus on technology programs that can dramatically improve the skills of individuals at the bottom of the social-class ladder. But they also focus on education, K-12 and higher education. Further, this chapter contains an analysis of the concept of *access* and *cyber-rights* and what they mean when applied to new media, the information superhighway, and the Internet.

The Internet itself has been around for more than a quarter of a century. Its origins are in Defense Department research done in the late 1960s. Primarily, it grew out of a network designed to link up the National Science Foundation's (NSF) five supercomputer sites at the University of California at San Diego, Cornell University, the University of Illinois at Champaign-Urbana, Carnegie

Mellon University in Pittsburgh, and the National Center for Atmospheric Research in Boulder, Colorado.

Called NSFnet, the network began operation in 1987 and provided high-speed connections between the super computer sites so that researchers and scientists could access the sites remotely from government agencies and academic institutions (Baran, 1996). Regional networks were connected to the NSF network, as well as to a similar network developed by NASA called the National Science Internet. Thus, the Internet grew into a international system of linked networks, allowing global access to electronic mail and databases, as well as to other Internet resources such as new groups and more recently, the World Wide Web.

According to government reports available August 1998, more and more Americans were on-line than ever before, but minorities still lagged behind. A study commissioned by Vice President Al Gore, from the U.S. Commerce Department's National Telecommunication Information Administration, entitled *Falling through the Net II: New Data on the Digital Divide* (1998b) provides the following snapshot. It shows the nationwide penetration rates in 1997: 93.8% for telephones, 36.6% for personal computers (PCs), 26.3% for modems, and 18.6% for on-line access. More importantly, it shows PC ownership increased from 1994 to 1997 to 51.9%; modem ownership grew 139.1%; and E-mail access expanded by 397.1%. Though 36.6% of all Americans owned computers in 1998, when broken down by race, the digital divide is apparent: 40.8% of Whites owned computers, 19.3% of Blacks, and 19.4% of Hispanics (U.S. Commerce, 1998).

An additional problem, historically, is that technology has not always served the interest of people of color in the United States, particularly African Americans. If one undertakes a review of technology's role in squeezing African Americans out of the job market once their labor was no longer needed, it would be easy to deduce why many African Americans remain suspicious of technology today.

FROM CIVIL RIGHTS TO CYBER-RIGHTS

In his book *The End of Work* (1995), Jeremy Rifkin analyzes the impact that technology has had on job creation and loss in America and describes the dawn of the "postmarket era." In a chapter called "Technology and the African American Experience," Rifkin traces how technology has historically marginalizd Blacks in the United States and made their labor obsolete. Speaking about automation, he writes: "Automation had made large numbers of Black workers obsolete. Today, millions of African Americans find themselves hopelessly trapped in a permanent underclass. Unskilled and unneeded, the commodity value of their labor has been rendered virtually useless by the automated technologies that have come to displace them in the new high-tech global economy" (pp. 79-80).

The U.S. economy has evolved from industrial to information, wherein the gathering, processing, and analysis of information are critical skills for obtaining employment. Given this technological shift, many minority leaders are aware of how technology has been used against the interest of Blacks and other racial minorities. Nonetheless, they are articulating the message that access to computer technology should be considered a "civil right." In the latter part of the 1990s this concept was advanced through the fight for what is referred to as "universal service." The previously mentioned Commerce Department's study for Gore (1998b) heralded the importance of universal access to both telephony and computer technology. The authors of the study stated in the introduction that the concept has broadened to include access to Information Services and that access to the computers and networks may be as important as access to traditional telephone services.

In this chapter, the political struggle to obtain access to computer technology and the Internet, along with the ideological theory that holds that access is a modern democratic right, is referred to as *cyber-rights*. The cyber-rights concept contains at least three interrelated components: (1) public policy: ensuring that the federal, state, and local governments do what they can to keep information technology widely accessible to the greatest number of citizens; (2) financial: keeping computer technology affordable so that low-income individuals, schools, and nonprofit entities can purchase the technology. The financial aspect of cyber-rights also involves establishing provisions for minorities and women to own systems and applications related to new media technology; and (3) education: making sure that technology is used to educate the nation—from children to senior citizens. This aspect of the cyber-rights concept involves fully using technology to develop human potential. It includes using computer technology to help inner-city youth learn to read, write, compute, and do arithmetic, as well as analyze problems and think critically. It also involves using technology in lifelong learning contexts to train and retrain Americans and, to some extent, the world's work-force, to open up avenues of communication between disparate groups that don't communicate because of racial or ethnic polarization and social stratification.

Some who are advocating for racial minorities to shift their focus from civil-rights to cyber-rights say the economy has changed to an information-based market where the gathering, analysis, and dissemination of information, increasingly within the computer-mediated environment, will continue to predominate. Their conclusion, regarding the shift in the U.S. economy, is supported by information released by the U.S. Commerce Department in the first quarter of 1998. The report indicates that information technology, including business on the Internet, is growing twice as fast as the overall economy. In its report entitled "The Emerging Digital Economy" (1998), the government found that the information technology industry employs 7.4 million workers, some among the nation's highest average salaries. In an unrelated survey in 1998 by the American Electronic Association, one of the first to track Internet-related jobs, salaries for Internet- and Web-related jobs range from $39,500 to $120,000 per annum. All jobs surveyed—positions like Internet strategist, $121,200; Web publisher, $78,500; and Web editor, $47,400—outpaced the private sector wage average of $28,582.

The Commerce Department also reported in "The Emerging Digital Economy" that traffic on the Internet has doubled every 100 days and, that by 2002 commerce among Internet businesses will surpass $300 billion. Commenting on the rapid growth among Internet users, the report also states that in 1994 a mere 3 million people were connected to the Internet. By the end of 1997 some three years later, 100 million people were using it. This included 5 million African Americans. These facts suggest that, within the next decade, if minorities can't compute, "cruise" the Web, or write in a computer language, there might not be enough low-skill jobs left over from the previous economy.

Referring to the importance of keeping computer and Internet technologies available to children and the poor, 1998 Federal Communication Commission Chairman Bill Kennard and some members of Congress advocated for "universal" or "discounted" computer and Internet service as a way of bridging the gap between race, income, and computer accessibility. In an Associated Press report, Kennard was quoted saying, "The discount must—let me repeat— must go first and foremost to those places where it is most desperately needed" ("FCC Chief," 1988). Discounts would be paid for through fees on telephone and other telecommunications companies. In 1998 the fund contained about $2.6 billion a year in Internet subsidies for schools, libraries, and rural health care corporations.

Guaranteeing access and discussing cyber-rights as civil rights have implications for both public policy and education. Black leaders and educators say minorities should pay close attention, in particular, to the role the government plays in allocating public resources such as spectrum and funding. In early 1997, for example, the U.S. government added 64 colleges and universities to the National Science Foundation's high-speed computer network, which has become the backbone of the Internet 2 project. The expansion of the network is being supported by $12.3 million in federal grants. The 64 institutions hope to develop an improved Internet for a variety of academic uses. The colleges and universities will connect to what is called the Very High Speed Backbone Network Service, or VBNS. This network is considerably faster than the conventional Internet, carrying information as fast as 622 million bits per second, compared to 50 million bits per second for the current Internet network. This network is the latest state-of-the-art computer network. Participating institutions will be at the cutting edge of this fast developing field. None of the initial 64 institutions were a Black college or university. Further, of the most "wired" educational institutions using the Internet in 1997, there were no African American institutions listed, according to Yahoo Magazine.

In fact, only recently have educators, scholars, and professionals in the African American community recognized the need to be on-line. For example, in the summer of 1996 Dr. John Hopps, the provost of Morehouse College, said his premier institution was not, at the time, on-line (J. Hopps, personal communication, April 1996). An indication of how fast Black institutions are coming on-line is that by the summer of 1997, Morehouse had not only developed a large presence on the Web, but had hired a full-time staff devoted to educational telecommunications. Moreover, in April 1997, with the aid of a $120,000 grant from the Andrew W. Mellon Foundation, Morehouse inaugurated a program that put computers, modems, and printers in 20 churches in the metropolitan Atlanta area. In addition, Morehouse College students held workshops to teach members of the community how to use the technology, and children were given computer accounts so they could send and receive E-mail. The distance this historically Black college traveled in one year symbolizes the pace at which the African American community is becoming aware of the potential of new media. But there is still a disparity between Blacks and Whites in terms of computer ownership.

Several studies document increased computer ownership on the part of African Americans and other racial minorities (e.g., U.S. Commerce Department, 1998a, 1998b). These studies show that more minorities own computers today than in the five years prior to the report, but they still lag behind Whites. In 1996 *Emerge*, an African American-oriented newsmagazine, reported that only 12% of African American households owned computers, compared to 30% of White households (Curry, 1996). Of equal importance, the magazine reported that more than half of the African Americans with computers in 1996 were without modems, the device that is needed to access the Internet. The group that is hit hardest is poor and working-class African American families.

In the Vanderbilt Project 2000 Study, authors Donna L. Hoffman and Thomas P. Novak, associate professors of marketing at Vanderbilt University in the Owen Graduate School of Management, reported the results of their research project on race and the Internet (Hoffman & Novak, 1998). Their study was "the first . . . on the race and ethnicity of Internet users that can be used to make national estimates in reference to households with annual incomes below $40,000. Whites were six times as likely as Blacks to have used the World Wide Web in the previous week. The study also found that lower-income Whites were twice as likely (27.5%) to own a home computer as were Black households (13.3%). The survey's results were based on data provided by Nielsen Media Research in a poll of 5,813 people conducted from December 1996 through January 1997. The same study indicated that among Blacks with incomes over $40,000 a year, home computer ownership is roughly equal to that of Whites of comparable incomes.

On April 17, 1998, the *New York Times*, referring to the Hoffman/Novak study, reports, "The study is significant because it documents concerns [that] the recent exponential growth of the Internet might further exacerbate the gap between the nation's rich and poor. While it is no surprise that Americans with lower incomes are less likely to own a computer, the study highlights for the first time what may be the more disturbing role of race in determining who has access to digital technology" (as cited in "FCC Chief," 1998, p. E2).

The Gore study by the NTIA also found that minorities still lagged far behind in terms of computer ownership and Internet access. White households are still more than twice as likely (40.8%) to own a computer as are Black (19.3%) or Hispanic (19.4%) households. According to the Gore study, this divide is apparent across all income levels: even at incomes higher than $75,000, Whites are more likely to have PCs (76.3%) than are Blacks (64.1%). The Gore study further shows that the rates for on-line access are nearly three times as high for Whites (21.2%) as for Blacks (7.7%). The study concludes that the digital divide between racial groups in PC ownership increased since 1994 by about five percentage points: 21.5% in 1997, to 16.8% in 1994 (U.S. Commerce Department, 1998b).

As far as education is concerned, the gap between African American and White children is even wider. Only 39% of Black students in public schools have access to computers at school, compared with 56% of White students, a difference of 17 percentage point (White, 1996). In some regions, the problem may be worse. The *Atlanta Journal-Constitution* (AJC) reports that "schools with substantial minority populations, though numerous in Georgia, are virtually absent from the list of schools with home pages" (White, 1996). In 1996 the AJC reported further that most African Americans surveyed were unaware of the Internet and its uses (Poole, 1996). These reports suggest that the biggest threat to the African American community's participation in the information revolution is the lack of access to computers in the home and classroom.

Some Black entrepreneurs, however, want to prove that there is a large Black presence on the Web to demonstrate the existence of a viable Black market that can be reached by advertisers and businesses selling products and services. In 1997 Everything Black started a nationwide campaign to verify that more than 1 million African Americans are on-line (recent research shows that in 1998 about 5 million Blacks are on-line). Calling itself a "comprehensive directory of Internet Web sites of particular interest to persons of African descent," Everything Black sent out a message to African American Web users urging them to stand up in cyberspace to be counted. "Are there 1 million Black Internet users? We have been told by major advertising executives that there are not "that many" Black persons on the Internet. We are conducting a research experiment to prove that there are at least 1 million regular users of the Internet who classify themselves as African American, African, Pan-African, or Black. The purpose of the research is to justify to the major media, advertisers, content developers, hardware and software manufacturers, and others that we are a viable audience that cannot be ignored" (Patrick McElroy, Personal Communication, February 1, 1997).

Another example of the influence of Blacks on-line is F. Leon Wilson's SpectraLinks. Wilson, an entrepreneur in Columbus, Ohio, has an E-mail list he believes is of special interest to people of color. In part, he is trying to prove that although people of color are not developing Web sites in proportion to their numbers in the general population, they are, nonetheless, highly engaged with the Internet in the more "interactive spaces" like E-mail lists and chat rooms. SpectraLinks is designed, in his own words, to "map Cyberspace in full colour" (Guernsey, 1997). Wilson sends out Web addresses of recent articles on a new trend in Black demographics or tips on new software. More than 3,500 people subscribe to his automatic E-mail system, which is archived at St. John's University in New York. Wilson hopes his archives will chronicle how people of color have used the Internet. "We will have [a] fully documented archive of the triumphs and downfalls that created our story," he adds.

CASE STUDIES IN TECHNOLOGIES FROM ATLANTA

Atlanta is an important city, both nationally and internationally, in terms of Black empowerment and information technology. It is the birthplace of one of the world's greatest human rights leaders, Dr. Martin Luther King Jr. In 1996 Atlanta played host to the Centennial Olympic Games, wherein the Games' Host Broadcast Center was the largest broadcast center ever constructed. In 1998 Atlanta mayor Bill Campbell cochaired a committee of local computer and information technology business leaders who were interested in finding a nickname, like Silicon Valley or Research Triangle, for Atlanta's high-tech corridor. As chair of the U.S. Conference of Mayors Transportation and Technology Committee, Campbell's voice is often heard nationally, advocating for technology to be used to solve problems in education and society. In *Government Technology*, a magazine that focuses on solutions for state and local governments in the information age, Campbell says in response to an interviewer's question: "It [the digital divide] is the greatest issue we face. It is the absolutely greatest issue because nothing in recent memory, other than the civil rights struggle, had the potential to either unite or divide our country the way access to technology can . . . Either we are going to use technology as the great equalizer, or it will be the thing that divides this country along class lines."

Atlanta has been a world center of information technology largely because of CNN's worldwide news network; the Georgia Center for Advanced Telecommunications Technology; Scientific Atlanta, a world manufacturer of high-tech communication equipment; and Bell Laboratories. As it relates to technology, there have been several historical firsts achieved in Atlanta. In 1975 Scientific Atlanta developed the first Cable satellite connection; in 1979 Bell Labs in Atlanta created the world's first application of a fiber network; in 1987 a mobile satellite uplink was developed by Scientific Atlanta; in 1992 the first telephone call over a cable TV network was transmitted by Cox Enterprises; and in 1995 the world's first Internet Bank, the Security First Network Bank, was launched in Atlanta.

Atlanta also has a long history of citizen participation and alternative media activism. In 1971 WRFG, a community radio station, was incorporated. It went on the air two years later and still broadcasts today. In 1973 the Atlanta branch of the National Association for the Advancement of Colored People (NAACP) and the American Civil Liberties Union (ACLU) of Georgia successfully challenged the licenses of the Cox Communication-owned WSB-TV and WSB-AM-FM radio and television stations. The challenges resulted in a settlement that provided funding for the establishment of a community-based media program—the Atlanta Media Project—designed to train the community in producing community-oriented film and video programming.

In 1980 Black Atlanta took advantage of another opportunity to participate in the telecommunication explosion when cable television came to town promising and delivering to the African American community 25% minority ownership, 35% of the cable jobs, five neighborhood access studios, and nine public, educational, and government access channels. Atlanta was the first major urban city to receive a state-of-the-art, multiple-hub-site cable system. It became the blueprint for the rest of the nation. MediaOne in Atlanta today is rebuilding the system with fiber to all of its new hub sites.

Atlanta's community television program was also a model for minority participation (Kagan, 1983). In 1986 over 6,000 residents were certified to use the public access facilities. The station, still in existence, is now in its 18th year of operation. The authors wrote about the new medium of public access television in Atlanta in an article entitled, "Taking Cable to the People, Taking the People to Cable" (France & Simama, 1982).

Public access programming does more than reveal to the public its problems and potential solutions. Through encouraging citizen participation, public access helps foster self-discovery within the creative process. Herein lies the key, that distinguishes access programming from other forms of local television: access programming encourages and, in fact, requires citizen participation (France & Simama, 1982).

A number of significant initiatives under way that include projects that help bring computer technology and training to Atlanta's public housing complexes. Research being conducted at the Georgia Center for Advanced Telecommunications Technology could dramatically reduce the problem of computer accessibility for the poor. An innovative "race in cyberspace" Mentor-protégé program exists between a freshman English class at the Georgia Institute of Technology (Georgia Tech) and Martin Luther King Jr. Middle School, a predominantly African American, working-class public school in Atlanta's inner city. There are a race and ethnicity Web site and college course designed to foster greater cooperation between scientific-engineering-based colleges, historically Black colleges, and community-based organizations.

Youth Educational Town

Staff is making sure that kids at Martin Luther King Jr. Middle School in Summerhill don't get left behind on the information superhighway. Aaron Sampson, who has since left his position, was the former director of Youth Educational Town (YET), an after-school computer enrichment program for fifth and sixth graders that teaches them all about the wonders of computers and the Internet. "In 10 years, if you don't have computer skills you won't be able to do anything. I don't think that message is getting through to the majority of teachers, many of whom don't have computer skills themselves," laments Sampson, pointing to the necessity of programs such as YET.

Six months into the project, Sampson estimated that YET had already exposed some 500 youth, who would not have otherwise gotten any computer training, to computers and the World Wide Web. In addition to 35 on-line computers, YET had a CD-ROM library of 100 disks. With the help of six full-time staffers and several volunteers, kids learned everything from basic computer skills to downloading files from the Internet, using E-mail, and creating Web pages. YET received a grant of more than $1 million from the National Football League Charities, which sets up similar programs in cities that host the Super Bowl. YET operates out of a brand-new 6,500-square-foot facility attached to a 14,000- square-foot gymnasium that used to be part of the old Smith School. The operating budget in 1997 was shared by the United Way and Exodus/Communities in Schools; the Sony Corporation and Digital Corporation donated the equipment.

Sampson was introduced to computers when he was about ten years old. He believes it is imperative that the African American children who attend Martin Luther King Jr. Middle School, ages 11-13, travel down the information superhighway with all deliberate speed. In addition to computer training, YET offers an after-school enrichment program that includes classes in a plethora of subject areas like Microsoft Word, photography, cooking, and musical instruments. But the heart of YET's program centers on what young people learn to do with computers.

Though the formal program operated only during after-school hours, except in the summer, computer use is up because teachers can, and often do, bring their classes to YET during the school day to receive computer and Internet training. Staff members provide free training for Martin Luther King Jr. Middle School teachers. Volunteers who teach classes on subjects unrelated to computers are asked to identify, if possible, a computer nexus. "We try to figure out a computer interface. Almost any class you teach can make use of computers if you're creative," adds Sampson. The staff hopes adults in Atlanta will offer their skills and make a commitment to mentoring kids during the tough adolescent stages of their lives.

Mentor-Protégé Programs in Computer Technology

Steve Spence, 34 at the time this research was conducted, is a White college teacher who believes that those who have been privileged, such as himself, can render an important service to society by having his technically oriented students work directly with low-income kids like those at the Martin Luther King Jr. Middle School, close to where Sampson's YET program is located. Spence asserts: "This technology [the Internet] should be encouraging people to see themselves as participants and creators and not just recipients or consumers of culture. We have the potential to bring more voices into the conversation . . . We need to start using the Internet to connect people who would not otherwise connect" (Steve Spence, Personal Communication, April 10, 1997).

One way to ensure that the next generation of African American youth is not lacking in computer skills is to begin training them in how to use computers and navigate the Internet at an early age. Making such training a part of public schools' curricula is imperative, but resolving the problem of the national shortage of teachers who themselves are trained in the technologies might prove to be a larger problem. To address this latter problem, Spence and other college professors set up Mentor-protégé programs wherein college students were paired with elementary, middle, or high school students to tutor and serve as mentors to them in the areas of computer and Internet technology.

Another program devised by Spence involved his students from his Race and Cyberspace freshman writing class at Georgia Tech and students at the Martin Luther King Jr. Middle School. The college and public school students, coming from separate stations in life, stayed in communication with each other through the use of electronic mail. The older mentors encouraged the middle school students to probe into their own identities through discovering more about the neighborhoods around them. The public school students wrote about their experiences and published their essays on the World Wide Web.

The college students benefited from the Mentor-protégé program because it created an opportunity for them to become more in touch and involved with the larger community. Program participants say that students were better able to retain what they learned because they used the knowledge immediately. Another benefit of the Mentor-protégé program is that when middle-class college students work in close proximity with working-class public school students, they usually became a bit more sensitive to the realities that working-class families face on a day-to-day basis. This sensitivity might make the college students more empathic to the problems of working-class families. This could pay dividends in the future when Spence's college students make their way into positions of power.

Public Housing and the Information Society

Public housing complexes have traditionally been tough environments to maintain viable programs that positively impact the community. Some programs are beginning to have a positive effect on public housing environments. The Capitol Area Mosaic (CAM), a community center that has been in existence since 1958 in downtown Atlanta, works with professors who want to share their skills with residents of Capitol Homes, a public housing complex near the Georgia State Capitol. In 1994 an anonymous benefactor provided funds to create the Capitol Area Information Center. The center opened with four computers, an extensive CD-ROM collection, and a small lending library. In 1995 the IBM foundation donated 11 more computers, which enabled the center to triple the number of machines available to the center's children. In 1996 the Atlanta-based Internet service provider, Mindspring, donated an account for residents' use.

In a proposal to the BellSouth Foundation to fund "instruction to 100 underprivileged children, ages 7-17, in computer literacy, information retrieval, and publication on the Internet," authors of a CAM proposal wrote of the significance of the Internet:

The explosive growth of the global information infrastructure places a powerful tool within the reach of these children. The Internet—the ultimate "open" computer network—makes available millions of documents and worlds of possibility that were once restricted by cost and geography. Both global and inexpensive, the Internet promises to level the playing field among those literate in the basic skill of network navigation. Unfortunately, in Atlanta and in the nation, the Internet is not keeping its promises. (Capitol Area Mosaic, 1997)

Unfortunately, BellSouth rejected the proposal request. BellSouth's rejection surfaces a larger problem: corporations like IBM and BellSouth are often willing to make donations of excess or outdated computers, but they are less eager to fund personnel for instruction and program development. Without adequate staff, organizations like CAM cannot reach the number of children who need training. Spence, a CAM volunteer and former professor at Georgia Tech, speaks to this problem in a grant proposal he helped write: "While children line up to use the computers, they most often play games that offer little beyond basic keyboard and mouse coordination . . .These programs need supervisors and one-to-one training."

Stan Motley, director of Fulton County Parks and Recreation Department (FCPRD), says his department is trying to change its old image as a "baby-sitter of children after hours, once school is out" (Stan Motley, Personal Communication, April 11, 1997). His department now pays college students to train public housing residents to use computers and navigate the Web. "They [the community] are asking for training in computers," says Motley. "Nowadays there is no line between fun and training. We still offer fun in after-hours recreation, but increasingly we are mixing fun with something that has educational value."

Fulton County Housing Authority (FCHA), in conjunction with the FCPRD, provides training to adult residents of the Red Oak and Boat Rock communities, two of the county's largest public housing complexes. As in Capitol Homes, a community group initiated this project. Several Red Oak families formed a community action group to work with Georgia Tech in converting vacant apartments for use as family resource centers. For years, the Department of Housing and Urban Development (HUD) has cited public housing authorities for the high incidence of public housing vacancies. Many of the vacant structures had become havens for drug distribution and prostitution. The conversion of vacant public housing apartments into computer resource centers is important in several regards. First, it demonstrates how public housing tenants can empower themselves by refusing to give in to the criminal elements within their respective communities. Second, it shows how neighborhood liabilities (i.e., vacant, blighted properties) can be converted into assets that benefit the entire community.

The first lab opened at Boat Rock in the summer of 1996 with 15 residents completing a three-month course. The centers now are fully equipped, and the parent group has formed a partnership with Georgia Power and Alumax, Inc., the third largest U.S. aluminum producer. Betty Davis, director of the FHA, remembers how her agency became motivated to move into the computer age: "One of the things I realized in the last 5-10 years was that of the many programs we had, we did not include any technology. This related to the fact that we have not had access to computers in the community. We felt that at the Housing Authority it was important that our residents not get left behind as far as technology is concerned" (Betty Davis, Personal Communication, April 3, 1997).

According to a report issued in 1997 on FCHA's Computer Training Program, 50 residents had gone through the formal training and, "more than 100 residents had used the labs on an individual basis to prepare resumes, cover letters, and practice typing." The centers were fully equipped with six computers each. Tyronda Williams-Minter, family self-sufficiency coordinator at FHA, says the agency planned to purchase 12 new computers that would be powerful enough to access the World Wide Web (Tyronda Williams-Minter, Personal Communication, April 14, 1997). This would then bring the total number of computers available to residents at the two housing complexes to 24.

Patricia Ballard, a resident of Boat Rock, completed the training and said she learned much in a "relatively short period of time" (Patricia Ballard, Personal Communication, April 14, 1997). She now works in Red Oak as a Vista volunteer. "The training has helped me in what I am doing today," says Ballard. "I use computers to help residents obtain jobs, type resumes, create fliers, and type letters. I'm really looking forward to going on the Internet." Ballard believes her enthusiasm for the Internet has been bolstered by the interest of her 17-year-old daughter, Shalonda, who was first introduced to computers at West Lake High School in Fulton County. Ballard says she is not "afraid of the technology," and that is due largely to her daughter's positive experience with computers.

Patricia Farley, a resident of Red Oak, says she, too, has benefited from the computer training provided by FHA. She speaks intently of the implication of computer training for finding a job. "At first I didn't even know how to turn on the computer," she admits. "Now I can operate it on my own . . . A lot of jobs will require you to know a little about this technology" (Patricia Farley, Personal Communication, April 14, 1997). Like Ballard, Farley said she, too, learned additional things about the computer from her two children, who were seven and eight years old at the time. Observers say that parents' learning about computers from their children is a positive development, particularly if it empowers parents to better assist their children in doing their homework.

The Boat Rock and Red Oaks collaboration initiatives are similar to other ones like the Campus of Learners initiative being promoted by the Department of Housing and Urban Development. As part of this federal initiative, "public-housing communities 'connect' with a university or technical college to create their own centers of technology" (Crik, 1997).

Telemouse

To address the problem of computer shortage within the African American community, some engineers are experimenting with the possibility of providing access to the Internet and other on-line technologies via telephones and television sets. Senior research engineer Dan Howard, with the Broadband Telecommunications Center in Atlanta, is working on a solution to the computer accessibility problem by using cable and telephone technologies interfaced with a computer. The technology is called Telemouse, and it involves using a portion of the cable television spectrum to view images and data created on the Internet. With this technology, one can use the numbered buttons on a regular telephone to manipulate a mouse on a television screen. For example, the 4-key on a phone moves the mouse cursor to the left, and the 6-key to the right. "It will be dirt cheap, $50 to $100 bucks or less," says Howard, the center's associate director. "Making this technology accessible to low-income people is the focus of the project. The entire focus of the Broadband Telecommunications Center is on the homes, both low and high incomes." (Dan Howard, Personal Communication, April 15, 1997).

One place where the center plans to implement the Telemouse technology is at the rebuilt Fowler School in Atlanta. There, Howard is proposing to place a single computer in the basement of an apartment building and allow residents to share access to it, using the Telemouse concept. According to an E-mail message, the project's main purpose is to "integrate low wage/welfare residents with higher wage residents over a high tech telecommunications infrastructure which connects them to each other."

In Athens, Georgia, the center is also using the Telemouse technology in a distant learning project that makes innovative use of a public access cable channel. Students use the World Wide Web to create Web pages. Parents who don't have access to computers at home can use the Telemouse technology to view their children's Web pages on the public access channel. According to Dr. Michael Hannafin of the University of Georgia Learning and Performance Support Laboratory, the Telemouse technology defines a "model for moving the school from 'behind closed doors' into the community at large" (Georgia Center for Advanced Telecommunication Technology [GCATT], Personal Communication, April 14, 1997)

"With the use of an inexpensive keyboard and a mouse, the TV can become a personal computer and provide infinite educational possibilities, such as distance learning and, eventually, interactive TV," reports the GCATT (cited in *Georgia Tech Alumni Magazine 73*, [October 29, 1997], 27). If such technology can be efficiently developed involving the television set, a technology Black people are very familiar with, some believe the sociological impact could be great in terms of leveling the information playing field.

The Internet and African American Studies

Making computer technology available to the African American community and training Black youth to cruise the World Wide Web are important objectives. But some say the African American community must be able to develop, at the same time, a capacity to study, critique, and analyze the impact that new media and information technologies have on the African American community. There is very little scholarship on this subject. Few, if any, college courses are offered on race, ethnicity, and new media. In January 1997 I developed and taught what is believed to be one of the first college courses in the nation that focused exclusively on race and the Internet. In September 1997 I offered a second course at Georgia Tech in the School of Public Policy on race, pedagogy, and new media. In these courses, I fleshed out many of the salient aspects of new technology and located them in the context of African American studies. In these courses, I was particularly interested in educational uses of computer technology, as well as how African Americans and other racial minorities were using the Internet and new media in areas such as environmental justice, public education, community organizing, and the media and society.

From the courses, the following can be concluded:

- Teaching a race and Internet course forces technically oriented and nontechnical students to work together in ways those traditional courses would not permit. This helps to undress technology's mystique.

- The creation of a virtual community in cyberspace reinforces links in and with one's actual community.

- Technology affords the community the opportunity to use the Internet as a communication network that bypasses the gatekeepers and censors of traditional media.

- Using technology drives home the point that technology's greatest potential is its ability to provide information to marginalized communities.

- No technology can replace a mercurial thirst in an individual for knowledge and information.

When teaching, it is always useful to start with a general demographic overview of who is in the class. Both classes were racially diverse, but African American students made up a majority of the students. Black students dominated class discussions, though Whites were almost as active on-line. When we asked one White student why he didn't discuss his views more often in class, he said, "I don't believe Black students are really interested in my views on race." His response, though candid, was telling. He obviously saw the class as a place to come and obtain knowledge, but he didn't see it as a place where he could give much. But what was most interesting about this student is that he strongly articulated his views in the class' electronic discussion group, where his identity could have been, but rarely was, kept anonymous.

In the January 1997 class that dealt with racial imagery and the Internet, 23 students registered. Forty-three percent were engineers (i.e., computer, civil, electrical, environmental, industrial, or material). Five were majoring in cultural studies, and the others were majoring in a variety of subjects like biology, math, management, and economics. Of the ten engineers in the class, all except two rated themselves as being excellent or superb in Web authoring and design. Thirty-five percent (eight) of the class were female. Of the students who said they had no Web experience, or only a small amount of it, 60% were females. No female student rated her Web authoring skills as being excellent, and only one said they were superior.

By looking at the breakdown of the class, one can ascertain how closely it mirrors society in terms of who has computer skills. Women and racial minorities in society, as the preceding percentages indicate, are at a distinct disadvantage. One of the first things we did to help break down the mystique of the engineer was to divide the class into groups. We made sure that no more than two engineers were placed in any one group. We also divided up the class based on who had experience in Web authoring and design. Each group became a subcommunity in and of itself, and Web CaMILE, our Internet listserv, became a distinct community in cyberspace (View Web CaMILE at http:// prada.cc.gatech.edu/cgi-bin/lcc4875/lcc 4875. Use case-sensitive user name, User 1; no password required).

The graduate course offered in September 1997 comprised graduate students majoring in cultural studies, public policy, math, and engineering. Cultural studies students predominated. Their research projects ranged from investigating how the state funds technology at inner-city versus suburban schools, to defining the aesthetics of Black Web sites.

The creation of a virtual community in cyberspace is largely dependent on one's ability to create interaction. On-line chat groups are popular forums for interaction among young people who want to vent or provide spontaneous reaction to current events. However, what works best for educational purposes, in subject areas requiring reflective dialogue, is an Internet discussion list that focuses on specific topics. In both race and new media classes, a new software program created by a Georgia Tech professor called Web CaMILE was used. Web CaMILE assigns to each discussion list its own URL (Universal Resource Locator). Web CaMILE allows for direct links to other Web sites of relevance to topics being discussed. For example, if a student posts a response to a class discussion on W.E.B. Du Bois, that student can include in his or her posting a direct link to another Web site on Du Bois. Class discussion lists such as Web CaMILE work best if professors check them regularly and post on them about 25% of the time, the research shows.

In a ten-week quarter, students posted approximately 120 times, an average of four times per student. Other than a handful of assigned topics, students could post reactions to any issue they believed to be relevant to the African American experience. The following list identifies the top seven issues from the first class:

Topics	Number of Posts
Racism in media/television	20
Racial stereotypes in society	10
Hip-Hop Music/Death of Tupac	11
Shakur and Notorious B.I.G.	8
Ebonics	8
Blacks lacking access to computers/Technology	5
Blacks/Internet and New Media	5

Students posted reactions to 40 different issues ranging from why more "love films" aren't made by and about African Americans, to adjustments that students believed they had to make when entering the business world. One student who was a computer engineer major (and who landed four job offers before the end of the quarter) responded to a White student who asked: "I would like for someone to clarify for me . . . specific ways in which Black people have to give up their culture to be successful":

Allow me to comment from my own experiences, as I've been interviewing with a number of companies here on campus. The business world does not accept any part of the culture of African Americans (good or bad). When I go to interview with a company, I have to consciously suppress all notions of race and ethnicity that might otherwise seep out without my knowledge . . . I am well aware that White employers do not like the way I walk . . . I have to cut my hair as short as possible. Sometimes I feel they assume I can't speak proper English and when I show them that I can, it's a pleasant (and sometimes not so pleasant) surprise. (Student Personal Communication, January 31, 1997)

An Internet discussion list allows students to ask questions and respond to each other in highly personal ways. This type of intimacy is rarely accomplished in face-to-face interaction. Students share deeper and more private emotions because an Internet list is generally only for those who choose to subscribe. In actual communities, many people land where they are by an accident of birth (particularly, poor people). But individuals who share interests in particular subject matters and who often share a value system establish cyberspace communities. By analyzing students' posts on a discussion list, one can discern the special sense of community that exists. One student posted an emotional elegy to a culpable brother entitled "My Biggie." It came from an African American female majoring in economics. She tried to elucidate to her younger brother what future might await him if he didn't turn his life around. Using the occasion of the death of the Notorious B.I.G. to confront him, she posted:

When I heard about Biggie's death, I called my little brother. He's 16 and wants the fast life of Biggie. He hangs around all the wrong people, had dropped out of school, and gets in trouble daily. I had shed so many tears over him, worried so many times about him, that I had slowly begun turning away from him. But, on Sunday, I cooked him dinner, we watched movies, and I made sure he knew that I loved him. I told him it wasn't too late to live his life right and that I always believed in him even when I didn't agree with him. He has a good heart and I believe that he is worth the effort . . . [H]e's my Biggie. (Student Personal Communication, March 4, 1997)

Ironically, two female classmates responded to this emotional post, which occurred near the end of the quarter. One female student wanted to know if anyone was still "listening." It is interesting that this student chose the word "listening," as if the Internet provides an auditory, instead of textual, narrative voice. The other female student simply penned her response, "Hold on." Sharing a grief as deep as in "My Biggie," she wrote: "It is very important that you hold on. Like you mentioned, you may not have known Biggie personally, but we all have one in our family. The world is full of Biggies and it important that we stay close to the ones in our lives. My Biggie was my cousin who a couple weeks ago [much like Biggie and Tupac] was shot and killed in cold blood outside of a club in New York" (1997).

Students posted deep emotions and private thoughts because they felt a sense of community with the others on the list. The list was "secured" (i.e., you had to have a password to enter it), which enabled students to be more confident that their vulnerabilities wouldn't be exploited. It is clear from working with Internet lists that they have potential for serving as a network for people who need information as well as access to each other. But Web CaMILE could have been more powerful if the students in the class, some of whom were studying to be engineers, had spoken directly to youth from the inner city about the importance of studying math at an early age.

In addition to the new media's creation of a Black virtual community in cyberspace, it makes producing, publishing, and distributing of information much more economical and efficient for those who are on-line. In the race and Internet and race and pedagogy classes, Web projects undertaken by students all held pertinence for the African American community. In the race and Internet class (divided into five groups of five), students developed Web sites that dealt with the following topics and issues:

1. Images of African American women in music video

2. Blaxploitation films in the 1970s

3. African Americans in television commercials

4. African studies courses, programs, and departments in higher education in Atlanta

In the race and pedagogy class, students developed Web projects or wrote research papers on such topics as

5. Environmental justice and the Internet

6. FutureNet: an infrastructure of information to low-income communities

7. State lottery funds and educational technology

8. The aesthetics of African American Web sites

Space does not permit a detailed ratiocination of all these sites, but it might prove useful to explicate the two Web sites that dealt with African American studies. First, let's explain the process of how students built a Web site. Hypertext Markup Language (HTML) and Java are the two languages most commonly used in Web construction. As a class project, it is good to have students work collectively to develop Web sites. This process is egalitarian and diminishes the unhealthy aspects of competition that are so often a part of the culture of higher education. Learning the skills associated with team building also can be important in terms of future employment. In the Information Society, many professional jobs require employees and managers to work collectively in networked environments to solve complex problems.

In the race and Internet class, without prompting from the instructor, students divided themselves into discrete job functions related to Web construction. Once in a group, some students elected to conduct research on their selected topics. In the case of the African American studies courses, students first obtained catalogs from all the schools involved. After they identified key people, they wrote letters to provosts, deans, and department chairs to introduce the project. They followed up the letters with phone calls. While this occurred, other students took on the task of thinking visually about the design of the Web. They had to consider such matters as what colors to use, whether or not to employ tables, and how many pictures and graphics to include to visually embellish the text. Another important feature of HTML is that it makes it relatively easy for students to perform hypertext links. Students were challenged to search for the best links and to make sure all links were relevant to their subjects.

For the African American studies project, students created links to all Atlanta universities and colleges, Black studies departments, if they existed, and other topics relevant to African American studies. Finally, all the students coded the material with the proper commands, placed it on a server, and uploaded it to the World Wide Web. Even students who lacked prior experience in Web authoring learned from working in this type of collaborative environment.

The technical process of constructing a Web site in a cooperative environment is an important component of what Web authoring offers. But the greatest potential of a Web site, once on-line, is that it creates new ways for the community to interact and access information. For example, the comprehensive listings of African American studies courses offered at Clark Atlanta University, Emory University, Spelman College, Morehouse College, and Georgia State University included course descriptions, syllabi, bibliographies, and a list of student exams and projects. Students listed on-line nearly 200 African American studies courses offered at the institutions on their Web sites. Now students wanting to take courses at other campuses have a convenient way of finding out what is offered without leaving their physical campuses.

The race and pedagogy class was taught as a seminar for graduate and advanced undergraduate students. Because the class was smaller in size (ten students), students worked on projects individually. In order to give students an opportunity to test their subjects, they were first required to present a 30-minute seminar at midterm on their proposed topics. Students were required to integrate technology in some way in their presentation. Most students chose to use the Internet as an aid in their presentation. For an example, the student who selected a project on environmental racism and the Internet walked the class through several Web sites and links relevant to environmental justice. Her main concern centered on how, if at all, the Internet was being used for information and as an instrument for organizing local communities concerned with environmental issues. The student even found a Web site listing that was thought to contain information on how one grassroots community used the Internet in its struggle against environmental racism in a neighborhood near the university. Unfortunately, the Web site was no longer active.

The study of issues like environmental justice and associated Web sites helps to drive home the point that to really understand a given Web site, one has to understand how the Web site is used in a community. One cannot merely undertake a formalist or structuralist analysis of the Web site. It is important to know a Web site's social function, and how effective it is in providing quick and accurate information to a given community. An effective Web site must also be easy to use, and have clear objectives and a definite audience.

Web sites could further help to tear down the boundaries between the respective educational institutions and facilitate exchanges of students who now can work together on projects beyond their individual campuses. One interesting finding that came out of the race and Internet class was that among the 200 African American studies courses offered by the institutions surveyed, none except ours dealt with race, the Internet, and new media.

There are some encouraging signs. In 1996 the *Chronicle of Higher Education* reported on a program spearheaded by African American studies scholars in the Afro-American Studies Program at the University of Maryland. The director of the program wanted to put her Afro-American Studies Program in the forefront of research on the use of technology among African Americans, "building on scholarship in the field while reaching into the Black communities to familiarize more people there with computers" (Floyd, 1996). Her program supports the premise that one has to simultaneously embark upon the path of research and scholarship while working to expand the technology and knowledge of computers to the African American community. In her description of the curricular changes under way as a result of the Afro-American Studies Program's new emphasis on technology, Bianca Floyd, a writer with the *Chronicle of Higher Education*, writes of the University of Maryland's program:

This year, the program has added a technology section to the multicultural-curriculum course it offers to teachers in the predominantly Black public-school system of Prince George's County, MD, a Washington suburb. The section will introduce teachers to multimedia resources, such as CD-ROMS, which can be used in the classroom. In addition, faculty members have started research projects on the subject of minority people and technology, and the department is considering more such courses for undergraduates. (Floyd, 1996)

Programs such as the one at the University of Maryland will have the potential to transform traditional approaches to African American studies and lead the nation in research and innovative approaches to race and new media. African American studies departments have been slow to embrace new media—in part, due to economics, and, in part, due to tradition.

The Internet, like television before it, has the potential to serve as a low-cost community communication network to enable the community to send and receive information, images, and messages free from the influence of the gatekeepers of traditional media. But having the potential is one thing; having technology benefit the African American and other marginalized communities is an altogether different thing. The question of whether new media technology will be committed to the betterment of all of society is a question of power—political, economic, and cultural. At the present time, there is much tension between educational and public uses of the Internet, on one hand, and commercial and corporate uses, on the other. Will Black government officials be the ones to lead the fight at the local, state, and federal levels for requirements that guarantee universal access to the Internet? Will African Americans with

Internet and other new media skills begin the daunting task of educating Black elected officials about the importance of the information revolution?

It is incumbent upon the African American community to seize the opportunity to become involved in the information revolution, because the technology is changing so rapidly. If African American youth don't learn the computer skills at an early age, they may very well become extinct in the job market in the years to come. The African American community can leverage its political and economic power to ensure that the new information technologies avoid a cyberwasteland. Their contributions to new media democracy could include demarcating historical, economical, and cultural boundaries that have segmented the poor, women, and racial minorities to the extreme margins of technology and society. The struggle for cyber-rights is part of a long struggle the African American community has engaged in to fully participate as shareholders in American democracy. It is a struggle for self-determination and self-actualization. It is a struggle that must be won—now.

REFERENCES

American Electronics Association (1998). *Cyberstates update: A state-by-state overview of the high-technology industry.* Washington, DC: Author.

Baran, N. (1996). Privatization of telecommunications. *Monthly Review, 48*, 59-69.

Capitol Area Mosaic (1997). Proposal to Southern Bell for netcamp=97. Available on-line: www.mindspring.com/~caic/.

Crik, K. A. (1997, October 29). Access granted. *Georgia Tech Alumni Magazine, 73,* 27.

Curry, G. (1996). Editor's note. *Emerge, 7,* 6.

FCC chief says needy should have Internet. (1998, April 17*). Atlanta Journal Constitution*, p. E2.

Floyd, B (1996, December 20). Program in Afro-American studies explores the racial gap in access to technology. *The Chronicle of Higher Education, 43,* A 19.

France, A., & Simama, J. (1982). Taking cable to the people, taking the people to cable *Still Here, 49,* 67.

Government Technology (1998). Mayor Bill Campbell building the new smart city. 11, 46, 41-44.

Guernsey, L. (1997, July 23). Entrepreneur's E-mail service highlights resources on Black culture. *Daily On-line Report from Academe Today*. Available on-line: www.chronicle.com (archives).

Hoffman, D. L., & Novak, T. P. (1998). Vanderbilt University Project 2000 Study. Available on-line: www2000.orsm.vanderbilt.edu.

Kagan, P. (Ed.). (1983, January 11). Cable TV programming. *Paul Kagan Associates Newsletter*, 5.

National Telecommunications and Information Administration (July 1998). *Falling Through the Net II: New Data on the Digital Divide.* [On-line]. Available: http://www.ntia.doc.gov/ntiahome/net2/.

National Telecommunications and Information Administration (July 8, 1999). *Falling Through the Net: Defining the Digital Divide.* [On-line]. Available: http://ntiant1.ntia.doc.gov/ntiahome/fttn99/contents.html.

Poole, S. M. (1996, November 3). New window on the world. *Atlanta Journal Constitution*, p. P1.

Rifkin, J. (1995). *The End of Work: The Decline of the Global Labor Force and the Dawn of the Post-Market Era.* New York: G. P. Putnam's Sons.

U.S. Commerce Department (1998). *The emerging digital economy.* [On-line]. Available: http://www. ecommerce.gov/emerging.htm.

U.S. Department of Commerce (July 1995). *Falling Through the Net: A Survey of the "Have-Nots" in Rural and Urban America.* Washington, DC.

U.S. Commerce Department, National Telecommunication Information Agency (1995, July). Falling through the Net: A survey of the "have-nots" in rural and urban America. [On-line]. Available: http://www.ntia.doc.gov/ntiahome/fallingthru.html.

U.S. Commerce Department, National Telecommunication Information Agency (1998b). *Falling through the Net II: New data on the digital divide.* Available on-line: http://www.ntia.doc.gov/ntiahome/net2.

White, B. (1996, January 7). Web sites with class. *Atlanta Journal Constitution*, p. B1.

PART V

The Cultural Dimension

The technological advances of the emerging Information Society provide for an explosion of media about the cultures of American society. But how is cultural information about African Americans presented at the beginning of twenty-first century? "The information media have been dominated by white images and messages primarily for the white community since the inception of this nation," Dhyana Ziegler writes in Chapter 12. She cites new technologies such as CD-ROMs and the Internet as vehicles that African Americans must use to change the images of African Americans and their culture. In Chapter 13, Todd Steven Burroughs points out that while these technologies are mainly owned and controlled by the majority community, such technologies offer an opportunity for Blacks to gain worldwide media self-determination through self-definition.

On the global level, the African American community has always shared a common culture with its homeland. Too frequently, however, the global media have worked to paint negative images of Africans on the continent and in the diaspora in order to exploit differences and separate these people. In Chapter 14, Emmanuel K. Ngwainmbi addresses the issue of whether global information systems will enable African Americans and Africans to enhance their cultural similarities or whether they be used to emphasize their differences. He points out several cases where these technologies are being used to create a computer-mediated global Black community that may connect African and African American cultures and disseminate positive images and messages about Africans on the continent and in the diaspora.

Chapter 15 is where some conclusions are drown about the position of African Americans in the Information Society in America. John T. Barber and Alice A. Tait point out reason why the Black community can be viewed as an information community. At the same time, they outline the challenges that must be overcome for Blacks to gain parity with Whites in the various dimensions of the Information Society in this nation.

CHAPTER 12

Afrocentric Information Content: Historical Developments and Economic Opportunities

Dhyana Ziegler

INTRODUCTION

Mass media have the ability to influence mass consciousness and have the responsibility to inform, educate, and persuade the public and to transmit culture. However, the mass media have fallen short in their function in regard to the transmission of culture. Historically, the information and entertainment media have been primarily dominated by images and messages designed specifically to promote the White community as the dominant race and culture, while the contributions of other races and cultures have been basically ignored. Mass media have packaged and displayed every aspect of White culture as a mirror and ideal model of American society that should be emulated. While this narrow reflection of what exists in American society is not a reality, this trend of promoting Whites as the dominant culture in the packaging of information content has unfortunately existed since the inception of this nation. "When radio was born, stereotypical 'Amos and Andy' was the top hit. When television was born, the mammy show 'Beulah' was our representation. If we don't control our images and information in this new communications era, what will be our next representation?" (Pescovitz, 1996, p. D3). These images have followed African Americans throughout history and have had a profound impact on the perceptions of society toward African American culture in particular.

While mass media are not responsible for all the ills existing in society, they have contributed to the adoption of stereotypical images of a variety of races and cultures. There is little argument that African Americans have been historically portrayed negatively in the mass media, reaching back to the days of print advertisements used to sell African Americans into slavery, and to the broadcasting eras of *Little Black Sambo, Beulah,* and *Amos and Andy,* just to name a few. African Americans' struggle with the mass media to provide

Afrocentric content to the masses that clearly depicts a balanced view of the African American experience has been a long, uphill battle. African Americans have never been portrayed as a positive contributor to the American dream (Gray, 1989; Ziegler & White, 1990). This reality exists in the print and broadcast media, regardless if it is news, fiction, nonfiction, or drama.

Evidence of the mass media's neglect to provide the public with positive images that fairly portray the African American experience was demonstrated during the Civil Rights movement of the 1960s. The movement created daily headlines and broadcasts on the plight of the struggle and brought the mass media's coverage into question for unbalanced reporting and painting a rather negative picture of the African American struggle for equal rights. The Afrocentric content packaged and disseminated for public consumption became a focal point during the movement, which prompted President Lyndon Johnson to appoint a commission in 1967 to study the media's coverage of the riots of the 1960s and to determine the role of all forms of mass media in promoting negative opinions and perceptions of African Americans to the rest of society.

The Kerner Commission Report was issued in 1968 and held that the news media failed to portray accurately the scale and character of the race riots. The commission further stated that television, in particular, had been guilty of "flaunting before non-White Americans the affluence of most of the White society" and called the American media "shockingly backward" in their hiring practices and urged an immediate change in policy. The commission believed that until the management and ownership opened up, "ethnic groups would continue to perceive mass communication as a tool of the White power struggle" (Report of the National Advisory Commission on Civil Disorders, 1968). The conclusions of the Kerner Commission clearly support the notion that the mass media promote Whites as the dominant culture. Although there has been some progress over the decades, there is still a need for the mass media to educate themselves and raise their consciousness on how to package Afrocentric content as well as that of other cultures that contribute and participate in this so-called American dream.

Much of the criticism that the mass media received from the Kerner Commission Report still rings true today; African Americans are still being depicted as "symptoms" of society, while White Americans are still touted as "symbols" of society (Ziegler, 1991, pp. 2-3). Mass media create these "symbols" of culture in the arrangement and packaging of information content. Despite the many years of criticism, the mass media have continued to provide Afrocentric content and images that, more often than not, portray African Americans as criminals, uneducated, poor, lazy, and without any moral or ethical framework, rather than educated, moral citizens of society who not only understand but practice family values. This process of packaging and disseminating information on race and culture has far-reaching effects and contributes to the promotion and cultivation of racist attitudes among some members of society. According to Tan and Tan (1980), "The stereotype portrayal becomes real, and behavior in real life is guided by expectations drawn from the stereotype" (p. 309). This agrees with the mass media enculturation theory, which is defined as "the influence of mass media on individual perceptions and attitudes formed from information, symbols, and ideas received during a transmission of culture" (Ziegler, 1991, p. 2). "Enculturation differs from acculturation inasmuch as it is not concerned with the adaptation to culture but rather involves the processing of information about culture received and assessed through the mass media. Enculturation can result in a positive or negative form of feedback depending on how the information is packaged by the source and assessed by the receiver during the communication" (Ziegler, 1991, p. 2). Individuals who receive most of their information about African Americans from the mass media are receiving a rather myopic view of the culture.

According to Agee, Ault, and Emery (1988), communication in its simplest form "is the act of transmitting information, ideas, and attitudes from one person to another" (p. 21). The conscious or unconscious neglect by the mass media to provide Afrocentric content that reflects the true contributions of African Americans, coupled with the disparities existing in our educational system, has resulted in the cultivation of a perceived reality for some members of society that results in a narrow view of African Americans in general, and, in many cases, the view is less than positive.

Thus, the goal of achieving parity in the mass media arena in relation to the packaging of information and/or entertainment has been, and still is, an ongoing struggle. Although Black Entertainment Television (BET), *Essence Magazine*, *Black Enterprise*, *Emerge Magazine*, Johnson Publications, and other African American-owned and -controlled mass media have definitely made their contribution to the promotion and packaging of positive images portraying African American life as a whole, African Americans still need to own, control, and have a greater participation in, the packaging and dissemination of Afrocentric content to a global society (see Chapter 6 of this book for a detailed description of the contributions of BET).

The introduction to this chapter discusses some of the historical barriers that have influenced the plight of African Americans in the evolution of mass media and communications. The remainder of the chapter highlights some of the contributions African Americans have made to the Internet as information content providers and some of the entrepreneurial activities that have evolved. Lastly, the chapter explains how some African Americans are finding new avenues in the information age to help level the playing field that are/were not available in the mass media.

MERGING ON THE INFORMATION SUPERHIGHWAY

Because there is a dearth of mass media ownership by African Americans, primarily due to a lack of capital, few are controlling information or packaging

Afrocentric content in traditional forms of mass media (print, radio, television [TV], and cable). Although there are limited opportunities and avenues available to provide Afrocentric content to the world that would change perceptions and promote harmony through a transmission of culture in these traditional forms of mass media, new technologies have provided other avenues for inclusion and economic prosperity for African Americans who are ready to get on board.

Jerry Landay (1996) asserts that society has experienced a "one-way mass media that has, for a century and a half, conditioned us to be still and just listen, and we have increasingly held our tongues" (p. 18). He further suggests that society's silence has affected the democratic process and believes that technology may offer opportunities for more voices to participate in the community process. Based on previous research, it is evident that Afrocentric content has never found itself as a real priority in mass media except in media that cater specifically to African Americans. It appears as if the general public as well as advertisers and underwriters have been satisfied with the packaging and marketing of mass media products to the status quo. However, the information superhighway offers new outlets to level the playing field (Preparing information, 1996). New technologies have made it possible to open new doors and create opportunities for ownership, content development, marketing, and distribution of software and other innovative business ventures. But while there are many opportunities in the information age at every level, African Americans must be prepared to be major participants in this technological revolution.

According to Stephan Adams, chief executive officer (CEO), Adamations, "This is the first time in history where we actually get an opportunity to have true consumption of our history, using the tools of technology" (Preparing information 1996, p. 70). The editors of *Black Enterprise* also stress the importance of African American involvement with technology:

The African American quest for equality in the United States has reached a pivotal juncture, and technology is the reason why. Technology will either help narrow or widen the gap between Whites and Blacks in this nation. Take a look around—advanced technologies are present in practically every part of our lives today, from voice mail to electronic banking, and the influence it has in our lives will only increase as time passes. What we do to embrace technology will make the difference between the economic empowerment or marginalization of African people worldwide (Preparing information 1996, p. 66)

This is, indeed, a good time for African Americans to set a steady pace on the information superhighway and be a driving force in the adoption and adaptation of new technologies and seize the opportunity to gain economic prosperity. Before getting into the fast lane, however, African Americans will definitely have to understand the driving needs of society in regard to the application of technology and must be able to assess these needs and develop creative ways to participate in addressing these needs. Technology can be used as a means to help level the playing field and to narrow the existing gaps between cultures. This is the challenge for now and the future.

However, roads are being built and new avenues are now open to deliver Afrocentric content in a variety of venues. For example, Microsoft and BET have a joint partnership and are producing interactive TV and CD-ROM products that cater to the needs of African Americans, and both companies are reaping an equal share of the profits from the MS/BET multimedia venture (Tedesco, 1996, pp. 8-9). The companies share a vision and are serving a need as well. "The ideas for the alliance grew from a desire to avoid a society of information haves and have nots by providing the 5.5 million African Americans who have cable television with a compelling reason to go on-line. 'It will ensure that Black and urban consumers will be full participants in the information and economic opportunities provided by the converging communications industry,' says Bob Johnson Chairman, and CEO of BET" (Jones, 1996, p. 24). The Microsoft/BET deal is just one example of how African Americans can get involved with the marketing and distribution of Afrocentric content in the information age. (See Chapter 13 of this book for a discussion of BET's latest Internet venture).

This is an opportune time for African Americans to merge onto the information superhighway to adapt and adopt new technologies, and "to actually have the ability to control distribution of content, and that content can be anything from a database of information to a product that's going to be sold on demand" (Preparing information, 1996, p. 70). These new technologies not only can help level the playing field economically, but can provide a window of opportunity to control and distribute information to the masses. African Americans can be the source that influences mass consciousness through the production and distribution of Afrocentric content to the world. This is the challenge for the future, and that future is now.

INTERNET CONTENT PROVIDERS

Understanding the application of technology today will assist African Americans in capturing a corner of the new marketing opportunities that will continue to unfold in the twenty first century. The Internet is definitely the premier vehicle for the flow of information on-line. It is estimated that nearly one-third of all Americans were using on-line technology by the end of 1997 (Steele, 1997, p. 4). That number has been steadily increasing. The Internet represents a new era in communications and a unique way to do business regardless if one is a mass media giant or a small business.

Some African Americans have found a niche and are making inroads as information providers on the Internet, some are driving in the fast lane. NetNoir was one of the first African American-owned on-line companies providing Afrocentric content. NetNoir's philosophy is clear. "NetNoir aims to spread the beauty of Afrocentric culture to the masses while making a little money too. The company hopes to profit not only by generating traffic on America Online (AOL), but also by selling attractive content to other parties for use on corporate

Web sites or future interactive television channels" (Pescovitz, 1996, p. D3). E. David Ellington, chief executive of NetNoir, believes "on-line distribution to be one of the strongest forces drawing African Americans to the Net" (Pescovitz, 1996, p. D8). NetNoir has networked with other companies and is receiving content from *VIBE Magazine*, Perspective Records, Motown Records, AmeriCares, and Blue Marlin, which is a "specialty athletic apparel company based in San Francisco that is providing information on the Negro Baseball Leagues, etc." NetNoir distributes information in Spanish and French and has positioned itself as a "crossover" on-line service (McKissack Jr., 1995, p. 13).

While innovative efforts such as the MS/BET partnership and NetNoir are making their mark in this technological revolution, several small and medium-sized companies are also making an impression as content providers on the Internet. The Universal Black Pages provides an extensive listing of Pan-African Web pages (http://www.gate-ch.edu/bgsa/Blackpages.html). The Network Journal is a site that provides information to small businesses and also links to other African American sites (www.tnj.com). Black on Black Communications (www.i-media.com/BOBC) offers information from an Afrocentric perspective; and the World African Network (www.worldafricannet.com) offers a variety of information on the African experience. MelaNet (www.melanet.com), AfriNet (www.afrinet.net), CPTime (home.earthlink.net/~afrolink/), the Black Informa-tion Network (www.bin.com), and the aforementioned sites are just a small sampling of Afrocentric content available on the Internet. Currently, 100,000 or more Web sites with the African diaspora, and the number of sites is increasing rapidly. Search engines such as Yahoo, Altavista, or Excite will lead a person to more sites and links catering to Afrocentric content. In addition to Web pages, African Americans are also communicating on-line through chat rooms, news groups, list servs, and bulletin boards (Cadet, 1996).

Several entrepreneurs have been quite successful at merging on the information superhighway. The brains behind many of IBM's successes have been African Americans. For instance, Mark Dean headed up the design team that created the PCAT architecture, "which set the standard for all computers from 1986 to present" (Muhammad & Coward, 1998). Sandra Johnson Baylor was part of the team that developed "the prototype for the IBM Scalable Parallel Processor, the base machine for Deep Blue." Many other African Americans are CEOs of their own companies and have found the information superhighway quite a lucrative business enterprise.

African Americans, in general, are utilizing on-line services. In fact, a 1996 informal survey conducted by *Black Enterprise* yielded responses that suggest that African Americans are more "technologically savvy" than they are given credit for (Muhammad, 1996, p. 39). A large majority of the sample reported they wanted to read more stories on new technologies and specifically listed topics such as the Internet, small office/home computing, software, educational applications, computer upgrades, and new developments. Most used a computer at home or the office, and almost all of those who returned the survey had some knowledge of the Internet. The research clearly indicates that African Americans are interested in technology, although the sample was selective, and one can argue that it does not represent the opinions of all African Americans from various education and economic levels. Nonetheless, the Internet offers an opportunity for everyone to interact with the world and serves as a new viewfinder for the transmission of culture. In fact, the information superhighway may offer African Americans the best opportunity to change the negative images perpetuated in the mass media that have had a profound impact on the self-esteem and identity of African Americans in general. However, technology is only a tool. The challenge lies in providing good content.

CD-ROM PRODUCERS

While the Internet has provided opportunities for African Americans to merge onto the information superhighway, it is not the only way for African Americans to stake a claim in this technological revolution. Delivering information on CD-ROM, for example, is one avenue enabling African Americans to enter the fast lane and become involved in software development and reap economic rewards.

CD-ROMs debuted in 1985 and were used primarily by publishers and catalogers who engaged in business-to-business marketing. By the early 1990s the entertainment industry and the field of education found the technology quite effective for multimedia productions that included audio, video, and text ("Will New Technology," 1994). The market continues to grow. As Richard Cross (1996) explains, content delivered on CD-ROM has a lot of strengths in this new technological environment.

CD-ROM technology stands out from its sister interactive technologies in its ability to combine print, video, and audio messages in a package that can also act like a random access database. The CD-ROM can also be used in combination with other communications media to add even more content. For example, the CD-ROM can be used in combination with commercial on-line services and the Internet to retrieve updated and complementary material. It is, in a sense, not just one medium but a multimedium. (p. 14)

Most of the newer computers are equipped with CD-ROM drives, which widen the market for the distribution of products. With 15 million or more CD-ROMs available to Americans at home and at work, it is quite obvious why Cross finds it attractive. It is indeed a profitable enterprise.

CD-ROM development is a viable way that African Americans can become involved and participate in the production of information or software for distribution to mass audiences. There are many advantages to producing information on CD-ROM. It can store an enormous amount of information at a relatively low cost. The storage capacity for CD-ROMs is 680 megabytes, roughly about 340,000 doubled-spaced pages or 500 best-selling novels.

"CD-ROM is the least expensive way to transport large amounts of information from one place to another" (Beiser, 1995, p. 102). Production costs of a CD-ROM can range anywhere from $25,000 to $250,000. But while production costs may seem high on the front end, mass quantities of CD-ROM discs can be manufactured for less than a dollar per disc.

The market for CD-ROM development and distribution is wide-ranging. CD-ROMs are used for education, and entertainment. Games are quite popular on CD-ROM, and several businesses are using the technology as an advertising, marketing, and promotional tool for business. At the time of this writing, thousands of African American CD-ROM products were advertised on the Internet. These CD-ROM products are diverse and cover a variety of Afrocentric content and subject matter. There are CD-ROM products such as "African Americans in the 1870 Census," which is an electronic database from the American Genealogical Lending Library; "The Faces of Science: African Americans in the Sciences," which profiles African American men and women who have contributed to the advancement of science and engineering; "African American Pioneer Women and Men Inventors," which includes 163 years of inventions contributed by African Americans; and "The Struggle for Freedom," which examines the extent of slavery in the seventeenth, eighteenth, and nineteenth centuries and how Black slaves began their struggle for freedom. These are only a few of the titles that currently exist on the Internet, and many more are in various development stages.

CD-ROMs can also be used in education as a supplement or learning tool for any subject matter and offer opportunities for faculty and students to engage in creative activities. Several universities are experimenting with CD-ROM development. A project at Azusa Pacific University is experimenting with CD-ROMs as a tool to promote diversity and intercultural interaction (Pacino & Pacino, 1996). "Art and Life in Africa" is an interactive CD-ROM that recontextualizes African art in the cycle of life that includes over 10,000 images of 600 objects and 750 field photographs, 107 ethnographies, and 27 ethnographic maps, 1,400 entries in a bibliographic database, 11 chapters, 36 essays, and video and music clips; and "The Trans-Atlantic Slave Trade: A Database on CD-ROM" has been produced by the Obermann Center for Advanced Studies at the University of Iowa and is published by Cambridge University Press. Louisiana State University Library has introduced "The Faces of Science: African Americans in the Sciences," highlighting biochemists, biologists, chemists, physicists, engineers, entomologists, geneticists, and inventors. Florida A&M University, in partnership with the Commissioner of Education's African American Task Force and the African American Studies Summer Institute, proposes to develop a CD-ROM and a companion Web site that will permit access to content and multimedia resources in African American studies for use by prekindergarten to twelfth grade teachers and other interested stakeholders. CD-ROM development is just one example of the opportunities available in the information age to deliver content to mass audiences. The aforementioned are just a sample of the applications and options available for content delivery on CD-ROM in the education arena.

As technology continues to evolve, more African Americans will have an opportunity to become major players as information content providers by delivering products or services on CD-ROM, the Internet, and/or other multimedia venues. However, CD-ROM development is clearly one open avenue for African Americans to enter the information superhighway. No one person has cornered the market on information technology, and no one knows where it's going or how fast. However, in this technological environment, one thing is certain: technology will be a constant in our lives. Interactivity is definitely here to stay, and there are many avenues to explore and new roads to pave.

MEETING THE CHALLENGE

As discussed earlier, there are many opportunities available to African Americans to become a viable factor in the evolution of the information age and to take a firm stand in the control of information content. Although gaining access to capital has always been an obstacle for African Americans seeking to engage in entrepreneur activities and other business ventures, some business executives are being very creative in their approach. For instance, some are setting up "virtual corporations" that do not employ an in-house staff but instead hire freelance people "who communicate by phone, fax, and computer" (Cook, 1996, p. 264). This allows members of the staff to share in product development and receive a percentage of royalties as opposed to paying exorbitant salaries to maintain high-level, skilled staff. These innovative and cooperative efforts can bring high rewards. Several African Americans have found their niche through the forming of partnerships and utilizing "a team approach" to create and develop software products and services. Additionally, software developers have discovered that they can "bypass wholesalers by marketing a game, for example, as shareware on the internet and computer bulletin board systems" (Cook, 1996, p. 264). This enables the software developers to promote a sampling of their product to millions of customers free of charge, and then users can pay for the upgrades of the product. These are just a few creative approaches African Americans can apply to networking, producing, marketing, and distributing Afrocentric content in the information age.

To survive long-term in the multimedia industry, African American-owned firms will need to execute a number of innovative strategies. "Small companies are at the heart of growth in this industry," says Gary Schultz, principal analyst and president of the Sunnyvale, Calif.-based Multimedia Research Group. "However, Black companies and others will find it harder and harder to fight for shelf space as competition grows fiercer. New and established companies will need to partner with others on marketing and development, look for niche software markets, create new channels of distribution, and be able to distribute their titles on multiple platforms like CD-ROM, the Internet and interactive television." (Cook, 1996, p. 267)

The research indicates that African Americans will have to develop and apply a variety of strategies in order to compete in a new era of doing business. Additionally, African Americans must utilize, support, and consume the information content that is being provided on the Internet and CD-ROMs. Regardless of this challenge, African Americans who are successfully driving on the information highway emphasize the importance of African American involvement in the packaging and delivery of information content for mass consumption.

While African Americans are surfing the Net and enjoying other new technology applications, research suggests that it is essential not only to learn how to use technology but to play a major role in the packaging and delivery of Afrocentric content that will be delivered and consumed through technological channels of distribution. As Cook (1996) states: "As technology becomes increasingly influential in our everyday lives, African Americans must strive to be not merely end-users of multimedia and other information but producers of the software and hardware that will propel the digital revolution. Only in this way will we impact the way information is disseminated and what is told and to whom" (p. 267). In other words, African Americans must control and package content for mass consumption that does not distort reality regarding the culture but rather strives to achieve a balanced view of African Americans in general. It's time for African Americans to tell their own story in new Afrocentric content and form. The information age opens the door of opportunity.

CONCLUSIONS

Since information is power, African Americans have a big investment and an enormous responsibility in the information age. In other words, African Americans must develop and transmit information content that offers positive viewpoints and images of the culture and should attempt to provide avenues for others to gain access to that information. This technological revolution cannot be taken lightly. As indicated, technology can divide society into the haves and have-nots. I appeal to African Americans to take control of their destiny and control the packaging and dissemination of Afrocentric content. While these words may be repetitive, history has proven itself to be redundant in the negative packaging of images depicting the African American experience. It seems clear that the only way to combat these negative stereotypes and gain some economic control in this new era is to take control of the reins and ride in the chariot of success.

As with everything that exists, there are the good, the bad, and the ugly. The need for African Americans to become information content providers is great. It is important to combat the mistakes of other information providers in the past who have been the producers and promoters of negative stereotypes about the culture. African Americans must continuously strive to produce Afrocentric content that both offers quality and represents something to promote African American pride and culture. Don't commercialize and compromise the transmission of culture for profit. There's a world of opportunity available to African Americans to have a profound impact on mass consciousness and do it in a positive manner, as many have done already. The opportune time is now. While several have made significant contributions to providing Afrocentric content on the Internet, it is time for more African Americans to seize this opportunity and join the drivers on the information superhighway and begin traveling in that same direction. Otherwise, African Americans will end up in a traffic jam or fighting over parking spaces.

REFERENCES

Agee, W. K., Ault, P. H., & Emery, E. (1988). *Introduction to Mass Communications.* New York: Harper & Row.

Beiser, K. (1995, September/October). CD-ROM by the numbers. *Online, 9,* (5), 102-105.

Cadet, R. (1996, July). Where Blacks are on the Net. *Black Enterprise, 26,* 12, 33.

Cook, G. (1996, June). Entering the world of multi-media technology. *Black Enterprise,* 262-267.

Cross, R. (1996, February). CD-ROM technology forges direct links to buyers. *Direct Marketing, 58,* 10, 14-17.

Entman, R. M. (1992, Summer). Blacks in the news: Television, modern racism and cultural change. *Journalism Quarterly, 69,* 2, 341-361.

Gray, H. (1989). Television, Black Americans, and the American dream. *Critical Studies in Mass Communication, 6,* 367-386.

Jones, J. (1996, May). Bob and Bill's excellent (ad) venture. *Black Enterprise, 26,* 10, 24.

Landay, J. M. (1996, June 28). Put the masses back into mass communications. *Christian Science Monitor,* p. 18.

McKissack, F., Jr. (1995, September). Black culture on the Net. *The Progressive, 59,* 9, 13.

Muhammad, T. K. (1996, December). Black Enterprise readers are cyber-ready. *Black Enterprise, 27,* 5, 39.

Muhammad, T. K., & Coward, C. (1998). The Black Digerati. *Black Enterprise, 28,* 8, 49-58.

Pacino, M. A., & Pacino, J. L. (1996, January). Multimedia and cultural diversity. *T.H.E. Journal,* 70-71.

Pescovitz, D. (1996, June 3). The soul of the Internet. *Los Angeles Times,* p. D3.

Preparing information (1996, March). *Black Enterprise. 26,* 8, 66-74.

Report of the National Advisory Commission on Civil Disorders. (1986). New York Times Edition. New York: Dutton.

Steele, B. (1997, Spring). Ethics in new media: The protocol approach. *Poynter Report*, 4.

Tan, A. S., & Tan, G. (1980). Television use and self-esteem of Blacks. In J. S. Tinney & J. J. Rector (Eds.), *Issues and Trends in Afro-American Journalism.* Washington, DC: University Press of America.

Tedesco, R. (1996, February 12). MS/BET deal: Content's the thing. *Broadcasting and Cable, 126*, 7, 56-57.

Will new technology change the marketing role? (1994, October). *Direct Marketing, 40*, 14-19.

Ziegler, D. (1991, Summer). Multiculturallism: An opportunity for broadcast educators. *FEEDBACK*, 2-4.

Ziegler, D., & White, A. (1990). Women and minorities on network television news: An examination of correspondents and newsmakers. *Journal of Broadcasting & Electronic Media, 34*, 2, 215-223.

CHAPTER 13

Old Voices, New Drums: Black News and Information On-Line

Todd Steven Burroughs

Black newspapers, nineteenth- and twentieth-century products of the abolitionist movement against slavery and the fight against Jim Crow segregation, have historically been local and regional publications, with certain periodicals—the *Pittsburgh Courier*, the *Baltimore Afro-American*, and the *Chicago Defender*—having national and other outside-region editions during the height of the Black press' impact from the 1930s to the start of the modern Civil Rights movement in the mid-1950s. Racial desegregation of major, White-owned and –oriented newspapers and the dominance of local and national broadcasting and Black magazines in the 1960s and 1970s eroded Black newspapers' agenda-setting power. Although in 1999 there were at least ten national Black-oriented magazines, with the exception of *The Final Call*, the organ for Louis Farrakhan's Nation of Islam, America has no national Black newspaper. The advent of cyberspace, however, has not only considerably changed the playing field of news publishers but changed how large the field can grow. The on-line explosion of the mid-1990s has had a somewhat unexpected benefit to African American communities and, more specifically, to Black newspaper publishers and "wanna-be" Black newspaper publishers: the development of a worldwide Black press.

This chapter has three purposes. The first is to discuss Black news and information Web sites and their development as a means for African Americans to manage and control the global distribution of messages and images of themselves. The second is to point out the contradiction inherent in many of these Web sites' being owned by Whites. Finally, it proposes that Blacks should overcome the challenges of White control and use new communication technologies such as the Internet to achieve self-determination through self-definition. This chapter is in five sections: (1) Black newspapers on-line, which discusses the on-line editions of established (meaning currently in print) Black newspapers; (2) Black on-line newspapers, which were specifically created on the Web for its users, (3) Black-oriented Web sites and other Black forums, (4) contradictions of Black news and information institutions on-line, and (5) conclusions about challenges and opportunities facing African American news and information services on-line.

BLACK NEWSPAPERS ON-LINE

Since the development of the World Wide Web, established Black newspapers have posted their content on-line. The first Black newspaper to publish on-line was the *Baltimore Afro-American*. The newpaper's site (www.afroam.org), AFRO-Americ@, in 1994.) contains news articles, op-ed pieces, and editorials from the previous week's editions of the *Baltimore Afro-American* and *Washington Afro-American* newspapers. It also has a children's section, with games and world folktales. It has a culture section complete with chat rooms and art galleries. It also has a history section, the Black History Museum, with "exhibits" (articles) on Jackie Robinson's desegregating major league baseball, the Afro's coverage of World War II, and the Black Panther Party.

Between 1994 and 1999, at least ten other established Black newspapers came on-line. They include the *Baltimore Times*, the *Final Call*, the *Philadelphia Tribune On-line*, the *New York Beacon*, the (*Brooklyn, New York*) *Daily Challenge*, and the *Dallas Examiner*. Nnpa.org—the official Web site of the National Newspaper Publishers Association, the Washington, D.C.,-based Black newspaper trade organization and news bureau representing and serving approximately 200 of the nation's estimated 300 Black newspapers—has links to at least five of its members, including the *Chicago Standard News*, the *Florida Sentinel Bulletin*, and the *Toledo Journal*.

Most on-line editions of established Black newspapers examined for this chapter contained the following items: (1) top news from the paper's last edition, including photos; (2) editorials; (3) op-ed pages, (4) subscription information to the "off-line" paper, (5) archives of previous editions, and (6) biographies and mission statements of publishers. Although most of the Black newspaper Web sites feature news, some are just postings promoting the individual paper. The emergence of Web editions of local Black newspapers is an extremely important advance in African American newspaper publishing because it has made *local* Black news accessible to *all*. With the exception of Black press wire services such as Claude Barnett's now-defunct Associated Negro Press and the NNPA Wire Service, there had never been a way to read *local* Black news, in depth, from across America. With the advance of cyberspace, however, the planet Earth has become one big local newsstand, with local Black news linked by computers across the nation and the oceans.

BLACK ON-LINE NEWSPAPERS

With the advent of Web publishing, Black publishers and other entrepreneurs started creating Black news Web sites. Those sites, constructed with the format of newspapers, provide national and international news features and commentaries. They also provide standard features of Web pages, including chat rooms and links to other Web sites. These sites were created to perform typical newspaper functions: to inform and entertain on a regular, updated basis. These news Web sites allowed for *central locations* of news affecting Africans and the African diaspora to be placed for a worldwide audience. (Many of them even provide links to each other, allowing a browser to see a variety of Black Web sites without having to go through a search engine.) Three of the most prominent Web sites for Black news and information are *www. BlackVoices.com*, www.politicallyblack.com, and *The Black World Today* (www.tbwt.com.)

BlackVoices.com. BlackVoices.com was created in 1995 by Barry Cooper, an editor of the on-line edition of the *Orlando Sentinel* newspaper, a member of the Tribune Co. (the Tribune Co. is the parent corporation of the *Chicago Tribune*). *BlackVoices.com* started on America On Line before going to the World Wide Web in 1997. Although *BlackVoices.com* provides a brief compilation of news from the Associated Press, its main attractions are its chat rooms, career information center, and shopping stores. In 1999 it was reported that the site has more than 200,000 registered members ("Tribune funds," 1999).

Politicallyblack.com. Politicallyblack.com was started by two Washington, D.C.,-based Black entrepreneurs, Charles D. Ellison and Roderick Conrad. The site provides political commentary, links to federal government and legislative sites, and a "Minority News Daily" wire, compiling all articles of interest to people of color from major newspapers and magazines such as, the *Miami Herald*, the *Washington Post*, and *U.S. News and World Report*, and wire services such as Reuters. The site also carries links to more than 50 African American, African and Caribbean news sites.

The Black World Today (www.tbwt.com). Don Rojas, a former executive editor for New York's premier Black weekly newspaper, the *New York Amsterdam News*, created *TBWT.com* in 1996. *TBWT.com* provides national and international news from Reuters and the IPS wire service, the latter organization covering the Third World. Its most prominent feature is its collection of politically left to radical Black commentators, most of whom are distributed to Black newspapers for free.

BLACK-ORIENTED WEB SITES AND OTHER FORUMS

Communication is now more interactive and specialized, and old formats intersect with new technology. The new technology has suggested new forums. For example, although *BlackVoices.com* was included in the previous list, its construction suggests that it is more a Black-oriented Web site than a Black on-line newspaper. *BlackVoices.com, NetNoir.com.* and other Black-oriented Web sites function more as electronic town hall meeting places than news organs. (Some sites, such as *Everythingblack.com,* serve primarily as links to the scores of Black-oriented Web sites.) *BlackVoices.com* and *NetNoir.com,* for example, make extensive spaces for chat rooms and places for shopping and personal ads, not for news. Although *TBWT.com* and *Politcallyblack.com* are also interactive, their news and commentary functions are more dominant and prominent.

Another example of the old-forum, new-technology innovation is the E-mail newsletter. Newsletters have always served specific publics. E-mail newsletter publishers send the periodical right to your E-mail file instead of your door. By 1999 I had received both "The Minority Wire," a digest of news about communities of color, and "The 6*1*9 NewsQUEST Report: A Multicultural Review of the Media" on a regular basis. The first newsletter, "The Minority Wire," lists bylines, leads, and headlines of race-related stories. It carried its own "Feature Commentary" op-ed column, usually done by a nationally syndicated Black press columnist. "The NewsQUEST Report," produced by Tom Jacobs, an advocate for the numerical parity of nonwhites in the nation's White-dominated mainstream news media, is a compilation of articles (or article sites) or commentaries dealing with media "issues of interest to people of color" who "are still largely ignored by the mainstream media." One issue featured article headlines such as "Competition for BET?," "Spotlight Feature— Hollywood Continues to 'Ignore' Minorities," and "Quick Takes—Black vs. White Viewing Habits Getting Closer?" (The 6*1*9 Report, 1999).

THE CONTRADICTION: BLACK NEWS IN WHITEFACE OR WHITE NEWS IN BLACKFACE?

The most glaring contradiction in this new development of Black news media is that much of it is not "Black" at all. Historically, Black media were defined as advocacy-oriented institutions owned and operated by Blacks and targeted to Black audiences. As Black media, most "Black" Web sites would not fit all of these criteria.

- *BlackVoices.com* is owned by a White corporation and provides news about Blacks from major White mainstream newspapers and wire services.

- *Afrocentricnews.com* depends on Black news from the White-owned and – oriented wire service United Press International.

- *Politicallyblack.com's* "Minority News Daily" is a digest of articles from the *Washington Post* and other major White mainstream sources.

- Even *TBWT.com*, which provides a strong dose of African and Third World news, uses Reuters and IPS, two White-owned wire services. It also uses the White-owned Africa News Service and other non-Black agencies.

Many of these Web sites do provide strong Black perspectives via individual commentaries but provide established White-filtered perspectives on local, national, and international news. (An exception here could be made for on-line editions of Black newspapers, many of which provide self-generated local news and national and international digests from the National Newspaper Publisher Association (NNPA), in addition to major White wire services.) The "Black news" provided on Black on-line sites, then, is "Black" by topic only. *None* of these Web sites have their own national and international reporters. *None* carry investigative reports or hard-hitting editorials. At this writing (October 1999), *TBWT.com* national editor Herb Boyd is planning to beef up *TBWT.com's* content with the hiring of selected national freelancers who would write exclusively for the site (Don Rojas, telephone interview, September 1999).

CONCLUSION: CHALLENGES AND PROMISES

The Challenge: Financial Backing

Black news and information Web sites need strong financial support, such as that which Black-established newspapers provide for their on-line editions, or corporate sponsorships, such as those that the Tribune Co. provide for *BlackVoices.com* or that America Online and other investors provide for *NetNoir* Black Web sites that do not have financial backing from a parent institution are having trouble surviving. Even having strong corporate parents sometimes is not enough: *Our World News*, a Web site featuring Black news, folded within two years of its 1996 launch, despite the fact that Dow Jones Co., publisher of the *Wall Street Journal*, was one of its partners. *Our World* editor Joel Dreyfuss said he couldn't raise the money to keep going. Independent on-line newspapers such as the *Black World Today* are struggling to remain afloat. *TBWT.com* publisher Don Rojas was rejected by every venture capitalist he approached in three years. (Ward, 1999b). One Black Internet advertising agency executive suggests that a way to create a strong Black Web site is to "create a national Web network of the 250 U.S. newspapers targeted to Blacks" However, he was pessimistic that advertising alone would and could get a new Black Web site up and afloat, instead saying that fee-based services would have to be provided (Ward, 1999a).

The Promise: Convergence+Black Media=Worldwide Media Self-Determination through Self-Definition

In August 1999 Robert L. Johnson, chairman and chief executive officer of Black Entertainment Television (BET), announced the scheduled November 1999 launch of *BET.com*, which he hoped to be the premier Web site for African Americans, with a large expansion of traditional Web site features such as entertainment, chat groups, news, and shopping. *BET.com* has $35 million in investments from Microsoft Corp. and other media corporate partners, such as Rupert Murdoch's News Corp. and USA Networks (Henry, 1999; Li, 1999). BET is a cable television network begun by Johnson in 1979. It primarily provides entertainment programming in the form of music videos and recording artist showcases. BET also owns a string of nightclubs as well as jazz and movie pay-per-view channels and two magazines, *BET Weekend* and *Emerge*. The *BET.com* announcement was part of Johnson's plan to make BET a "one-stop" brand name for African American consumers in the Walt Disney Co. tradition of market saturation. (This chapter was written prior to BET.com's launch.)

Other Black Web site executives said the announcement of *BET.com* is proof positive that their ventures are valid. NetNoir cofounder David Ellington said the BET site could generate more targeting to Blacks by Internet companies (Li, 1999). *TBWT.com* founder Rojas agrees: "Rather than eliminating the competition, I think the move will improve our chances of getting recognition, respect and support from the investment and advertising communities" (Boyd, 1999).

What is left out of this primarily marketing-related dialogue is an important fact. With the coming convergence of print and broadcasting into the computer and on the Web, Blacks worldwide will be able to define their reality, via media, by and for themselves to a worldwide audience. If self-generated news and information are added to the entertainment and marketing mixes, Black people will no longer have to complain about the "White media," because the White media will be irrelevant to the political, cultural, and social reality in which they live in the twenty first century—a century without "mass" media. Technology has made it possible for Black people to set their own political, social, economic, and cultural agendas for the new century without White interference or control. It is already known that they will try to do this; whether they succeed depends on resources and will.

REFERENCES

Boyd, H. (1999, August 30). Will BET dominate the black Net? *The Black World Today*, www.tbwt.com/views/hboyd/hb_08-30-99.asp.

Henry, S. (1999, August 12). BET plans site for African-Americans. The *Washington Post*, pp. E1, E13.

Li, K. (1999, August 12). BET's big bet. *The Industry Standard,* www. hestandard.com/articles/article_print/0,1454,5888,00.html.

The 6*1*9* NewsQUEST Report: A Multicultural Review of the Media, (1999, May 19). No. 4.

Tribune funds expansion of BlackVoices on-line community. (1999, May 22-28). Press release in the *Washington Afro-American.*

Ward, J. (1999a, July 12). Beyond the black portal. *The Industry Standard,* www.thestandard. com/articles/display/0,1449,5587,00.html.

Ward, J. (1999b, July 12). Outside looking in. *The Industry Standard,* www. thestandard.com/articles/display/0,1449,5426,00.html.

CHAPTER 14

Black Connections and Disconnections in the Global Information Supermarket

Emmanuel K. Ngwainmbi

INTRODUCTION

As Blacks attempt to break through the shackles of slavery, colonialism, racism, and economic hardship, the media, in an effort to document the lives of Africans on the continent and in the diaspora, continue to generate misunderstanding, exploit differences, and promote conflict among these peoples. Newspapers, magazines, video/audio recordings, books, and television and radio networks in industrialized societies continue to depict Africans everywhere in a negative light, thereby furthering psychophysical separatism among them. This electronic colonization of African people might reach a new level with the introduction of the global information supermarket.

The use of the Internet, beeper, cordless phone, facsimile, E-mail, new telephone lines, and other high-speed communication links like video telephones and movies-on-demand in hitherto unreached regions has generated the potential for increasing the pace of communication, hence, creating a context for the manifestation of better living standards. Will Africans in the continent and the diaspora benefit from this technology, or will they miss the information revolution as they did the Industrial Revolution? Will the information technology (IT) connect them—bring them together—or will it continue to emphasize their differences? Will it generate psychocultural and economic activities between Black communities—Africans on the continent and in the diaspora? If so, who will design and supervise policies and by whose standards? To what extent will IT improve intracultural relations in African communities? Could one expect a Black cyber-mediated community, or will the gathering, processing, and dissemination of electronic messages only increase electronic colonialism and confusion?

These issues cannot be fully articulated without an examination of linguistic discourse, political structures, and contiguous historical circumstances in Black communities. In this chapter, community is explored in two contexts: (1) college-educated Africans and African Americans living in Africa and the United States, respectively, and (2) membership in computer-mediated communication—those who use or are capable of using computers in communicating. The first section of the chapter will dwells on the spatial aspect of community; it examines community as a physical entity determined by historical circumstances and complexities. The latter part deals with community as performer. It considers community as a holistic construct and describes certain conditions necessary for using cybercommunications in advancing international polity, economy, and understanding among Blacks.

OVERVIEW OF GLOBAL COMMUNICATION

The global information supermarket means using fiber-optic systems to generate, process, retrieve, store, and disseminate huge amounts of information around the world in a faster and cheaper way for the advancement of socioeconomic and educational needs. It was the brainchild of a United Nations Education, Scientific, and Culture Organization (UNESCO) conference in Paris in November 1978. African representatives joined the rest of the world to acclaim, among other objectives, "the declaration of fundamental principles concerning the contribution of the mass media in enhancing peace and international relations, in promoting human rights and in countering racism, apartheid and in preventing the incitement to war" (Kasoma, 1994, p. 77). Representatives of this meeting posited a New World Information and Communication Order (NWICO) because they viewed information as a possible weapon in the war against social, political, economic, and cultural inequalities around the world in general and in the developing world in particular. Even though the Third World was seeking a NWICO, the West, led by the United States, opposed it. Following a 1983 United Nations (UN)-UNESCO NWICO round table conference held in Igls, Austria, on communication technology, U.S. secretary of state George Schultz stressed the need for world regions to maintain human rights and the free flow of information.

During the Reagan and Bush administrations of the 1980s, conservative journalists, diplomats, and publishers organized meetings in Europe to denounce the NWICO (Kleinwachter, 1994, p. 16). Such opposition intensified bipartisan congressional opposition to UNESCO for attempting to promote a new information order (Macbride & Roach, 1994, p. 8). Indeed, the Heritage Foundation, World Press Freedom Committee, the International Federation of Publishers, and the Inter-American Press Association joined these governmental institutions in rejecting any program or proposal that sought to control or regulate the distribution of ideas and information. Although UNESCO attempted to resuscitate NWICO's image at the 23d Conference in 1985 by adopting a resolution that sought the promotion of communication development in underdeveloped regions and the creation of a better context for balancing ideas with action, it still failed.

According to Kleinwachter (1994), its failure was predicated upon the following: (1) a shortage of material and financial means and (2) the control and reduction of publications and seminars in favor of the NWICO. That resistance to a global communication process gave the United States and other Western media an unequal advantage over underdeveloped countries in Africa and communities with limited access to communication technology like African Americans. Meanwhile, Western countries with strong economies continued to invent sophisticated mass communication technologies and used them to construct and distribute news and ideas about their societies, based on Western social philosophy.

Newspapers, magazines, reference books, video equipment, television, and radio networks in industrialized societies treated Black issues in a negative light, thereby fostering psychosocial separation among Blacks. Historical studies have shown that African Americans have been portrayed in the audiovisual media as dangerous, subservient, and dysfunctional people. In their comparison of Black and White family behavior on television, Greenberg and Neuendorf (1980) also showed that conflict was a major source of interaction in the Black family. Although recent studies have found a shift in the portrayal of Blacks on television from stereotypical roles to positive middle- and upper-class roles (Gutierrez, 1988) as competent people (Stroman & Merritt, 1993), the change has been slow and limited. Stroman, Merritt, and Matabane (1989) have posited that the casting of African American characters on television is generally governed by myths about African Americans. They either were portrayed in all-Black, comical settings or were more likely to be cast as maids or handymen in the 1960s and 1970s (Stroman, Merritt, & Matabane, 1989, pp. 44, 46). Such portrayals of African Americans belittle their public image, especially in an emerging global society that has cultivated the habit of using television programs as its primary source of information.

A significant portion of information disseminated by African-based media networks contains Eurocentric values because African media personnel receive their training primarily from European educational systems. Also, there is a surging interest in Western programming among African media audiences initiated by early Voice of America and BBC broadcasts, as well as Peace Corps and popular magazines like *Playboy* smuggled into many African countries.

These technologies have influenced the world economy and the nature and sources of power and have increased the potential for industrialized nations to advance their economic interests. Similarly, the right to, and practice of, constructing news and ideas for other regions have led to the creation of an information supermarket that advances commercial and educational interests.

In the 1990s the Clinton administration said that the creation of a national information superhighway could chart the economic and social course of the United States (Jones, 1995). While the West has used information technology to advance its sociopolitical, economic, and military interests around the world, Blacks (Africans living in Africa and African Americans living in the United

States) have been deluged not only by their portrayal in the media but also by the unidirectional flow of information—from industrialized areas to developing areas.

NWICO has led to rapid development of regional news and information services like the Pan African News Agency (PANA) and Pan African Telecommunications (PANAFTEL). Moreover, international organizations like the International Association for Media and Communication Research (IAMCR) and the African Council for Communication Education (ACCE) have been established. Nevertheless, the emergence of the Internet has created an imbalance in information supply and consumption and made communities lacking this technology to be politically and economically dependent. However, these new information sources are an opportunity to move toward a new equilibrium, establish equality in the flow of information between the North and South (Europe, America, and Africa), and establish a common medium for the promotion of sociocultural and economic agendas.

In order for the IS to reflect UNESCO principles, two conditions must exist: (1) an information superhighway must be accessible to all, and (2) groups or individuals must be able to use the IS to promote their interests, including diplomatic and business relations. In order to assess the effective operation of Blacks within this highway, the following issues must be examined: the complexity and effects of Black history on their contemporary views of the world, how to address or resolve cultural differences in order to ensure better understanding among Blacks, the choice of an appropriate language for effective communication among Blacks in cyberspace, and the criteria for selecting and training IT personnel.

THEORETICAL FRAMEWORK

This chapter examines the ideological and operational aspects of communication technology within the Black communities in question. It assumes that information technology can bring change. Hence, agenda setting, uses and gratifications, and diffusion theories generally used in analyzing economics, infrastructures, and development matters may be considered for this study to determine how Blacks use the global information technology. The chapter further assumes that individuals or groups linked to specific communication channels may use such channels to create a social system. Katz, Lewin, and Hamilton (1963) suggested that people with a given system of values and who are linked to communication channels accept specific ideas, items, and practices over time. In conceptualizing the role of information technology in the Black community, other factors must be considered: the availability of media technology and its expectation to bring change and constraints among social groups within that community in using that channel for interacting purposes. Ogburn (1927) considered change as an important part of development by arguing that new technological forms (in those days, automobiles, telegraphs, and wireless radio sets) would break up the society because the rich ones would have more interactions than those who could not purchase such equipment.

Through this new technology, the rich would interact only with their kind and expand their socioeconomic and educational interests, while poor people would be deprived of such benefits, hence creating two distinct communities: the superclass (developed) and the underclass (underdeveloped).

That dichotomy creates a context for social inquiry for new scientific methods in analyzing social issues, as seen in the writings of Harold Lazarsfeld, John Dewey, George Mead, Kwame Nkrumah, John Langer, and other prominent, world-class social scientists. As I have stated elsewhere, newness means change, which entails using one's mind to think freely (Ngwainmbi, 1995, p. 20); it is the idea of affecting values, opinions, beliefs, and attitudes in order to integrate and improve lives (p. 18). Change has also been described as the introduction of new systems of interactions for better self- and community adaptation (Langer, 1979). Hence, technological diffusion and the diffusion of social practices are complementary to community spirit; however, the management and use of social technologies rely on shared systems of belief or shared values.

There are several ways of understanding continuity or rationale for using information technology. Hanson and Narula (1990) have identified them as "technological determinism" and "technological liberalism" (p. 39). The former, they argue, is a motivating force for change in society, and the primary effect of technology—technological liberalism—is moral, uplifting, and inherently good. Whether or not they are suggesting that both terms mean chance or choice, the concepts form a basis for examining the innovation, adoption, and use of information technology. Hence, cultural practices, work habits, linguistic orientation, and values are necessary for understanding the social context of communication technology. Here, communication should be seen as the most effective context through which individuals and communities can share their values, improve an understanding of each other's customs, and promote bilateral international relations.

THE COMPLEXITY OF BLACK HISTORY

Black history is charged with complexities and confusing information, which somehow limit the ability for Blacks to mediate community spirit and to progress through global information technology. The moral and social development of Blacks occurred under conditions of slavery, linguistic differences, imperialism, colonialism, and racism. For over 300 years, these conditions have created linguistic, psychological, and social problems among Blacks, suppressed community spirit, and provoked so much misunderstanding among Blacks that sociologists, historians, and politicians articulate the genesis of Black thought—the nature of gender politics and Black worldview—differently. Black aesthetic manifestations, experiences, values, beliefs, social structures like power and government, material objects, language, and erotic and spiritual relationships are not interconnected but are products of global historical circumstances. African historian A. Mazrui (1987) has said that the history of Black connections can be best seen in two contexts: territorial and labor imperatives. Mazrui (pp. 36-37) defines labor imperative as the period that produced slave trade and resulted in the emergence of Black America, while territorial imperative refers to the period in which the West considered territory as Africa's most important resource. These emerging imperatives of global purchasing power and investment in Black assets—land, language, and human potential/resources—could not have been realized by the cultural other—colonial/slave masters—alone. The slavery and colonial periods have provided the basis for latent sociocultural and economic interconnections among Blacks in that they underwent oppression from Europeans.

Political Implications

Arguably, the political context for Pan-Africanism started as a psychosocial activity and progressed into an institution. In 1775 Prince Hall, an immigrant from Barbados to Massachusetts, sought to improve the minds of Blacks through research (Fisher & Quarles, 1967). This activity set a precedent for a barrage of political coercion among African diasporans and Africans. From the mid-twentieth century, Pan-Africanism flourished in Central America, the United States, Europe, and Africa. A Francophone writer from Martinique, Aime Cesaire, (1968) revolted against the domination of the French language in his work "Return to My Native Country." In Africa, Kwame Nkrumah was advocating a culture of nationhood; in Europe, there was a strong hatred against Blacks, but that only helped them to recognize the values they had in common. These attitudes only prepared the context for a global expression of Blackness. Black studies scholar Molefi Asante (1987) further articulates this new Pan-African spirit:

The spiritual distress that settled over France after the first carnage of Europeans at the turn of the century, the racial discrimination practiced by the French in the Caribbean, and the economic crisis in Europe called into question old values, as well as the place of Africans in colonial territories. DuBois and Sylvester Williams had begun Pan-African conferences, Price-Mars had founded the Haitian Indigenist Movement, Harlem had a Renaissance, and in France, Leopold Senghor, Leon Damas, and Aime Cesaire started with what they had available and created the Negritude Movement. (pp. 111-112)

This resistance to Eurocentric values was not practiced collectively but among isolated groups; hence, they could not be sustained. The lack of a fast communication medium like telephone, fax, or Internet, common language, and the distance between Black communities have made them susceptible to other cultures and have complicated communication circumstances.

Despite these setbacks, the political activities of the 1960s and 1970s helped to promote a sense of communalism among Blacks. The Civil Rights movement, the independence of African nations, apartheid, and racism happened simultaneously in Africa and America. Although both entities used different measures to manage their predicaments, these conditions affected both Black Americans and Africans deeply. Information about racism in Africa and the United States was transmitted primarily through Fulbright exchange programs, books, newspapers, magazines, radio, television and travelers. However, America's influential economy and the availability of electronic media there made information more accessible to the Black American audiences than to Africans.

Radio and television (TV) played the greatest role in covering the predicaments of Blacks on both sides of the hemisphere. Through their coverage of atrocities, those media may have been promoting separation from, and discouraging interactions between, Africans and other Blacks. This phenomenon of using electronic media to influence public opinion and activity is not unusual, given that viewers cannot spread information verbally with as much magnanimity and force as the former. Long-running American TV programs like *Amen*, *Sanford and Son*, and The Jeffersons, dramas like *Roots* and *Shaft*, and movies like *I'm Gonna Get You Sucker*, which cast Blacks in subservient roles, were sold to African TV stations at very low cost. As a result, African audiences learned to underrate Blacks. Although most of the American TV programs projected Blacks in a negative light, most of the subsequent programs sponsored or directed by Blacks attempted to rejuvenate the battered Black image. For instance, Eddie Murphy's 1986 blockbuster movie *Coming to America* and Bill Cosby's long-running sitcom *The Cosby Show* depicted an aristocratic, value-driven, functional Black family.

A new perspective on Blackness spread in Africa and the diaspora when John F. Kennedy's administration implemented the Peace Corps and economic assistance programs in Africa. Through these programs, Afro-Americans (as they were known in Africa) and Africans became exposed to each other's customs. Americans lived in African villages, ate African food, wore the same clothes as Africans, and spoke the same languages as the natives. Africans emulated dress patterns of "Afro-Americans," from keeping Afro hair, to wearing broad-edged trousers—*patte de l'elephant*, as Francophones knew it. This diplomatic gesture further exposed Blacks to each other's lifestyles and helped them to identify physiological and cultural similarities.

The most influential activities that advanced Pan-Africanism in the 1990s were the African, African American summits held in the Ivory Coast, Gabon, and Senegal. Arranged mainly through telephone calls, fax machines, E-mail, and regular letter writing, these conferences brought together top resources from Black communities—policymakers, business and military personnel, scholars, athletes, medical professionals, and entertainers—and charted new directions for the manifestation and advancement of common interests between Africans and African Americans.

Similarly, foreign radio programming has been more effective in its coverage of Pan-African issues than African radio networks. Washington-based international radio, Voice of America (VOA), covered Blacks on both sides of the hemisphere in a timely manner. Although only a few daily programs dealt with Africa, VOA's selective broadcasting of political events in Africa provided Africa's educated elite with critical information, which could not be heard in African radio networks due to government censorship. Conversely, the African American educated elite was more likely to retain information about Africa through television exposure. Both groups received limited news about each other's community, as Black issues were not a priority in America's media agenda.

Nevertheless, because of its affordable purchasing cost, its ability to reach more listeners than television, and its ability to transmit international broadcasts, the medium-wave radio set may have influenced the thought processes of many Africans. On the other hand, the PanAfrican News Agency was started by the Organization of African Unity (OAU) to "rectify the distorted image of Africa, created by the international news agencies" (Wauthier, 1987, p. 66) and placed under the control of the OAU's Conference of Information Ministers (Bourgault, 1995, p. 175) in order to generate and report news about Africa correctly. Additionally, the source and coverage of local news are still strictly controlled by one-party or military regimes that make the gathering, dissemination, credibility, and consumption of information about Blacks almost inaccessible. The reason for this handicap is, that" Africa is told by the West that most of its news agencies cannot be used in Western media because it is mainly political propaganda" (Kasoma, 1994, p. 77). Conversely, the negative coverage of African affairs by foreign media has created among Blacks and other sympathizers a context for harnessing confusing views about their place in history and their actual role in world politics. Aesthetic manifestations describe the nature of connectedness among Blacks.

The Liberal Arts

Music and language form the bases for identifying culture and for tracing its origin and presence in time and space. African aesthetic constructs can be traced in Black American livelihood (Lomax, 1968; Richards, 1985; Asante, 1978, 1987; Asante & Asante, 1985) not only because Africa cradles world civilizations but also because Black Americans are descendants of slaves imported from Africa. Their speech, dress, music, and dance patterns are largely carryovers of ancestral African ways.

Through their interactions with Whites during slavery and colonization and through interracial marriages, linguistic evolution, and their experiences with modern technologies, Blacks have acquired new customs that have rendered their identification with a set of preferred values difficult. The racial activities between Blacks and Caucasians over time have created a hybrid or third Black community that comprehends the evolution and value of Euro technology, further splitting the Black community into three sociopolitical groups: the African or remote conscience, the African American, and the educated Black. The

African adores everything African but has limited or no knowledge of the existence of Black America. The African American who lives in America thinks of the self as Black, but this person has limited knowledge of the African continent and the African worldview. The third caste—educated Blacks—puts Africa at the center of his or her thoughts but also uses Eurocentric values, like technology and thinking methods, to address economic situations. This portrait of Blacks shows a psychosociological interconnectedness expressed through aesthetic manifestations and historical circumstances.

Music

Music is an integral part of Black culture because it organizes Blacks in political and sentimental stages. The importance of music to Blacks was first documented in the English language in the seventeenth century through a trade mission. Southern (1983) says that the Company of London Adventurers sent English sea captain Richard Jobson to Africa in A.D. 1623 to explore Africa's potential for trade; there Jobson saw music as Africans' ornament. Music, like other oral traditions, offers reliable clues to the past and intersperses every individual and communal activity (Southern, 1983, pp. 6-7).

Also in Africa music constructs a common social agenda because every festival, ceremony, rite, dance, or group activity uses it. The Negro spiritual and chant in the Black church are comparable to the dirge and panegyric in African funeral sites and festivals. Musicians and songwriters have successfully used lyrics to communicate social, economic, and political messages. Jimmy Cliff and Bob Marley (Afro Caribbeans), B. B. King and James Brown (African Americans), and Franco and Fela R. Kuti (Africans) of the old school raised an Afrocentric consciousness among Black youth in the 1960s, 1970s, and 1980s by singing about racial injustice and the ineptitude of Black political leaders. Through their music, African youth became aware that the problems in their community were similar to those faced by Blacks in the United States and the Caribbean. Moreover, the distribution of their records to other regions of the world helped to spread a sense of camaraderie among Blacks. This Pan-African activity set the pace for a better understanding of other issues facing Blacks.

Through aggressive marketing and distribution of their music internationally, Miriam Makeba, Suny Okosun, Manu Dibango, Hugh Masakela, Clarence Carter, Francis Bebey, The Temptations, Shaba Ranks, Michael Jackson, Marvin Gaye, and Pepe Kalle—sought to intensify Black connections. The messages in their lyrics ranged from social problems, to love and other universal matters, making them famous worldwide. Consequently, Black pride was represented in their fans' dress and dance patterns. African youth wear Michael Jackson T-shirts. Nightclubs still play disco and reggae music. That tradition intensified among African youth in the 1990s with the massive importation of American popular culture via electronic technology like television and cable programming (movies, news, docudramas, and comedy), video text, and videotapes. Among urban African youth, social acceptability is measured by physical appearance and the ability to rap, that is, speak street language. They wear baggy clothes and earrings and dance to rap music. Conversely, African American youth are not equally exposed to the former's popular lifestyle because they lack the same communication tools.

The strongest connections among Blacks may have been established through the exportation and distribution of music from Africa to the United State and vice versa. In the 1960s, when African countries were at the threshold of their independence from colonial rule, and Blacks in the United States were involved in Civil Rights movement, Black music became a construct through which Blacks shared a common agenda. African students returning home from Europe brought English music magazines like *Hit Parade*, and *Rolling Stone*, which contained articles about major artists like James Brown, and shared them with others. Passengers returning to Africa or traveling to Europe as well as exchange students took along records produced by Black artists in both communities. Decca, a British record company operating in Paris, and Makossa Records, based in Brooklyn New York (still in business), were the main distributors of Black music around the world. Quincy Jones and Harry Belafonte also facilitated the Black connection by promoting African music in American theaters. South Africa's Hugh Masakela and Miriam Mekaba, brought to the United States by Belafonte, communicated African ethnomusic and apartheid conditions to the Black community in the United States. According to G. Collinet (telephone interview, February 28, 1996), Africa's jazz artist Manu Dibango was sponsored in the United States by Decca because of the success of his gold album, *Soul Makossa* (V. Mbarga, interview, February 25, 1996). Dibango's performance at Madison Square Garden, his connections with the world-renowned music group the Temptations, and the camaraderie between African and African American musicians not only turned their songs into popular hits, but created vistas for the circulation and consumption of new Black music in the United States and Africa. Major city nightclubs, bars, and music stores across the United States and Africa carry Black music, including rap, rhythm and blues (R&B), soul, makossa, reggae, zaiko, and zouk. This caliber is suitable for middle- and lower-class Black youth aged between 14 and 40 because it communicates identical emotional and political needs.

Aesthetic connections were further strengthened when the radio station VOA (the Voice of America, received around the world) and its personality Georges Collinet interviewed Black artists and played Black music regularly. Listeners tuned to Collinet's program *Now Sound* to hear James Brown, Aretha Franklin, Clarence Carter, KC and the Sunshine Band, and Brass Construction or watched music programs like *Soul Train*, produced by Don Cornelius. James Brown's songs "Say It Loud, I'm Black and Proud" (1968) and "This is My Country" (1968) by the Impressions not only were popular in African nightclubs but became a political statement used by African youth to identify with "Afro-Americans" and to find solutions for change in their community. Musicians from both communities visited each other's turf to promote and share Black culture. In the 1970s James Brown visited Yaounde, Cameroon, and performed at Stade Omnisport before 30,000 youth. Earlier, Nigeria's Babatunde Olatunji, one of the first African artists who studied in the United States in the 1950s, became a formidable drummer. Olatunji was especially known for the piece "Oya" (1982). The artist's success created a conducive climate for the exchange and/or manifestation of Black culture; indeed, such Pan-African activities set the pace for a better understanding of Black political issues.

CONTRADICTIONS AND CONNECTIONS WITHIN BLACK HISTORY

One cannot clearly understand how a cybercommunication system that connects Blacks can be efficient without identifying two critical factors: the oratorical discourse and political movements. Such a system began among the slaves in the New World who used folktales, song, dance, and other oratorical forms in the plantations to retain their heritage. Some of the slaves fused African languages with a few English words to facilitate interaction with their owners and with each other. Since they had limited access to their owners, the slaves maximized an interest in retaining African languages and telecommunication systems like drums and flutes, which they eventually used to communicate messages only among themselves. Their owners quickly suppressed frequent interactions by separating the slaves into "house niggers" and "field niggers" and trained the former to think they were superior to their counterpart. Not only did their natural fascination with this new language demonstrate an increased appreciation for its subtleties and potentials, but it became a source for managing their political interests. The separation was not very effective at the family or cultural level since slaves did not come from Africa as house or field niggers but were made so by circumstances beyond their control, particularly the new environment and the policies of their owners. Hence, one cannot successfully argue that one caste— field niggers—had superior communication skills than the other because of its physical environment. However, members of this caste (field niggers) used numerical dominance and proximity to each other to develop codes for protecting themselves against the harshness of their masters and to maintain group spirit.

Although electronic media sped up the pace of communication, such technology was not available among the slaves. While African villagers used additional information technology like bells during this period, the pace of interaction was not much different than that of the slaves in America. Heavy communication took place only among regular residents, not between residents and village authorities. These political environments could be modeled for the designing of electronic, educational, economic, and linguistic messages.

Language

Language has always been an effective communication tool despite its complex intrinsic qualities. The ability for communication technology to decentralize message production allows multilingual participation. Today, it is not uncommon to notice French, English, and Spanish being used by Usenet groups in the Caribbean, North America, and Africa. Ferdinand de Saussure, Noam Chomsky, and other linguists have described language as having cognitive components. However, words cannot influence minds, decisions, and actions unless their users attach meaning to them. Hence, the ability to recognize images, and perceive structures as having meaning and the act of assigning meaning to words, signs, and actions constitute language; yet language becomes inaccessible to everyone when political and economic values are attached to it.

One of the major political and economic ramifications of language used in the Internet is the writing of pages for the World Wide Web. Cognizant that the Internet is one of the fastest sources for communicating messages, the control of Internet language and the setting of grammar rules to create Document Type Definitions (DTDs), the upgrading of browsers for new documents, and formatting of files are crucial in determining market size and user behavior as well as the meanings of information on the Web. For instance, Hypertext Markup Language (HTML), the most popular Web document format run by Netscape Communications Corporation, provides access to documents. Combined with Standard Generalized Markup Language (SGML), an older, internationally used standard organization page-description format, HTML will have more control in formatting documents and in setting language rules for the creation of documents.

That situation may create ownership problems for the Black market, which is more consumer-oriented than producer-oriented. If Black entrepreneurs and/or Internet users want to optimize its use for socioeconomic and educational development, they must have some control over the writing, editing, and formatting of Web documents; allowing such control in the hands of others would eventually affect the content of their messages negatively, as have slavery and colonization. Foreign control would dictate what Blacks write and how they write it and may even restrict their access to Internet services, especially when browsers have been upgraded. Conversely, Black entrepreneurs may not change HTML rapidly because they are more likely than Whites to show sympathy to fellow Blacks due to their limited economic resources and purchasing power. From a global perspective, this brethren concept of transacting business would be less rewarding than Caucasian and Asiatic business systems because Black culture is governed by communal principles—sharing—while its counterparts are laden with individualism. (The latter have a metrical view of life.) Action is based on individual growth. Moreover, nations that practice self-reliance have used linguistic autonomy to build economic, political, and military power to control other nations.

Hence, the New World economic order demands the use of a dominant language for continuity and easy communication. While indigenous languages are agents of local power, wealth, ethnic identification, prestige, and continuity, they lack cash value, unlike international languages. Here, cash value refers to the political and economic motives for learning an international language at the expense of preserving indigenous ones. When a language is perceived as having low cash value, its corresponding culture eventually loses its significance and becomes susceptible to any language with a high cash value. African people educated in European languages made more money and were given more authority than blacksmiths and traditional rulers. This new aristocracy bought and owned more property and trained others, who upset the economic and political structures of their ancestral community. No culture can be sustained when a new way of life brings humiliation and alienation. Since language permeates every aspect of life, it must be chosen carefully, based on its grammatical and semantic simplicity, to promote understanding and interactions between multicultural Black communities.

Linguistic imperialism may become a critical deterrent to the mobilization of an Afrocentric information community since over 1,000 languages are used in Black communities around the world. Put differently, it is difficult to select an appropriate language for every user of cybercommunication technology without putting members of one region at a disadvantage economically and socially. Users of English do not face that problem because it is the medium currently used by corporations, governments, and millions of people in the world. English has become the dominant international language for technology, commerce, finance, science, and travel. The use of this language has spread at a dramatically fast pace for numerous reasons:

1. America has military influence over other nations. Since the end of World War II, America has been given the authority to have "an army of occupation" in troubled regions. This has led to the spread of English.

2. The world's strongest economies emanate from English-speaking world powers.

3. Entertainment and news content are disseminated around the world through three of the five major information agencies based in English-speaking nations, namely, UPI, AP (America), and Reuters (London, England).

English is the major language of instruction and economy in most educational and popular settings in the world.

The use of English around the world makes it a veritable medium for communicating in an IT society; however, its intrinsic and extrinsic components have disoriented nonnative speakers and acculturated them. African tribes and slaves colonized by Anglo-Saxons never held a detailed conversation in their own native language without mixing in English words, and that has forced them to inculcate Anglo-Saxon ways. Since African languages have been infiltrated, there can be no original Afrocentric cybercommunity.

African languages are not likely to be used on the Internet because there are too many language groups. Selecting one language might cause political uprisings; one language/ethnic group might boycott the Internet. If Swahili or Black English, used by poor Blacks, is selected for use on the Internet, instructional materials must be translated into English to accommodate educated Blacks seeking connections with their own race. For either Swahili or English users, there is an obstacle: they must first transliterate the message of the new language into their own language, and internalize it before contextualizing or articulating it, in order to communicate efficiently with experienced users. Also, since hardware technology does not belong to any language but is available for use irrespective of racial, ethnic, religious, or sexual origin, Blacks can create new codes to execute their activities. Is it necessary to use only one language for cybercommunication given the polylingual nature of the Black community? There can be no cybercommunication without language. Thus, Blacks need to agree on a set of communication rules to avoid confusion and to increase possibilities of tackling socioeconomic issues collectively, unless language translators are built into the communication systems as intelligence agents.

The problem is further complicated by the fact that French-speaking countries have advocated the application of French on the Internet to counter the dominance of English. Although this process can unite Francophones in Africa and the diaspora, it may confuse English-educated Blacks, who form the majority of the Internet community, who are not familiar with the French idiosyncracy.

THE INFORMATION REVOLUTION

Communicating first through spoken messages, then through pictographs, the written and the printed word demonstrates people's desire to share information with one another. The storing, carrying, and retrieval of information is not only essential to understanding today's mass communication but also necessary for the assessment and control of political, social, and cultural institutions. Computer technology, which processes and transmits information more efficiently than mechanical devices (Biagi, 1996, p. 20), is responsible for many changes affecting today's society. The thought of a global society for Blacks seems frightening only to those in small civil societies whose culture may be quickly infiltrated by cybermedia, which continue to attract consumers in developed and developing areas. For example, Usenet, a popular network linking an estimated 4 million users, now reaches more than 90,000 sites across five continents (Reid, 1993). These sites are primarily research laboratories, engineering, telecommunication companies, government sites, and universities (Baym, 1995, p. 138). Usenet and Internet (E-mail) are building an Information Society among industrialized nations. Usenet users subscribe to groups of their choice.

OTHER OBSTACLES TO BLACK CONNECTIVITY

The presence of, and recent innovations in, information technology in Africa are limited. Only a few countries have complete access to IT. In 1994, for instance, the University of Dar es Salaam, Tanzania, produced its first journal on CD-ROM technology and Micro CDs for librarians, archivists, researchers, documentalists, and other information specialists. In the 1990s some African American firms designed distance learning programs to enable Black students in Africa and the United States to receive lessons from each other's region. Despite those advancements, the continent's bleak economic landscape has forced it to become a minor participant in the global information supermarket. On most university campuses, there is no computer terminal for students and university professors to retrieve research material because of its high cost. The IBM PC with a 386-16 megahertz processor became outdated in 1989 and was replaced by the Pentium model; it costs about 1 million francs, CFA (approximately U.S. $2,000), or higher, depending on the African currency. CD-ROMs and Internet services are being introduced only in selected African universities and are available only to scientists. BITNIS, an electronic mail service, facilitates automatic searches for the National Library of Medicine in the U.S. databases, but it does not transact E-mail directly from source to receiver (Ngwainmbi, 1996). This makes computer-mediated communication difficult between African and other Black scientists around the world because the former may not be able to afford the cost of Internet services due to their low per capita income level.

Another obstacle is the African's fear of technology. Traditionally, Africans have been raised in a culture of secrecy. Information for public interest is normally disseminated through state-controlled media channels: government media, government-paid journalists, or traditional rulers (Ngwainmbi, 1995). Information about the state comes through those channels, and it is normally censored to protect national security.

Weak economies and racial discrimination problems faced by Blacks could make their connectivity in the information supermarket almost inaccessible. There may also be a decline in personal interaction among Blacks if they continue to use IT to work, learn, shop, bank, share ideas, and converse without leaving the house, possibly diminishing the level of closeness and fun usually associated with interpersonal discourse. African users may become the greatest losers because their primary source for mediating messages and for constructing human relationships has been less complicated and less costly—face-to-face communication—compared to Western societies that have used advanced IT for decades.

SUMMARY

Historic-political circumstances, the content of media programs, and media practitioners have obfuscated international understanding of Black livelihood, just as the connections between Africans and African Americans have become less effective (unlike in the 1960s, 1970s, and 1980s) because of the intrusion of advanced information technology. This condition has created economic and knowledge gaps on a large scale between Africans and African Americans in general and educated Blacks in particular. Students and professors have virtually no reliable information about both communities on the Internet. Rather, information has been created, processed, and accessed by individuals who lack the expertise or funds to collect reliable and adequate information. The reluctance by certain Black policymakers, and the lack of Black educators, to engage in meaningful dialogue that would expedite the use of IS for their economic advancement has created a context for disconnecting cultural connections built by their predecessors (artists, musicians) prior to the information revolution. Despite this dismal picture, Blacks could benefit from the IT revolution.

SUGGESTIONS

The African American Communication Landscape

Although limited connectivity between Africans and African Americans has been caused by political problems, the African American elite can play the lead role in improving connectivity among Blacks because they have direct access to IT. Through the American Constitution, especially First Amendment rights, African Americans have the potential to purchase and use IT equipment freely. They can use their constitutional rights to create better opportunities than Africans who are still living under autocratic circumstances. With the many banks, other lending opportunities, and major private corporations, Black entrepreneurs can seek ownership of communication systems by investing in start up projects or by acquiring partial ownership with others. Anthony Williams, director of the FCC Office of Communications Business Opportunities, has estimated that the cost of participatory ownership may be too high for minorities because of different procedures involved (Scott, 1995). The auction price of a personal communications services license is approximately $18 million, but it is minimal compared to the total cost of building a wireless communications system. That is substantial capital for a Black business community; however, in order to have complete control and to compete for customers, Black entrepreneurs should raise funds not only to obtain their own license and build a powerful information system but also to operate, market and sustain it. Rather than invent telecommunication technology, which is more costly, they should offer more services and programming for the new media because more Black-oriented on-line services are being created every month. African Americans are setting up way stations on the IS where information on social issues, careers, and business opportunities are shared (Hayes & Sabir, 1995). Market research on outdoor billboards, television, newspaper and magazine commercials, and posters and business Black directories can be registered on-line at affordable rates. Certainly, Blacks can maximize business development opportunities and international understanding and eventually influence world politics if more Blacks continue to use the Internet and other information systems.

Communication is not limited to one-on-one E-mail or on-line correspondence. With the invention of satellite systems, special interest groups (SIGs) can have databases, discussions, and networking as frequently as desired. Some African American forums have five or more people discussing Black history and other world issues in cyberspace (Hayes & Sabir, 1995). Since cyberspace activity does not involve personal contact, the encoder and decoder can have an effective interaction because they do not know much about each other's background. Race, ethnic origin, social class, profession, gender, and other demographics may reduce the potential for a successful interaction because they make people biased toward each other. Since cybercommunication is largely governed by intuition, participants are encouraged to respect others' opinions, as racism and related issues could negate the benefits of taking part in the many ongoing discussions on the Internet. Conversely, if Black participants express their sentiments to racial slurs or consider some discussions a personal attack on their integrity, they may be limiting their use of the technology and, therefore, reducing their chances of benefits that Internet communication offers: information on careers, jobs, business, news, and research findings.

Networking in cyberspace can be seen as a form of group therapy. Participants share ideas, interests, feelings, and objectives. This new form of communication is more rewarding than the face-to-face model because initially members can learn much about how others think and what they know without knowing each other's demographics. On the other hand, personal discussion is laded with subjective concepts of people's capabilities. The Internet could be more useful to Africans and African Americans in breaking down cultural barriers and misunderstandings erected by Western media, colonization, and slavery than music, art, literature, exchange programs, and classroom lectures about Blacks. That a Black person can have direct access to information about each other should be a rewarding experience because nonmediated messages are more reliable.

Although Blacks and other private organizations in the United States have erected libraries in Black communities that carry material on Black heritage, poorer communities do not have enough electronic information systems or funds to manage them; hence, they are deprived of knowledge on world affairs. Not only should the 1996 Telecommunication Reform Act eventually give historically Black institutions and low-income areas access to electronically processed information, but wiring such areas would give these entities opportunities to generate, process, store, retrieve, and disseminate messages (Figure 14.1).

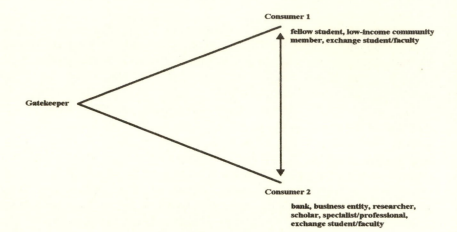

Figure 14.1
Cyber Communication Model for Black Users

Expected long-term results are economic empowerment through information circulation, business partnership, education, and understanding. Expected short-term results are social interaction: basic knowledge on shared social issues, like relationships, politics, religion, also advertising of Web sites, exchange and distribution of international business directory, job information.

The African Communication Landscape

While cyberspace communication is the best source of connectivity for Blacks. Africa's participation in the IS may appear difficult given its seemingly ephemeral politicoeconomic crises. However, the African elite (college-level person, academic, and other professionals trained in a universal language) can use this linguistic connection to create links with Black leaders elsewhere for the discussion of, and solutions to, problems affecting development in the Black community. The steadily increasing educated class in Africa, energized by the European colonial process, political independence, and the rising middle class in Black America, was brought into being by historical circumstances; slavery, emancipation, the Black Power movement, the National Association for the Advancement of Colored People (NAACP), the Civil Rights movement, African/African American summits, and the Nation of Islam can set a pace for better interaction among Black IT users by designing low-cost computer programs and Web sites and by funding the distribution of IS messages to universities, high schools, hospitals, clinics, and community centers in Black areas.

THE TOWER-OF-BABEL CONCEPT

Although the educated elite reserves the right to design and distribute messages is condescending and unrealistic ways, Black politicians and diplomats have not been able to bridge the economic and knowledge gap between Africans and African Americans, especially in the 1990s—the age of globalization. Since political independence, African leaders and artists have not taken significant steps to resolve such gaps. Hence, the African educated elite should enhance this relationship by advertising NGO programs on the Internet and by increasing information-oriented organizations to promote peace, unity, and educational objectives. Without an agenda that involves government input, the educated elite may not be able to present an acceptable platform to their African American colleagues. However, as more African governments privatize their Information Ministries, nonofficial groups could have more access to different information sources. Besides expecting objective news coverage of Africa when PANA expands its operations by establishing news bureaus in major international cities like London, Paris, New York, Tokyo, and Berlin, journalists around the world would have direct access to news about the continent.

Some African information agencies have been making progress in distributing information to different world regions. The ACCE (see note), PANA, and WALA and information supermarkets like PADISNET, AfriNet, and ZAMNET, as well as regional networks formed by African communities abroad like CAMnet, are contributing to information circulation in and beyond Africa. Cameroonians and their friends who share social tidbits and news about Cameroon use CAMnet. However, these agencies do not have enough funds to sustain operation. Internet information from African researchers is decoded and processed at sites beyond Africa; hence, its original form is polarized (Ngwainmbi, 1996). Despite these situations, Africans who are normally discreet with commercial and intellectual property should become open to suggestions, ideas, and public criticism, as these are common characteristics among Internet users worldwide.

A World African Business Network and a Black College Network would give Black administration, faculty, students, staff, and other business an opportunity to share information. This boss-boss, employee-employee, client-client, and top-down or down-top pattern would increase productivity among Blacks if such networks are established.

A computer-mediated global Black community is emerging. Of the 30 million Internet users, thousands of Black professionals and students are sorting, sending, receiving, and reading messages by other users. The Nubian Network—an infrastructure focusing on Internet research, management, and service,—and the Africa World Press are some of the important stations available to Blacks. Also available in the United States are accounts and way stations set up by Africans and Peace Corps Volunteers (PCVs) to help users retrieve information about Africa.

Among the 25,000 networks and/or 71 countries connected to the Internet worldwide, Africa has 150, with the majority of connections in South Africa.

Forty-six of the 51 African countries have Internet access, 30 of which use the fidoNet—a PC-to-PC dial-up network. Wresch (1995) has said that only Egypt, Ghana, Tunisia, Zambia, Zimbabwe, Kenya, and South Africa have full Internet connectivity and World Wide Web browsing capabilities. Tunisia has had E-mail services since 1987, connected through a leased line between Institute Regional des Sciences Information et des Telecommunications (IRSIT) and a French Internet node in Paris. With about 25 hosts and over 200 connected computers generating 1.3 gigabytes of traffic every month, Tunisia is prepared to interact with the Haitian community and the increasing French-speaking African population in the United States Angola, which has a four-year-old E-mail system that connects over 66 organizations, and South Africa, with over 140, will become primary partners with most African American users because English is the instructional mode there. This sort of connection will be easier when automatic language translation mechanisms become available in the computer.

Although the majority of the world's least developed telecommunication systems are in Africa, with a national density of two telephone sets per 1,000 and one computer per 1,000, the future of the IS in Africa is promising. The United Nations, World Bank, AT&T, and other international corporations are donating or selling computers, telephone services, equipment, and other technology to Africa's educational institutions and persons. The Africa One Program, a fiber-optic network expected to connect West Africa and the world by 1998, will help the continent in participating in the globalization process. The fact that African governments are privatizing the telecommunication sector, as evidenced by the ongoing Africa One project and negotiations with major telephone companies to supply more private lines, is itself a positive revolution, given that African governments have owned and controlled the mass media.

Finally, administrative researchers—uses and gratifications, agenda setting, and diffusion theorists—need to revisit and broaden such theories to include the dynamics of the information revolution.

NOTE

1. The ACCE was created out of IAMCR to address information and mass media issues facing Africa, to assess communication activities in Africa, to promote scholarly exchange, and to provide an alternative concept on Africa. Headquartered in Nairobi, Kenya, it holds annual meetings in African cities and publishes works by members. Its maiden publication, *Media*, and sustainable development containing 16 contributors address theoretical and practical issues related to the media and development in Africa. It now oversees the publication of *Africa Media Review*, an internationally acclaimed scholarly journal. ACCE is the most conspicuous communication association in Africa.

REFERENCES

Asante, M. (1978). Intercultural communication: An Afrocentric inquiry into encounter. In B. Williams & O. Taylor (Eds.), *International Conference on Black Communication*. A Bellagio conference. New York: Rockefeller Foundation.

Asante, M. (1987). *The Afrocentric Idea*. Philadelphia: Temple University Press.

Asante, M., & Asante, W. K. (1985). *African Culture: The Rhythms of Unity*. Westport, CT: Greenwood Press.

Battle, L. S., & Harris, O. R. (1995). *The African American Resource Guide to the Internet*. Columbia, MD: Demand Press.

Baym, K. N. (1995). The emergence of community in computer mediated communication. In S. Jones, (Ed.), *Cybersociety*. Thousand Oaks, CA: Sage, pp. 138-163.

Biagi, S. (1996). *Media Impact*. Belmont, CA: Wadsworth.

Bourgault, M. L. (1995). *Mass Media in Subsaharan Africa*. Bloomington: Indiana University Press.

Césaire, A. (1968). *Return to my Native Land*. Paris: Présence Africaine.

Davies, C. (1985). The politics of identification in the Trinidad calypso. *Studies in Popular Culture, 8*, 12.

Fisher, L., & Quarles, B. (1967). *The Negro American: A Documentary History*. Glenview, IL: Scott, Foreman.

Greenberg, B. S., & Neuendorf, K. (1980). Black family interactions on television. In B. S. Greenberg (Ed.), *Life on Television: Content Analysis of U.S. TV Drama*. Norwood, NJ: Ablex, pp. 173-181.

Gutierrez, F. (1988, September 11). Black TV roles reflect changed attitudes. *Atlanta Journal*.

Hanson, N., & Narula, U. (1990). *New Communication Technologies in Developing Countries*. Hillsdale, NJ: LEA.

Hayes, C., & Sabir, N. (1995, April). Surf the cyberspace. *Black Enterprise, 54*.

Jones, S. (Ed.) (1995). *Cybersociety*. Thousand Oaks, CA: Sage.

Kasoma, F. (1994). Ironies and contrasts. In G. Gerbner, H. Mowlana, & K. Nordenstreeng (Eds.), *The Global Media Debate: Its Rise, Fall and Renewal*. Norwood, NJ: Ablex, pp. 77-81.

Katz, E., Lewin, M. L., & Hamilton, H. (1963). Traditions of research on the diffusion of innovations. *American Sociological Review, 28*, 237-252.

Katzner, K. (1992). *The Languages of the World*. London: Routledge & Kegan Paul.

Kleinwachter, W. (1994). Three waves of the debate. In G. Gerbner, H. Mowlana, & K. Nordenstreng (Eds.), *The Global Media Debate*. Norwood, NJ: Ablex, pp. 13-20.

Langer, J. (1979). *Theories of Development*. New York: Holt, Rinehart, & Winston.

Lomax, A. (1968). *Folk Song Style and Culture*. Washington, DC: AAAS.

Macbride, S., & Roach, C. (1994). The new international information order. In G. Gerbner, H. Mowlana, & K. Nordenstreng (Eds.). *The Global Media Debate*. Norwood, NJ: Ablex, pp. 3-12.

Mazrui, A. (1987). The world economy and the African/Afro-American connection. In A. Cromwell (Ed.), *Dynamics of the African/Afro-American Connection: From Dependency to Self-Reliance*. Washington, DC: Howard University Press, pp. 36-53.

Mowlana, H. (1993). Toward a NWICO for the twenty first century? *Journal of International Affairs, 47* (1), 59-72.

Ngwainmbi, E. (1995). *Communication Efficiency and Rural Development in Africa*. New York: University Press of America.

Ngwainmbi, E. (1996, Fall). Africa in the global infosupermarket: Perspectives and prospects. *Africa Media Review*, 2.

Ngwainmbi, E. (1997). *Transferring Communication Technology to Developing Countries: Social, Political, Economic, and Educational Implications*. Lanham, MD: University Press of America.

Ogburn, W. (1927). *Social Change with Respect to Culture and Original Nature*. Chicago: University of Chicago Press.

Regis, H. (1995). Orientation and interest in popularity of the works of Caribbean musicians. *Howard Journal of Communication, 5* (3), 184-194.

Reid, B. (1993, August). Usenet readership report. Newsgroup: News Lists.

Richards, D. (1985). The implications of African American spirituality. In M. Asante & K. W. Asante (Eds.), *African Culture: The Rhythms of Unity*. Westport, CT: Greenwood Press, p. 20.

Scott, S. M. (1995, June). Quest to own the information highway. *Black Enterprise*, 55.

Southern, E. (1983). *The Music of Black America: A History*. New York: W. W. Norton.

Stroman, C., & Merritt, B. (1993). Black family imagery and interactions on television. *Journal of Black Studies, 23* (4), 492-499.

Stroman, C., Merritt, B., & Matabane, W. P. (1989). Twenty years of Kerner: The portrayal of African Americans on prime-time television. *Howard Journal of Communication, 2* (1), 44-56.

Vaughan-Nichols, S. (1995, May) Web language wars. Internet.

Wauthier, C. (1987, March-April). *PANA: The voice of Africa*. Africa Report.

Wresch, W. (1995, November). New lifelines. *Internet World*, 102.

CHAPTER 15

Is Black America an Information Community?

John T. Barber and Alice A. Tait

CONCLUSIONS

In this book we have presented a systematic discussion of African Americans' status in the Information Society and addressed some critical issues in determining whether or not Black America *is* an "information community." In our estimation, Black America *is* an information community. Black people are making strides in every dimension of the Information Society that we have examined here. Nevertheless, tremendous challenges face this group in excelling in a rapidly changing, information-based world. Now we turn to some conclusions on this central question and make some recommendations for continuing this line of inquiry.

Our analysis has shown that Blacks are consumers and users of information technology, adopt such technology sometimes at a greater rate than their White counterparts, use the Internet for a variety of purposes, and have concerns about the use of information technology by the majority of the community as a surveillance device to invade their personal privacy. African American women seem to be playing a major role in the technology adoption process in the Black community. African Americans, as stated by *Black Enterprise*, are more sophisticated information technology users than some may have assumed.

While Blacks are consumers and users of information technology, they are facing serious difficulties as owners and controllers of information industries. Political and economic systems that would aid Blacks in this area have been dismantled or failed to improve the Black ownership profile. The African American newspaper faces a decline in its utility and certain demise if it does not use its economic strength to adopt new information technologies and systems. African American newspapers are slow to adopt the systems that majority newspapers have put into place. With the recent sale of radio and television stations by Black broadcasters, the direction of ownership and control of broadcasting by African Americans has changed. A few years ago, Black ownership was small but increasing; as the information age goes into full swing, Black ownership is even smaller and diminishing. One of the positive outlooks for the Information Society is that new industries and business opportunities will form because of the proliferation of new technologies. One could assume that new industries that will open up will provide African Americans new opportunities to control emerging information industries. African American Personal Communication Services (PCS) businesses formed recently as a result of auctions of spectrum space by the Federal Communications Commission (FCC) are a case in point. The *Adarand* decision and other political moves are limiting the participation of Blacks in new information businesses.

Blacks are also facing a critical challenge in gaining the jobs in which information and knowledge are created, and Black educational institutions do not have the resources to produce Black information professionals. Training African Americans to move from information-processing and distribution occupations to those that involve the creation of information and knowledge may be one of the greatest challenges to this community in the next few decades.

As the world of work concentrates on the production and distribution of information, Blacks are poorly represented in research and development, mass media, and other high-end information professions. At the same time, Blacks are concentrated in greater proportions in positions such as post office workers and information machine operators than they are represented in the society in information processing and distribution.

Accessing major computing networks for the purpose of solving social problems is fundamental to participation in the Information Society. As the world moves toward electronic politics, accessing networks becomes tantamount to political participation. While Blacks are becoming more and more computer-literate and making their presence felt in cyberspace, they do not have the computing access of their White counterparts. This problem is being dealt with in programs and activities all over the nation, but these efforts are relatively small.

Information technology has put great power into the hands of African Americans to produce images and messages about African American culture. Moreover, it provides the opportunity for unified messages to emanate from Blacks around the world. This technology could change the negative portrayal of Blacks in this country and across the globe. Some steps are being taken in this direction in America and the diaspora as well as in Africa, but the problems are great and difficult to overcome.

In every era of development in this nation, African Americans have been actors in the dramatic changes that have taken place in America. The current era is no different. The editors of *Black Enterprise* summarized it this way in their March 1998 issue: "For African Americans especially, the Information Age is a time of great promise. 'The impending information and telecommunications revolution is possibly our best chance to become masters and creators of our own destiny,' says Technology editor Tariq K. Muhammad. 'We were locked out of opportunities during the Industrial Revolution by racism. This time, the only thing that will hold us back is our own lack of foresight'" (p. 13).

RECOMMENDATIONS

There are three areas in which recommendations for the assessment of Blacks' prosperity in the Information Society must be considered: political, economic, and scholarly. Black political leaders should form a global agenda for establishing policies that will aid Blacks in gaining a strong foothold in the Information Society. Reversing policies that are currently working against African American ownership and control of information industries, for example, should be at the top of such an agenda.

Corporate leaders should find ways to work with Black colleges and universities and school systems to help them obtain resources to train information professionals and intelligent consumers and users of information technology. The Black community has many hurdles to overcome to be a strong player in the Information Society. But information technology innovations offer this community great opportunities to excel. Information research and policy institutes should be established in the Black community to provide policy initiatives that support and assist African Americans in their efforts to prosper and achieve excellence in the twenty first century.

THE FINAL WORD

The Black community is not a one-dimensional sector of American society. To unilaterally state that Blacks are falling through the Net or being left behind is inaccurate and irresponsible. While this view seems to receive a lot of attention in the media, we find that the picture is much more complex than that. Blacks are not only using the Internet for a variety of purposes, but using it to conduct business. Not only are many Blacks using telephones, but they are also contributing huge sums of money in long-distance and other fees that are helping to finance the construction of the information infrastructures. At the same time, the Black community is a sector of society that is struggling to achieve parity with other communities in the Information Society. In this area, it may need assistance from those in the majority society. Those who observe and measure its progress in the years to come should view the Black community in this way. This book hopefully is a helpful tool in that regard.

Index

About the Editors
and Contributors

JOHN T. BARBER is Assistant Professor and former Acting Chairman in the Department of Communication Studies at Morgan State University in Maryland. His research interests include the press portrayal of African American congressional representatives, the creation of a multicultural news paradigm, and the impact of communication technology of African Americans. He is a former Congressional Black Caucus Senior Research Fellow. He received the top three papers award for research in political communication from the Eastern Communication Association. He has published in the *Howard Journal Communication* and contributed to the book *Mediated Messages and African American Culture: Contemporary Issues.* He is a member of the Research and Policy Committee of the National Association for Minorities in Communications. He has been a research consultant to HBO on marketing programming to African Americans.

TAFT H. BROOME is Professor of Engineering in the Civil Engineering Department at Howard University in Washington, D.C. He publishes regularly in vibrations and ethics literatures. His research interests span three fields: engineering, philosophy, and social science. In those areas, he has published articles and book chapters on continuous and combined dynamical systems, ethics and philosophy of engineering, and character development. He has published in numerous journals and periodicals, including *Journal of Engineering Mechanics, Research in Philosophy and Technology,* and *Science Communication.*

TODD STEVEN BURROUGHS is a student of Black media history and twentieth-century popular culture. A former media critic whose column "Drums in the Global Village" was syndicated nationwide in Black newspapers from 1992 to 1999, he is currently a contributing columnist for *The Black World Today* (www.tbwt.com). He also is working on a journalistic biography of death-row journalist Mumia Abu-Jamal.

OSCAR H. GANDY, JR. is Herbert I. Schiller Information and Society Professor in the Annenberg School of Communication at the University of Pennsylvania. His research interests involve the political economy of information. He is the author of *The Panoptic Sort, Beyond Agenda Setting,* and *Communication and Race: A Structural Perspective.* He has published more that 75 articles and chapters exploring the ways in which information is used to shape public policy and social practice. His research on racial comparative risk was supported in part by a Freedom Forum Media Studies Fellowship (1993-1994). His current work is engaging the ways in which instrumental rationality shapes the life chances of various social groups.

GLORIA P. JAMES is Professor of Communication at Clark Atlanta University. She is the Executive Director of the Telecommunications Institute and Media Alliance (TIMA). In this position, she oversees WCLK-FM Radio; CAU-TV, Atlanta's University Channel; and the Broadcast Training and Electronic Field Production Center. Under her leadership, in 1993 the university developed and implement the Olympic Host Broadcast Training Program (HBTP), which gave minority students the opportunity to work with national and international media professionals and Atlanta Olympic Broadcasting Group in covering the Spring 1996 Centennial Olympic Games. She has authored major evaluation reports on the assessment of expenditures by historically Black colleges and universities. She has written reports in the field of communications for the Library of Congress, Congressional Research Service, and the Department of Education.

STEPHEN JONES is the Director of the SUCCESS program at Drexel University in Pennsylvania. Previously he was Assistant Director for the Academic Achievement Program at the Philadelphia College of Textiles and Science. He is also Chief Executive Officer of Stephen Jones & Associates and has more than 14 years of experience as an administrator of academic support programs in higher education. Since 1983 his firm has provided educational and computer training for schools, colleges, and corporations. His firm provides services that strengthen individual and group communication and teamwork.

JOSEPH P. McCORMICK II is Associate Professor in the Department of Political Science at Howard University in Washington, D.C. His current research focus is on the sociopolitical attitudes of men who attended the historic Million Man March. He was the co-principal Investigator of the Howard University Million Woman March Collaborative Survey Research Project. He was also Faculty Coordinator of the Million Man March Public Opinion Project. He has written numerous articles, book chapters, and monographs on various topics, including the political-fiscal-racial crisis in the District of Columbia, the dual traditions of race relations politics and African American politics and opinions from the Million Man March. His work has been published in *The New Afrikan Journal, National Political Science Review, PS: Political Science and Politics*, and other publications.

EMMANUEL K. NGWAINMBI is Visiting Professor of Communication at Elizabeth City State University in North Carolina. He is also an expert on internal communication. He is the author *Communication Efficiency and Rural Development in Africa* and *Exporting Communication Technology to Developing Countries*. He has taught at a number of colleges and universities in the United States and abroad. He serves on the editorial boards of several African news and issues publications. He has been Technology and Development editor for African Access Magazine, based in Canada. He has published numerous books and articles on development communication.

JABARI SIMAMA is the director of Marketing and Communications for the city of Atlanta. He is also an Adjunct Professor in the School of Public Policy at the Georgia Institute of Technology (Georgia Tech). Previously, he taught at University of Cincinnati, Morgan State University, and Clark Atlanta University. He is a national award-winning journalist who has written for several newspapers and magazines. In 1996 he won the AAN editorial award for his series on race and politics in Atlanta during the Olympics Games. Prior to then, he served as a member of the Atlanta City Council, and the Metropolitan Atlanta Olympic Games Authority and as the Director of Community Television for Prime Cable of Georgia.

WILLIS G. SMITH is Principal of the media marketing research firm W. G. Smith and Associates. He has worked extensively in the area of cable television and telecommunications and held a variety of media positions, which have provided him with a board range of operational and management experience while on-site in major U.S urban markets. He has also worked with the National Cable Television Association in their Research and Policy Analysis Department. He won the Alan Bussell Research Award and was published in *Resources in Education*. He has published in industry trade journals, such as *Communications Technology, C.E.D.*, and in the *Proceeding Manual for Technical Papers* for Cable Tech's Expo, where he was also a speaker. He also served on the Adjunct Faculty of Howard Unversity and Prince George's Community College. In 1994 he was recognized by *Dollars and Cents* magazine as one American's Best & Brightest Business Professionals.

GEORGE SYLVIE is Associate Professor in the Department of Journalism at the University of Texas at Austin. He has several years of experience in daily and weekly newpapers, and as a reporter and editor he has developed a research interest in media management issues. He has studied various aspects of newspaper management, publishing articles on intergroup relations, market impact on department cooperation, and technological impact on management behavior and on content. He also studies media concerns of African American; he has written studies about the impact of competition on coverage of racial matters and about newspaper coverage of race and politics. He is currently studying change and the Black press, newspaper technology, Internet market analysis, agenda setting and the early Civil Right movement, and the effect of real time newspaper on newswriting style.

ALICE A. TAIT is Associate Professor of Journalism at Central Michigan University. Her research taps into a number of areas such as the Civil Right movement, disabilities and the mass media, and the portrayals of African American in television. A few of the publications for which she has written include *Western Journal of Black Studies, New Computer Journal*, the *Handbook on Mass Media in the United States, Michigan Academician*, and *Negro Educational Review*. She has been the Chairperson of the Michigan Academy of Arts and Sciences.

G. THOMAS WILSON II is Assistant Professor of Communication at Morgan State University in Baltimore, Maryland. He has more than 18 years of experience in broadcasting, cable, file/video and theatre production, and public relations. He was Senior Producer and Narrator of the 1987 Emmy-winning production, Descendants and was the Jazz and Information Host of the Year(s) 1975 and 1976 for the San Bernardino, California, metro area. He is a Telecommunication and Print Media Consultant, Educator, and Lecturer specializing in management, ownership, policy analysis, economic development, and balanced images.

DHYANA ZIEGLER is currently Assistant Vice President for Instructional Technology/Academic Affairs at Florida A&M University. Prior to this appointment, she was the Garth C. Reaves Eminent Scholar Chair of Excellence at this university. She served as Professor of Broadcasting at the University of Tennessee Knoxville for 13 years. She is also a television producer and on-air personality. She has produced programs for several media outfits and television stations. She is the author of *Molefi Kete Asante and Afrocnetricty in Praise and in Criticism*. She has coauthored a book entitled *Thunder and Silence: The Mass Media in Africa* and written numerous book chapters. She has published articles in several periodicals and journals, including *Journal of Black Studies, Journal of Broadcasting and Electronic Media* and *Journalism Quarterly*.